PRAISE FOR COWBOY FROM PRAGUE

"Charles Ota Heller's newest memoir, *Cowboy from Prague*, is a gripping and hauntingly beautiful exploration of loss, survival, trauma of losing one's identity, and triumph of discovering it once again. What begins as a generationally familiar pursuit of the 'American Dream' develops into a unique and fascinating tale of one man's reclamation of his life, liberty and Jewish soul. This is required reading for a generation that often forgets that the struggle is the most important part of the journey."

> – *Major General (Res.) Doron Almog, Israel Prize Laureate and Founder/Chairman of ADI Negev-Nahalat Eran*

"At a time when immigration is being restricted, Charles Heller writes his own story about why immigrants are vital participants in America's growth and prosperity. His family survived the Holocaust and arrived in the United States with almost nothing. They worked hard to build a life fulfilling the American Dream. Once you start reading *Cowboy from Prague*, you will not put it down."

> – *Gary Jobson, America's Cup Hall of Fame sailor; Emmy-award winning TV producer; author of* Gary Jobson: An American Sailing Story

"Grit and determination course through *Cowboy from Prague*—but also self-reflection, as Charles Ota Heller looks up from a whirlwind life as an immigrant overachiever to come to grips with what it means that nearly all his extended family died in the Holocaust before he set foot in America. Late in life, the question '*Am I Jewish?*' opens new connections and enriches his already expansive life."

> – *Sheilah Kast, journalist, broadcaster, and co-author of* Dracula Is Dead

"As you read *Cowboy from Prague*, you will realize how important it is to have your own imaginary compass. Heller certainly didn't lack one. At the age of 12, he fled a Communist country in the center of Europe for America. He had a dream like many other immigrants —to make it in a free country. But he never forgot where he came from."

> *– Judita Matyášová, Czech journalist and author of* Friendship in Spite of Hitler

"In *Cowboy from Prague*, Charles Ota Heller has written an engaging and deeply personal memoir that delivers two invaluable and timely messages: (1) an 'immigrant' is not a faceless concept but an individual whose story is woven into the fabric of our nation, and (2) exploring the intersection of one's personal experience as a part of history can be a transformative experience. Writing in an appealing, self-deprecating style, Heller covers his evolution as a 'real' (his word) American and his search for understanding the impact of the Holocaust in his life. In writing of his successes and failures in education, business, and sports, the touchstones are always his resourceful parents who left Europe and adapted to life in the United States and his own family. To read *Cowboy from Prague* is to meet Charles Ota Heller and delight in time spent in his thought-provoking, humorous, dynamic presence."

> *– Susan Moger, former Senior Editor at Scholastic and author of the novel* Of Better Blood

"Charlie Heller's story is one of a kind. He has been an active member at the US Naval Academy Golf Club for several years, and is one of the most unassuming members we have seen, despite his incredible life journey. His life experiences are lessons that will inspire readers from every generation; truly the American Dream personified!"

> *– Patrick S. Owen, Men's Golf Coach, US Naval Academy*

"*Cowboy from Prague* is a moving and inspiring memoir. Charles Ota Heller survived the brutal Nazi and Soviet occupations of his homeland Czechoslovakia, emigrated to the United States knowing only a few words of English, and persisted to become the youngest tenured professor at the US Naval Academy, a renowned entrepreneur, and an acclaimed writer. Readers will find this to be an uplifting account of overcoming daunting personal and professional challenges enroute to a gratifying and highly successful life."

> – *Hank Parker, author of* Containment: A Thriller

"In this brilliantly written book, Charles Ota Heller poignantly describes an immigrant's pursuit of the American Dream, which is as real today as it was in the 20th century; the challenges facing immigrants then are similar in so many ways to those faced by immigrants today. The American Dream is truly 'happiness and life fulfilled,' something that Dr. Heller has indeed achieved for himself and his family. This is a recommended read for everyone, and in particular those with ties to Central and Eastern Europe."

> – *Dr. Cecilia Rokusek, CEO of the National Czech & Slovak Museum & Library*

"Perfect timing. Heller's very personal story is a needed reminder not only of the steady contributions of immigrants to our country, but of the suffering and struggles that usually precede those contributions. A story of hopes, dreams, drive and resilience. It is a must read as we search for our way forward with immigration policy today."

> – *Paula Singer, former CEO of Laureate Global Products & Services and of Walden University*

"*Cowboy from Prague* is not only an immigrant's pursuit of the American Dream, but it is a thrilling and exciting story of a rich life written by an extremely gifted storyteller. The author takes you on a personal journey mixed with the histories of Czechoslovakia and the United States. Be prepared to be part of a life story full of turns and unexpected developments. You are going to return to read this book again and again."

> – *Jiří Stavovčík, Vice Rector for Internationalization, Palacký University, Czech Republic*

"Charles Heller's story is more poignant that ever today. The Soviet authoritarian government is rising again, and *Cowboy from Prague* shows us the pathway and opportunities that come from the courage to live free. His story shows the amazing generosity of Americans through friendships from coast to coast. With the eyes of an immigrant from a Soviet-style past, he shows us the promise of America and lessons that we should not forget. Our country's greatness comes from the intellect and work ethic of immigrants. America is the land of the free and home of the brave. We are the land of immigrants."

> – *Paul Tikalsky, Dean, College of Engineering, Architecture and Technology, Oklahoma State University (great-great grandson of Bohemian immigrants)*

OTHER BOOKS BY CHARLES OTA HELLER

Prague: My Long Journey Home

*Name-droppings: Close Encounters with the Famous
and Near-Famous*

*Ready, Fire, Aim! An Immigrant's Tales of
Entrepreneurial Terror*

Dlouhá cesta domů (in Czech)

CHARLES OTA HELLER

COWBOY

FROM

PRAGUE

*An Immigrant's Pursuit
of the American Dream*

atmosphere press

Copyright © 2022 Charles Ota Heller

Published by Atmosphere Press

ISBN: 978-1-63988-354-7

Cover design by Senhor Tocas

No part of this book may be reproduced except in brief quotations and in reviews without permission from the publishers.

atmospherepress.com

To my wife, Sue—my Sammy...

...To my son, David...

...For my grandchildren,
Sam, Sarah, and Caroline

...For my great-grandson, Cole,
and his mom, Bethany

TABLE OF CONTENTS

CHAPTER ONE

ESCAPE

We're dead!

Two soldiers emerged from the darkness and pointed their rifles at us. Were they Nazi SS murderers rumored to be hiding near the border less than three years after the end of the war? Or were they Communist border guards under orders to stop escaping "enemies of the state" like us? In either case, I was certain that I would not live to see my thirteenth birthday.

The previous day, I had been worried—but not frightened—when my father explained why we had left Prague in a hurry and driven a couple of hours toward the western border. After all, Papa had fought with the Czechoslovak Brigade of the British army and defeated the Germans. He would never let harm come to Mother and me.

"We're leaving the country," my father had told me in the car. "The Communists have taken away our factory, and they will harm us in other ways if we stay. So, we're going to start a new life, hopefully in America. But first, you'll have to be brave because we're going to cross the border tomorrow night, and it's going to be dangerous. The border guards may try to shoot us."

After spending the night in a hotel, the next day— Saturday, March 13, 1948—we got back in the car and rode out into the countryside. There, with no one in sight, Papa drove the Ford into a field. We took out our baggage, abandoned the car, and walked back to a small village we had passed. Mother went to a bus stop, while Papa and I continued to the other side of town. We went into a tavern and had a snack. My father whispered to me that we were taking separate buses in order not to arouse suspicion. An hour or so later, he and I went back to the stop and caught the next bus to the town of Aš, the country's westernmost large town.

We met Mother in Aš and walked to the railroad station. Papa bought third-class tickets to Rossbach, a village near the German border. The train, belching white smoke from the stack of the coal-fired locomotive, arrived a few minutes later, and we rode it without incident to Rossbach. The village station was tiny, and there was no one in sight. But a few minutes later, a horse-drawn wagon pulled up near the tracks.

"Mr. Heller?" asked the driver. "Come with me."

We piled our belongings into the wagon and hopped in behind the driver. He cracked his whip, and the two horses began to trot out of town. We rode for some time until we came upon a farm at the edge of a thick forest. The farmer motioned us inside.

"Make yourselves comfortable," he said. "You'll stay here till midnight."

I noticed that he never introduced himself, nor did we ever hear the name of his wife, who served us dinner. Had I realized that this would be our last decent meal for many months, I would have savored it more. I dozed off in a chair, while my parents sat quietly and spoke to one another only occasionally. A grandfather clock in the corner seemed to be in slow motion as its little hand crawled toward twelve. Finally, the clock announced that it was midnight.

"Get your things and let's go," we were ordered.

Sleepily, I put on my jacket and shoes and headed out the door. Just as I was about to exit the house, I heard my father scream at the farmer.

"Where is our suitcase?"

It turned out that the farmer had stolen one of our bags while we waited in the living room. He proclaimed his innocence, but how else could one-fifth of our worldly possessions as we headed for exile disappear inside his house? There was nothing my parents could do but go on, now considerably poorer than we had been when we arrived.

Outside, we were greeted by a spectacular, starry but moonless, sky. The farmer motioned for us to follow him, with Mother carrying one suitcase and Papa having two bags strapped together, one in the front and the other in the back. I carried a bundle of blankets which, I would find out later, contained valuable jewelry that would constitute the majority of our assets as immigrants. We walked across a field to the edge of the forest. There, the farmer stopped and pointed into the woods.

"Walk for about three hours in that direction and, if you're lucky and the border guards don't shoot you, you'll run into American soldiers. Good luck."

With that, he turned and sauntered off to the farmhouse. We began walking in the direction he had indicated, avoiding footpaths in order not to be detected. It was dark and scary in the woods, and I imagined being attacked by wild animals or worse, by German SS killers who were rumored to be hiding in the forests. My bundle was getting heavier with each step, and I stopped every few minutes to rest.

Occasionally, Papa referred to his compass in order to make sure we were heading west. He urged me to keep up with him. I kept tripping over roots, stumbling and falling, all the time frightened that I would give us away by making so much noise. I expected to hear gun shots at any moment, and my heart was beating wildly. The night was cold, but I was sweating profusely. I was totally exhausted when, after three hours, we reached the end of the forest.

Suddenly, out of the darkness stepped two men in uniform, shining flashlights into our eyes and aiming their rifles at us. We stopped in our tracks as they approached, calling out in a strange language.

We're dead! I thought as I gripped Mother's hand. I looked at Papa and found it difficult to believe that he appeared so calm.

The soldiers came closer. Papa spoke to them—in the same strange language. Finally, he turned to us and smiled.

"These are American soldiers," he announced. "We're in the US Zone of Germany. We're free!"

CHAPTER TWO

SINK OR SWIM

"Come on, swim to me!"

Water clogged my ears, and I could barely hear my father, who had thrown me into the middle of the Labe (Elbe) River in Czechoslovakia. It was the summer of 1945, and I was nine years old. I had not yet learned to swim, and I was terrified of sinking to the bottom and never resurfacing. Having spent much of the Second World War hiding from the Nazis, I had not had opportunities to participate in waterside recreation. But now the war was over, and my parents and I were catching up on life.

Our German shepherd, Alma, jumped into the water next to me, and I imitated her by paddling furiously with all fours against the current. Ever so slowly, we advanced toward shore. Finally, triumph! Papa wrapped his muscular arms around me and squeezed me against his chest while Alma barked happily.

"You're a swimmer now," my father said, a smile spreading on his handsome face. "Not only that—you're a brave boy."

I could not have been prouder of myself. My war-hero father, who had only recently returned from more than five years of fighting against the Germans, just complimented me!

My father, Rudolph Heller, was short and stocky, with the build of a middleweight boxer. His wavy, blonde hair and blue eyes camouflaged his Jewish ethnicity. He was an outstanding athlete who excelled in soccer, volleyball, table tennis, and kayaking. Born in Prague in 1910, he grew up in Kralupy, a small city about twenty kilometers down the Vltava River from the capital. His father, Leopold, had been drafted into the Austro-Hungarian army during World War I and was killed when Rudolph was six years old. He and his mother, Otilie, were taken in by her brother, Emil Neuman, who owned a large hardware store.

After completing elementary school in Kralupy, Papa began commuting to Prague—by bicycle or train—first to a gymnasium (high school for university-bound students) and later to Bergmann Business College. The fact that he was able to attain a college degree was attributable to Czechoslovakia's first president, Tomáš Garrigue Masaryk, who insisted that his young nation, unlike others in Eastern and Central Europe, must not have Jewish quotas imposed on higher education.

Following graduation, my father came to work for Labor, the largest manufacturer of women's dresses and men's work clothes in Central Europe, located in Kojetice, a village about fifteen kilometers from Prague. The founder of the company was my great grandfather, Gustav Neumann, whom I called Dědeček (roughly equivalent to "Grandaddy," although he was my *great* grandfather). While in the employ of Dědeček, Rudolph met the love of his life, Ilona Neumannová, the boss' granddaughter. The young lady who would become my mother was born in 1915 to Artur Neumann, a Jew, and Marie Kozušníková, a Catholic, in Vienna. Artur and Marie never married. After Ilona was baptized in a Catholic church, Artur adopted her and brought her home to Kojetice. Marie returned to her home near Ostrava.

Mother was known not only as the richest girl in the region, but also as the most beautiful. About five feet six inches tall and slender, she had brown eyes and her black hair was short and upswept in the style of the period. Her radiant smile revealed a gap between her upper front teeth and lit up every room she entered. My parents married in December 1934, and I was born in January 1936. Like Mother, I became a devout Catholic, baptized in the church of St. Vitus in Kojetice.

Germany occupied our country on March 15, 1939, and soon thereafter, a purge of the large Jewish population began. Our relatives began to disappear, one after the other. My father escaped with the intention of arranging an exit for Mother and me. Once in Belgrade, he bribed a Yugoslav diplomat to bring us out using false passports that identified us as the latter's wife and son. The diplomat pocketed the money and never came for us. Soon, Mother and I, along with *Dědeček*, were the only members of our family left in Czechoslovakia.

Papa managed to make it as far as Palestine, where the British army was forming a Czechoslovak Brigade. He was one of the first volunteers, and saw more than five years of combat before returning home a war hero in 1945.

The Germans evicted Mother, *Dědeček* and me from our home and took over our family's factory. The three of us were taken in by my parents' friends, Vladimír and Marie Tůma, whose farm was located in Kojetice, down the road from the factory. Mother worked in their fields, while my great grandfather and I helped around the farm, feeding pigs, chickens, cows, oxen, and geese. We became one another's best friends.

I was unaware of the fact that, under the Nazis' Nuremberg Laws, I was considered a Jew because I had three Jewish grandparents. After all, I was a devout Catholic boy. Moreover, the "party-line" I was fed by Mother was that I was not allowed to attend school or go to public places such as parks, movies and swimming pools was "because your father is fighting against the Germans." Telling myself that living with deprivation without complaining was my way of helping Papa fight the Nazis, I managed to cope.

In April 1942, *Dědeček* was taken away to Terezín, a transit concentration camp, and out of my life. After the war, we would discover that, six months later, he was transported to the Treblinka death camp, where the Nazis murdered him upon arrival.

The second calamity occurred two years later, when Mother was taken away to a slave labor camp for Christian wives of Jewish men. Unable to protect me any longer, she hid me on the farm with the Tůmas. Life in hiding was lonely and, on occasion—when the Gestapo or Czech collaborators came looking for me—frightening.

Thankfully, the war finally ended in May 1945. My parents and I were reunited; however, we were the only Hellers and Neumanns to survive the war. Twenty-five members of our family had perished.

Following a couple of happy post-war years, we escaped just two weeks after the Communist take-over of the Czechoslovak government. The Soviet quislings had declared my father an enemy of the state for having fought with the western Allies and both my parents for being "bourgeois capitalists." We evaded armed border guards and—for a terrifying three hours—stumbled through a dark forest into the US Zone of Germany, carrying our remaining worldly possessions inside three suitcases and a bundle of blankets. Once on the safe side of the Iron Curtain, we spent fifteen months in refugee camps while awaiting visas to enter the United States.

People who have never been forced to flee their homeland will never understand the courage and risk-taking required to leave behind family, friends, comfort of home, material possessions, language, and roots. No one abandons all these things on a whim. People become refugees because they were driven out. Whether escaping tyranny, murderous gangs, poverty or religious persecution, all refugees have one thing in common: they are seeking a better life. My parents had survived the war, mourned the deaths of their family in the Holocaust, and rebuilt their lives in Czechoslovakia, only to be forced by the Communists to escape from the country they loved. Now, with some trepidation, they looked forward to all three of us working hard to live the proverbial American Dream.

On May 30, 1949, Papa and I stood on the deck of an American Liberty ship, two of several hundred immigrants staring out at a beautiful lady standing on a pedestal, wearing a flowing robe and spiked crown, holding a book in her left hand and a torch in her right.

"That's the Statue of Liberty," Papa said solemnly. "Remember this moment for the rest of your life. That lady is a symbol of everything your mother and I want for you in America—happiness and freedom to be whatever you want to be."

"Do you remember how I taught you to swim after the war?" Papa asked after a long pause, as the New York skyline emerged from the morning mist. "We waded into the river and then I threw you into the middle. You had two choices: sink and drown or figure out how to swim back to me. You learned fast and you were brave. Life in America is going to be a lot like that. You're going to be thrown into the river and will have to swim in order to survive."

I was thrown into the metaphorical stream much sooner than I anticipated.

CHAPTER THREE

"SANK YOU"

Less than one month after landing in America with my two-word English vocabulary—"sank you"—my father hit me with a bombshell.

"Tommy is going away for three weeks to be a summer-camp counselor in a place called North Carolina," he said in Czech. "He's been able to work things out so that you can go with him as a camper."

Tommy was the elder son of our friends and sponsors, the Eisners, with whom we were living temporarily on Long Island. He was going to supervise a group of New York City kids at High Valley Camp near Canton, North Carolina, in the summer of 1949.

"But Papa," I protested. "I can't speak English!"

"That's the whole idea," he replied. "You won't be able to speak Czech. Being around nobody but American kids for three weeks will help you learn English quickly. By the time summer will be over, you'll be ready for school."

I ran upstairs to the room I was sharing with Tommy's brother, Steve. There, I buried my head in a pillow and cried.

Papa told me I'd have to swim for my life, I whimpered. *Now, he's throwing me in with a bunch of sharks. They may not eat me, but they'll be laughing at me because I won't understand them and they won't understand me. Why couldn't we have stayed in Czechoslovakia?*

A few days later, Tommy Eisner and I boarded a train south. Born in Prague several years before the war, Tommy remembered perhaps a hundred Czech words, so we were able to communicate on an elementary level as we headed toward North Carolina. The following day, we arrived in Asheville, where we and the other campers were picked up and driven to Canton.

At High Valley Camp, the kids were divided into groups of six, by age and gender, with each group assigned to one of several small cabins scattered along a hillside. Each cabin was supervised by a counselor. Mercifully, Tommy was the leader of our group of boys, aged twelve to fourteen. We were the second youngest kids; the oldest were boys and girls going into their final two years of high school.

After selecting our bunks and unpacking, we walked down the hill to the main building, which housed the dining hall and several recreation rooms. Once we picked up our lunches, the camp director addressed us. I think he explained the rules and the daily routine, described the facilities and made clear what was expected of us. Of course, I do not know that, since I did not understand a word. When he handed out written instructions, I stared at the hodgepodge of meaningless sentences and wondered how I could possibly fit into this alien world.

Tommy attempted to explain the contents of the hand-out, but his hundred-word Czech vocabulary failed him. Finally, he managed to give me instructions that I understood:

"Just follow what I do. If I'm not around, follow the guys in your cabin."

Much to my surprise, not only my cabin mates, but nearly

all the kids in the camp, came to my rescue. They did not laugh at my inability to converse, nor did they treat me as an inferior immigrant kid. They took me under their collective wing. They spoke to me in sign language, encouraged me to participate in camp activities, took me swimming and horseback riding, taught me the rudiments of the strange game of baseball. Most importantly, they made me feel welcome—just another New York City kid spending the summer in the Great Smoky Mountains.

One game my new friends did not have to teach me was table tennis. My father was an expert player, and, after the war, I spent many hours volleying back and forth with him in our garden in Kojetice, our hometown a few kilometers north of Prague. High Valley Camp had several tables, and, each evening after supper, white balls were flying back and forth in fierce elimination games. The winner of each match remained at the table to take on the next challenger, while the loser sat down. Evening after evening, I was the last one standing, having beaten all comers—campers and counselors.

One day, the camp director pulled me aside and, using a combination of words and sign language, informed me that we were going to drive to Asheville "to play ping-pong." I failed to understand the reason, but I was fine with it. I was happy to play, no matter where or against whom.

The following day, a number of us piled into a bus and headed for the city. When we arrived at a school gymnasium filled with ping-pong tables, I was surprised by the fact that all the other campers climbed into the stands, while Tommy led me to a desk where he filled out some papers. Soon, my name was called, and I began to play. Just as in the rec hall at High Valley, I kept winning, and new opponents kept on coming and going. All the while, my friends in the stands cheered. Following my fifth or sixth victory, the High Valley kids came streaming down from the stands. They picked me up on their shoulders and carried me to the front of the gym, where a man dressed in a gray suit handed me a silver trophy. I had no clue what he meant when he announced:

"Congratulations to Charlie Heller, the 1949 junior champion of North Carolina!"

I returned to camp a hero, although I was not quite sure why. But whatever it was that I had accomplished, I now felt that I had taken a major step toward my father's directive to become "a one hundred percent American." Not only that, but the thing I wanted more than anything was to be accepted—and to earn Americans' respect. This was a start.

Upon my arrival at High Valley, I would have given anything if someone had offered to take me out of the place and back to the safety of my Czech-speaking family. But now I did not want camp to end. I was sad that soon swimming, horseback riding, hiking, tennis, baseball, and table tennis with my friends would be replaced by the rigors of school, another new, foreign place.

When Tommy and I returned to New York's Grand Central Station in late July, I spoke passable English. So far, I had managed to swim. I found out that Papa, who had been owner and general manager of a major manufacturing firm in Czechoslovakia was back working in his industry—clothing. The only difference was that, instead of being the boss, he began at the very bottom, as a pattern-cutter. McGregor Sportswear, at the time the world's largest firm in its sector, compensated him with the princely sum of $37.50 per week ($415 in today's dollars).

While I had been at camp, my parents found, and moved into, an apartment in Morristown, New Jersey, a few miles from Papa's workplace in the town of Dover. Mother, who in both pre- and post-war years had been surrounded by servants, took a job as a cleaning lady at Oakleigh Hall, a boarding school for girls in Morristown.

One evening at dinner, Mother apologized to us for the quality and quantity of our meal.

"I'm sorry about the small portions and toughness of the meat. Ordinarily, I try to find the best piece of meat for the money I can afford. But today, I was so tired after cleaning all day that I just ran into the A&P and grabbed the first piece available at a low price and walked home."

"Please don't ever apologize," said Papa as he walked over to her and kissed her on the forehead. "We may be living on the margins of poverty, but it won't last long. We're free, we're together, and we're happy. That's what counts. And the dinner is delicious!"

Although I was proud of my parents for what they had accomplished in such a short time in America, as a callow teenager I was too self-centered to comprehend the obstacles they had overcome. It would be many years later that I would ask myself:

How many times can one begin all over? How does an immigrant start from nothing, learn a new language, learn new customs, earn a decent living, and provide for one's family? How did my incredibly brave parents do it?

Some things never seem to change. As I write this, I am filled with compassion, admiration—and awe—for desperate immigrants on our southern border, frantic Afghans attempting to flee to freedom, and refugees throughout the world, anguished people like my parents. How difficult it must be for them to face the unknown! What courage it takes to do this!

For me, life was a continuing series of explorations and discoveries. During the remaining weeks of summer and in the fall of 1949, my American education continued, primarily on the basketball courts and baseball fields across the street from our new home.

As a boy in post-war Europe, I had been a good athlete. I excelled in soccer, hockey, skiing, and tennis. No doubt, I inherited my father's genes. He was not only an outstanding competitive volleyball and table tennis player, but he and a friend were co-holders of the European distance record in one-man kayaks. Following my success at table tennis in North Carolina, it dawned on my 13-year-old mind that the quickest way to earn respect in America might be through sports. We were an athletic family, but I had never seen—nor even heard of—the most popular sports on this side of the Atlantic: baseball, American football, and basketball. Now I knew that I had to learn them quickly, and that I would have to work diligently to become good at them.

Our Franklin Village apartment was directly across the street from a playground with a concrete slab that had, at each end, a steel pole to which a rectangular wooden board was mounted with a net hanging down from an attached circular metal rim. After school and into the evening, I sat by the window watching as a group of boys dribbled a ball somewhat larger than a soccer ball and then tried to throw it through the rim and net.

"It's called basketball," my father told me one day upon his return from work. "You should go down and learn to play it. I'm sure the boys will teach you."

At first, I was hesitant. After all, I had always been the best player among my Czech friends in soccer, street hockey, and volleyball. I did not want to embarrass myself in this new sport. Finally, after a couple of weeks, I got up the courage to approach the court and stand on the sidelines. There, I learned a bit about the game by observation. Then some of the older boys began speaking to me and even invited me to play a few minutes at a time.

After several weeks of being the worst player on the court, I began to understand the game and, by the end of summer, I was good enough not to be the last player chosen by the captains when they selected their teams.

Beyond the basketball court, in an open area today occupied by Morristown Memorial Hospital, was a baseball field. One day, I spotted two boys playing catch. Each was wearing a leather glove, one on his left hand and the other on his right. Emboldened by my success at basketball, I walked up and introduced myself to the guys and asked if I could join in. The right-hander, the one with the left-handed glove, told me his name was Jim Gerber. He loaned me his glove. I tossed the ball back and forth with the lefty: tall, bespectacled Pete Brown.

I convinced my father that I had to have my own baseball glove. He accompanied me to Ken Mills' sporting goods store, where we purchased a light brown number. Pete and Jim taught me how to break it in, and the three of us met every afternoon for a game of catch.

One Saturday afternoon, Jim and Pete invited me to go with them to see a baseball movie about a guy from a nearby town at the Park Theater in Morristown. *The Larry Doby Story* depicted the life of a boy who had been a three-sport star at Eastside High School in Paterson, New Jersey. He signed a professional baseball contract at the age of seventeen and, almost immediately, became an all-star for the Newark Eagles. However, both his education and athletic career were interrupted by service in the US Navy during World War II. By war's end, young Larry knew that baseball was his best sport. He had played against major-league stars as a seaman and had no trouble hitting the game's best pitchers. Without a doubt, he could play at the highest level of the game.

There was only one problem. It was 1945 and major-league baseball was a lily-white game. Larry Doby was Black. His only future was in the Negro Leagues, a traveling roadshow of talented, underappreciated, and underpaid athletes. He returned to the Newark Eagles in 1946 and led them to the league championship.

Then came 1947, the year Branch Rickey of the Brooklyn Dodgers changed America's pastime forever by making Jackie Robinson, a brilliant athlete out of UCLA, the first African American to wear a major-league uniform. Less than three months later, Larry Doby was signed by owner Bill Veeck and became the centerfielder of the Cleveland Indians—the first Black player in the history of the American League.

My English was still limited, and I failed to comprehend some of the movie's dialog and nuances. But it mattered little. The story of Larry Doby—his successes on fields and courts, his patriotism and dedication despite the humiliation and rejection he suffered—captured me. As a "hidden child" of World War II who had been victimized by the Nazis and now was a refugee in a strange land, I identified with his struggles. By the time Pete, Jim, and I walked out into the afternoon sunshine, I had a new hero, one who would influence my life for years to come. I would wear Larry's number 14 on the uniforms of all sports I played. When it was unavailable to me as a college basketball player, I wore its reverse: 41. Many years later, while our company was computerizing major league baseball, I finally met Hall of Famer Larry Doby. He told me how touched he was by the effect he had on an immigrant boy, now the CEO of a software firm.

"I'm really proud to meet you, Charlie," he said, and I felt as if I had ascended to heaven.

As my first summer in America came to an end, I worried more and more about starting school. Up to that point, my formal education had been limited because I had not been permitted to attend school during the war. Later, in refugee camps in Germany, there had been no school. Now I was entering eighth grade, having experienced only two-and-a-half years in a classroom, while my new classmates had eight years, starting with kindergarten! On top of this, my English was still merely passable.

I came to Alexander Hamilton School, on the other side of Morristown, full of fear and trepidation. But one wonderful person made my transition far easier than I had expected. She was Miss Agnes Leonard, a tall, portly, gray-haired, gentle lady of about sixty, who took me under her wing from day one until my graduation from elementary school. On that first day, after she welcomed the class back from its summer vacation, Miss Leonard addressed the students:

"Children, I want you to meet Charles Heller. He comes to us from a country called Czechoslovakia, which is in the middle of Europe." She pointed to my native country on a world map. "Last year, his nation was taken over by some really bad people called Communists, and Charles and his parents had to escape. They came to America this summer. Charles is learning English, and I would like all of us to help him learn."

Thus, Miss Leonard set the tone for a magical first year in an American school. The kids really did help me, not only by speaking more slowly so that I could understand, but by teaching me basketball during recess. In the classroom, I got a pleasant surprise. I found that I was far ahead of the other students in math, science, and geography as a result of clandestine tutoring I had received during the war from a brave family friend, František Volt, whom the Germans would have shot had they discovered our secret sessions in his attic.

Although I had early language difficulties, I became one of the best spellers in the class. But the subject I enjoyed most was history. We studied the American Revolution, something totally new to me, and I began to understand what made this nation great. From Miss Leonard, I learned about the struggle that led to the founding of the United States of America, and I developed a deep and abiding love for my new country.

After only one year, I was told that I spoke English "like a native." Fourteen years old and full of myself, I felt that I was now accepted as someone other than a refugee, and thus I was embarrassed by the fact that Mother and Papa still spoke with a Slavic accent. I insisted that we speak English to one another both inside and outside our home, and my parents complied. Ironically, when we arrived in America, Mother and I knew no

English at all, while my father spoke it well due to his time in the British army. Yet, many years later, Mother's speech would have only a slight accent, whereas there was never any doubt that Papa's native tongue was something other than English.

My parents purchased a new 1949 Studebaker Champion car and a small house in Morris Township, about two miles north of Morristown. Both were earning small salaries, yet they were able to save enough money to pay cash for the car and to make a fifty-percent down payment on the home, while taking out a five-year mortgage on the balance. Papa, who had been a successful entrepreneur in Europe, had an aversion to owing money to anyone, and he was not going to borrow a penny more than he had to. The cost of the house was $14,500 (around $160,000 in today's dollars). While modest by our family's pre- and post-war standards in Czechoslovakia, it was our little piece of America. Papa would live in it for the remaining thirty-eight years of his life and Mother for fifty-one.

Our neighbors, one house removed, became our family's closest friends. Jack Geils was vice president of Bell Telephone Laboratories, the storied communications think-tank in nearby Murray Hill and Whippany. His wife, Lynne, was a pert lady with a memorable laugh. Their only child, John W. Geils, Jr., known as Jay, was ten years younger than I; from the time he was a little boy, he showed a talent for music and played a number of instruments. Some years later, this talent would bring him international fame as the leader and guitarist of the J. Geils Band.

In less than one year, my father rose through the ranks at McGregor and became a foreman in the cutting department. His salary more than doubled. Mother quit her cleaning job at a girls' school and took a better-paying position as a seamstress for brassiere manufacturer, Maidenform, which had a small operation on Morristown's Speedwell Avenue, above Shalit's drug store.

I was proud of my parents who never looked back, unlike many immigrants who seemed to wallow in self-pity because they found life in exile difficult. They were not only in love with one another, but grateful to be alive, and to be together. They had left everything behind and were certain that they would never return. During those early years in America, they were one another's safe harbor—and mine.

The Heller family was on its way toward achieving the elusive American Dream, and, so far at least, I had managed to swim.

CHAPTER FOUR

GODDAMN IMMIGRANT!

I entered Morristown High School as a freshman in September 1950, fifteen months after arriving in America. Each day began in Ditlow Scroll's Room 202, my home room. We recited the Pledge of Allegiance and the Lord's Prayer and then dispersed to our classes for the next eight periods. I was enrolled in the college preparatory program. In addition to all the standard courses such as English, history, and math, we were required to take either three years of one foreign language or two years each of two foreign languages. I chose two years each of Latin and French. Since my native language, Czech, had similar noun declensions, verb conjugations, and other complexities foreign to English speakers, I found both Latin and French rather easy. Sometimes, being an immigrant was an advantage. At other times, it was not.

One sunny morning in the fall of 1951—my sophomore year at Morristown High School—a friend named Layne and I trotted down to the football field, wearing our gray gym uniforms and white Keds sneakers. Because we would be playing touch football in gym class, I wanted to practice kicking field goals before the game began.

In those days, all placekickers approached the ball from straight-on and kicked with their toes. As a soccer player two years removed from Europe, I advanced to the ball from the left side and kicked it with the instep of my right foot. With Layne holding for me, I began at the ten-yard line and, after each successful kick, moved back to the next yard marker. When I drove the ball through the uprights from thirty yards out, I heard a voice behind me.

"Let me see you do that again, Charlie," said Eugene "Cap" Smith, our gym teacher and the school's track coach.

I took three steps, kicked the ball, and watched it sail over the crossbar.

"Wow!" yelled Layne, and I wanted to scream in delight, but managed to appear cool and nonchalant.

"Run over and get Coach Flynn," Cap instructed Layne.

Bill Flynn was the head football coach at Morristown High. A short, burly Irishman, he was a legend in New Jersey high-school football circles. He arrived at the twenty-yard line shortly, breathing hard.

"Bill, you've got to see this kid kick the ball," said Cap. "He's making thirty-yard field goals, kicking soccer-style, and in sneakers. I think you may want him on your varsity. Do it again, Charlie."

I did, with the same result. The ball flew through the uprights. Cap asked me to repeat it to prove his point. I did and again had to restrain myself from celebrating.

"What do you think of that?" Smith asked Flynn.

The football coach looked at me, turned back to Smith and launched a wad of saliva onto the green grass.

"This is pure bullshit!" he snarled. "Only goddamn immigrant freaks kick the ball from the side. This is America, and that's not football." With that, he walked off in the direction of his office.

I felt as if the squat little man had kicked me in the groin as hard as I had kicked the football. I stared at Smith quizzically in search of an explanation. Cap was watching the football coach wobble up the hill toward the school building. Finally, he turned to me, and I could see that his eyes were moist.

"I'm sorry, Charlie. Apparently, Coach Flynn is not very fond of immigrants. I'm afraid you're going to meet a few people like him in your life."

For the next three seasons following the Flynn incident, I watched from the stands on Saturday afternoons as the MHS football team never attempted a field goal because none of the straight-on kickers had a sufficiently strong foot to make one. Some of my friends on the team—Dick Keefe, Rudy Jenkins, and Bill "Slim" Morrison—tried to talk me into coming out for the team, but I had no interest in playing for Coach Flynn. After all, I was a "goddamn immigrant freak."

Ten years later, in 1962, on a visit to Morristown from California, I would stop at the high school to say "hello" to Coach Smith, who had been my favorite teacher. Our conversation eventually turned to the Flynn episode.

"Just think," Cap said. "If it hadn't been for that idiot Flynn, you could have been the first soccer-style kicker in football, rather than Gogolak."

Pete Gogolak was a Hungarian-born student at Cornell, who went down in sports history as American football's first "sidewinder" kicker. In 1964, he would sign with the Buffalo Bills and become one of the most prolific kickers in professional football. There has not been a single "straight-on" placekicker in the college or pro game in many years. And yes, I have often wondered wistfully if I, another immigrant, could have been the one to change that bit of sports history.

CHAPTER FIVE

AMERICAN BOY

While the Flynn episode constituted my first encounter with anti-immigrant bias in my newly-adopted country, a second gym-class incident was less dramatic and more humorous. Unlike the football incident, this one caused a great commotion throughout the school, if only for a few hours.

One of the track events in spring gym of my junior year was the sixty-yard dash. While I was not particularly fast by the standards of the varsity track team, I did well in all intramural track events in which every boy, from athlete to klutz, participated. One morning, after I won the sixty-yard sprint by a couple of steps, Cap Smith came running over to me with stopwatch in hand.

"Charlie, this is incredible!" he said. "Unless my watch is off, you just broke the national high school record for the sixty by a half-second."

He called over the student assistant who had timed the race also and checked the boy's stopwatch. It matched the time on Cap's watch.

During the school day, word spread like wildfire: Charlie

Heller broke the US high school record, and he did it in sneakers and gym uniform! In every class, my fellow students cheered me and pounded me on the back. But I had a nagging feeling that something had to be amiss. After all, I was not exactly Jesse Owens. During the last class of the day, I was called to the principal's office over the intercom. The other kids in the room thought I was going to be interviewed for a story in the sports pages and cheered, but I knew something else had to be up. Cap Smith and the principal were waiting for me.

"Charlie, I'm really embarrassed," said Coach Smith. "We had the right time this morning, but we had the wrong distance. Somebody measured wrong and placed the finish line ten yards closer to the start than it should have been. You ran a fifty-yard dash—not a sixty-yard dash. Not even close to a record. I'm sorry."

"Thanks, Cap," I said. "I knew something had to be wrong. I'm not even fast enough to run the dashes on your track team, much less to set any kind of record. No problem." Though disappointed, the immigrant kid had enjoyed his day of glory.

"Look!" my mother exclaimed in Czech one morning at breakfast. "Here's Charlie's picture on the sports page!"

She passed the newspaper to my father, who smiled his approval. Although he had been a fine athlete during his youth in Czechoslovakia, he was too busy scratching out a living to take an interest in my athletic achievements in America until now, when he saw me in black-and-white, arms raised in triumph, on the front page of the sports section of the *Newark News*, New Jersey's largest newspaper.

Actually, there were two of us with our arms in the traditional victory pose, as we broke the tape simultaneously in an apparent dead heat. The other runner was the state's greatest athlete of that era, Milt Campbell of Plainfield High

School. Milt had set New Jersey records in the high jump, as well as the high and low hurdles, and he was one of the top middle-distance runners as well. He was a star swimmer, and he had scored nearly 150 points as a running back on the football team. After high school, Campbell would play football for Indiana University, the Cleveland Browns, and the Montreal Alouettes. Most significantly, he would earn international fame as "the world's greatest athlete," by virtue of winning the gold medal in the decathlon at the 1956 Olympics in Melbourne, Australia. So, I was in a dead heat with this guy? Pictures sometimes lie.

The highlight of every high school track season in New Jersey was the State Relays, held in Long Branch, a town near the Jersey Shore. In May 1953, our team bus left Morristown early on a Saturday morning so that we could spend a couple of hours relaxing at the beach in Asbury Park before the start of competition. When we arrived, each of us was given a small allowance to spend on the boardwalk. Several of my friends and I went off to the penny arcades. We were sitting on a bench, eating saltwater taffy and waiting to board the bus, when Coach Cap Smith approached and pulled me aside.

"Charlie, I have a problem," he said. "Some of your idiot teammates went wading in the ocean, and the water was so cold that their legs cramped up. A couple of them can't run this afternoon."

What does this mean to me? I wondered. *I'm running one of the quarters of the mile relay. Maybe one of the other guys has cramped up, and we'll have to forfeit?* Wrong.

"Here's the problem," explained Smith. "Tony was supposed to run the half-mile leg of the medley, and now he can't go. I don't have any other half-milers available, and I need you to substitute. Can you go 880 yards in the medley?"

"Sure, Cap," I said, knowing very well that running two consecutive laps on a quarter-mile track was something I did not do well, even at a slow pace in practice. I was a below-average—bordering on mediocre—middle-distance runner. I was on the track team only to stay in condition for the sports at which I excelled: basketball, tennis, and baseball. But I was a team player, and an immigrant seeking approval from Americans. If the coach needed me to run a distance I had never attempted before, so be it.

The sprint medley relay back then consisted of four legs: 440 yards, 220 yards, 220 yards, and 880 yards, in that order. I would run the final leg. Plainfield was considered the heavy favorite in this race, while Morristown was predicted to be an also-ran, even with its regular team in place.

By the time I was handed the baton for the finishing leg, we were far behind all the other teams. I ran a slow first lap, preserving my strength in order to be able to complete the race. I lost more ground. As I approached the end of my first lap, I saw the officials stringing a tape across the track. At the same time, I heard the pounding of track shoes off my right shoulder. I looked back and saw the great Milt Campbell, his black body glistening with sweat in the sunshine. We hit the tape simultaneously. He threw up his arms in the age-old victor's pose as he crossed the line. I figured: *What the hell, I might as well throw mine up, too.* And I did.

That is how the future Olympic champion and I made the front page of the sports section and appeared to be in a dead heat. The only problem was that I had to run one more lap. It was the longest quarter mile I have ever run, totally alone after everyone else had finished, and embarrassed in front of a crowded grandstand.

I snatched the newspaper before my parents had a chance to read the caption under the photograph.

When I started high school, I learned that many American boys in my economic stratum—poor—took on after-school and weekend jobs in order to supplement their family incomes. My parents told me they had no need for my assistance, but if I felt that I needed more than the fifty cents a week I was receiving as an allowance, I should feel free to get a job. I wondered how I could work after school and still play both high school and club sports, so I sought the advice of one of the best athletes at MHS, Bruce Derrick. Bruce informed me that his older brother Don, known as "Duck," was a supervisor at a local printing company and that he might be able to arrange a job that would allow me to attend practices and games.

I met with Duck and got the job at Compton Press, with the understanding that I would keep sporadic hours, based on my sports schedule. The offices were located on the second floor of a building on Morristown's South Street. I was paid sixty cents per hour, performing various mundane duties in the print shop, and considered myself rich. My fellow workers were sports nuts, and I felt at home.

I had several classes with a stocky, bespectacled fellow named Peter Sheldrick. We found that we had a great deal in common, particularly a love for books and for basketball. Pete's parents owned the Red Spade Nursery on Mt. Kemble Avenue, about halfway between Morristown and Bernards- ville. We hung a basket in a barn on the property so that we could play at night and during inclement weather. At least once a week, I hitchhiked the six miles from our house to Pete's, and we spent hours playing one-on-one. Often after playing, I stayed for dinner with Pete, his younger sister Betsy, and their parents. Near the end of our freshman year, Mr. Sheldrick offered me a summer job at the nursery, at $1.25 per hour.

"Thank you, sir!" I accepted. It was more than twice what I was making at the print shop.

The work at Red Spade was hard, but enjoyable. I learned to plant trees and shrubs, to fertilize and spray plants, and to drive a tractor. Pete worked alongside me, and our friendship grew. Nearly every day after work, we retreated to the barn to hone our line-drive jump shots, their flat trajectories necessitated by the low ceiling. Occasionally, I let Pete beat me in a game of one-on-one or H-O-R-S-E, but I had to work at it. My game was improving so rapidly that I began to dream of playing college ball.

I went out for the high school team my sophomore year, knowing I had no chance of making the varsity, which was loaded with good players. I made the Junior Varsity and got my first experience in organized ball. Although I did OK, I discovered that I had a long way to go before I could become anything resembling a star. The boys against whom I was competing, opponents as well as teammates, had been playing the game their entire lives, while I had begun playing only two years earlier. I knew I would have to work harder. Accordingly, I became a "gym rat." When not playing in Sheldricks' barn, I spent my free time shooting baskets on playgrounds and in church gyms, often with my pal, Larry "Tim" Timpson. My game was improving to a point that I became top scorer for two club teams playing in Northern New Jersey leagues. More important to me than winning games was the fact that I was winning Americans' respect. My teammates, opponents, and spectators viewed me as a basketball player, not as an immigrant.

In the early 1950s, the New York metropolitan area was loaded with elite college teams, and Madison Square Garden was the game's mecca. City College of New York, coached by the legendary Nat Holman, won both the National Invitational Tournament and the NCAA championship. Long Island University was a national powerhouse under Coach Clair Bee. New York University, St. John's, Manhattan College, and New Jersey's Seton Hall, all were among the best teams in the nation, competing for top honors with perennial powers Kentucky, Bradley, North Carolina, and Oklahoma State. (Oklahoma State University was called Oklahoma A&M College until a 1957 name-change. I will refer to it as Oklahoma State, or OSU, regardless of timeframe.)

I was in awe of the stars of those New York teams: Irwin Dambrot, Ed Roman, and Al Roth of CCNY; Sherman White of LIU; Connie Schaaf of NYU. I dreamed of someday wearing the uniform of one of my heroes and playing before large crowds at the Garden.

Then it all came crashing down. Junius Kellogg, the first black man to play for Manhattan College, reported to his coach that he had been approached by gamblers and offered a thousand dollars to hold down the score in an upcoming game. Kellogg was instructed by police to go along with the offer and to lead investigators to the criminals. He did, and the result was a scandal which nearly brought down the entire college game. Seven CCNY players, including my three idols, as well as stars from LIU, NYU, Manhattan, Bradley, and Kentucky were implicated in outrageous acts of cheating. They had taken bribes to shave points such that final scores would be within spreads established by professional gamblers.

Almost overnight, the names and photos of college basketball stars migrated from the sports section to the front page. I was stunned and heartbroken. Until then, I had thought that nearly everything and most everyone in America—particularly the athletes I worshipped—were perfect. Reading and hearing about these crimes was a devastating experience. The sport that had become my passion was now tainted, and newspapers, radio and TV reported a new discovery of gambler infiltration nearly every day for months. Now there would be no way I would consent to play for a New York college team, even if I proved good enough to be offered a scholarship. I felt physically ill and began to question whether or not I wanted to play the game any longer.

Yet, the cheating scandal proved to be a positive turning point for me when a casual perusal of a magazine on my parents' coffee table brought about a life-altering moment.

Appropriately, the magazine was *Life*. I opened it to an article on two facing pages. The headline over the left page read, "Basketball at Its Worst," and consisted of photos of point-shaving players being led off to jail. The facing page was headlined, "Basketball at Its Best." It contained action shots of a team wearing white jerseys with a large orange and black letter "O" in the front, and a portrait of a stern-looking man named Henry P. Iba, the team's coach. The brief article spoke of the coach's tough-love approach, the fact that his program at Oklahoma State had been untouched by any of the scandalous activities taking place at other universities, and his insistence that his players attain good grades and graduate. I tore out the two pages and taped them to the wall above my bed. I looked at them each night before going to sleep.

"I want to go to Oklahoma State," I informed my parents one evening at the dinner table.

Ironically, my father had been nudging me gently toward OSU, although his prodding had nothing to do with sports. It just so happened that our Czech friend, Jan Tuma, who, along with his wife Hana, had been among our twenty-plus roommates in a refugee camp in Germany, was on the civil engineering faculty there. Professor Tuma had been my math mentor in the camp, and later by correspondence after we came to America. Papa thought that having him nearby to give me an occasional kick in the butt would cause me to study harder in college than I was doing in high school. Now my father was surprised by my sudden change of heart after months of expressing interest only in New York City universities.

"What made you decide that?" he asked me.

"I'm going to play basketball for Coach Henry Iba," I replied, knowing full well that my parents would have no idea whom I was talking about. Still steeped in European culture, they could not comprehend how or why American colleges and universities, whose purpose was supposed to be the education of young people, would support revenue-generating athletic teams and give scholarships to students who played on them.

"I'm gonna send newspaper clippings to Bob Harris and ask him to send them to Mr. Iba with a recommendation to give me a scholarship," I continued.

"Bob Harris? I thought *you* were Bob Harris," Mother laughed, referring to the fact that I had been playing under that pseudonym in a semi-professional league in order to maintain my amateur status.

"Mother, I took that name from the *real* Bob Harris. He plays professional basketball for the Boston Celtics. In college, he was a star at Oklahoma State. I met him after a Knicks game in New York, and he seemed to be interested in helping me. I have to use an assumed name because I get paid a few dollars for playing in the summer leagues, and I would lose my amateur standing if the high school or colleges found out. But I have to cheat like this because the high school coach isn't letting me get any visibility, and playing semi-pro ball is the only way I can get college coaches to find out about me."

"I see," said Mother. "But, do they really give university scholarships for playing sports?"

"Yes, Mother. That's how it's done in America. And if I don't get one, I'm going to go out for the team and try to earn one. If I make the team, my education will be free."

"That would be great," my father chimed in. "But don't count on it. We're saving money for your education. That and the money you make in your summer jobs should be enough to get you an engineering degree."

I had never been asked what I would like to study at a university. European parents of that era did not ask their children. They told them. After having conferred with Professor Tuma, Papa decided that I would major in engineering. A technical degree would guarantee me a good-paying job following graduation. Although I appeared to be a "one-hundred-percent American" to others, just as Papa had instructed me, at home I was still a Czech kid. And Czech kids did not argue with their fathers. They saluted smartly and said: "Yes, sir"—in Czech, of course.

By now, I had become a fairly accomplished player. However, my relationship with our high school basketball coach, Jim "Mac" McIntyre, was lukewarm, at best. Mac was known to play favorites, and for reasons unknown to me, I was not one of his chosen few. I suspected that, like his colleague Flynn, he considered me a goddamn immigrant freak.

I knew that Mac had been a member of the famous Original Celtics, and I had looked forward to his imparting his knowledge to my teammates and me. Thus, I was disappointed to find that he was not much of a teacher. In practices, he told us war stories of having played with such legends as Joe Lapchick, the head coach of the New York Knicks, and then, after a shoot-around, we would scrimmage. Other than screaming at me for missing a shot or failing to grab a rebound, Mac seldom spoke to me.

Although the strongest parts of my game were shooting from the outside and distributing the ball to others, Mac decided that I would be a forward, taking short jumpers and fighting inside for rebounds. At six-one, living proof of a later-day postulate that "white men can't jump" and not particularly fond of contact, I was not a happy player, and not nearly as effective as I could have been in my natural position, one of the two guard spots. But we had two outstanding outside players—Pete Many and Herb Lindsley—and there was no way I was going to displace one of them.

My greatest successes in basketball came away from high school, in Northern New Jersey amateur and semi-professional leagues. I joined a sports club, Twirlers AC, in Morristown. In basketball, we played a full schedule as we traveled around Morris County. Playing my natural position and with teammates who became my closest friends—Dominic Terreri, Rudy Jenkins, Tim Timpson, Bill "Slim" Morrison, and others—I thrived. During my junior year in high school, I averaged 23.6 points a game for Twirlers, while I struggled for playing time on my school's varsity.

At the same time, as "Bob Harris," I signed a simple contract to play in a semi-professional summer league that paid its star players fifty dollars a game and the supporting cast members twenty-five bucks. I fell into the latter category. Due to the professional nature of the league, high school and college students were prohibited from competing. The league consisted of players who had completed their high school or college careers and, unlike me, were not concerned about losing their amateur standing. Ironically, several of the players implicated in the cheating scandals—including Ed Roman of CCNY and Sherman White of LIU—played in the league.

As I had explained to Mother, I became "Bob Harris" because the real Bob Harris was another of my heroes. He had played for Mr. Iba at Oklahoma State and now was a starter for the Boston Celtics in the NBA. I played for two less famous teams, one called the Aces and the other Verilli's—the latter named for its sponsor, a bread company. Teams in the league were funded by various businesses and several resort hotels. Both my coaches had a *laissez-faire* approach that was a refreshing change from Mac's dictatorial style, and my game flourished. Incredibly, I was on the same courts with some of my fallen heroes from the cheating scandals, and often managed to hold my own against them.

The assumed-name game of the semi-pro leagues was well known by everyone who followed basketball in Northern New Jersey, and no one paid much attention to it. Although "Bob Harris" appeared in the newspaper box scores, nearly everyone knew that he was really Charlie Heller (or "Chuck Heller," as some insisted on calling me, much to my distress; I pictured a "Chuck" as a roly-poly kid with a crew-cut, wearing shorts, white sneakers, and black knee-high socks). I wondered if football coach Bill Flynn read the papers and if he realized that Bob Harris, who was averaging more than twenty points a game, was that goddamn immigrant freak he despised.

Playing with and against Black guys who had learned their hoops on the hardscrabble playgrounds of the ghetto, I learned many of their tricks: behind-the-back passes, between-the-legs dribble, and reverse layups. The miniscule "crowds" which came out to watch us seemed to enjoy seeing a white kid playing like a Black dude.

Growing up in Czechoslovakia, all I knew about African Americans—Negroes, as they were called then in polite circles—came from having read the Czech-language version of *Uncle Tom's Cabin*, and I was not burdened with the racial biases of many of my fellow white students at Morristown High. In the 1950s, college and professional teams in all sports had very few, if any, Black players. (Later, I would discover that there were quotas on their numbers.) Perhaps because my early life experiences caused me to favor underdogs, I always rooted for teams with Negroes. I pulled for the Cleveland Indians because they had Luke Easter and my most cherished hero of all, Larry Doby. I hated the lily-white, racist, New York Yankees and Washington Redskins. I cheered for college football teams from the west and north when they played against all-white southern schools. My feelings about race relations were very much shaped by sports.

Ironically, with only a couple of exceptions, the Black guys who played sports for Morristown High School teams never accepted me as an equal. In the hallways, on bus rides, and in the locker room, they simply ignored me. When I attempted to join in conversations with them, they acted as though I did not exist. One of the Black athletes, Josh Baum, was downright hostile, and we often fought, not only verbally, but physically. One of the fights was precipitated by his calling me "a fucking immigrant" during a pick-up basketball game.

I was distressed by this failure to connect with the Black

guys. I felt that we had much in common. They and their families were being subjected to discrimination—and treated like second-class citizens—just as we had been treated by the Nazis and Communists in Europe. So, why were they behaving this way toward me? As a callow teenager, I was not into deep philosophical thinking, so I came to a rather simple conclusion: Negroes were at the bottom of the economic and cultural ladder in 1950s America; they needed to find someone whose standing was even lower than theirs. They had found me—the immigrant.

In my senior year of high school, largely based on my play in the outside leagues, I received scholarship offers from two small colleges, Tri-State College in Angola, Indiana, and John Carroll University in Cleveland. Both were disguised as academic assistance programs, but they were offered by the basketball coaches. Another offer—this one an undisguised athletic scholarship—came from a perennial Division-I loser, Rutgers University in New Brunswick, New Jersey. However, I was determined to play and study at Oklahoma State, even if it meant having to walk on to the team without a free ride.

Before heading off to college, I had a moment of sports glory away from the basketball court. The *Newark News* sponsored an annual statewide tennis tournament each year. It was a true "open" in that anyone could enter. I was playing well on the high school varsity team, so I mailed in my entry.

New Jersey had a young, dynamic, tennis-playing gover-nor—Robert Meyner—who entered as well. Miraculously, out of some four hundred players in the tournament, I drew Governor Meyner as my first-round opponent. I was simul-taneously elated and petrified. Generally, the early rounds were played in obscurity and the results were reported in agate type near the back of the state newspapers' sports sections. But this was a match against the governor, and I had a sinking feeling that the match would receive more scrutiny and coverage. I worried about being embarrassed again, as I had been by the Milt Campbell incident on the track.

The match was scheduled for a Friday afternoon in a public park in Maplewood. My parents were working long hours and had little interest in my sports activities. However, since this would be a momentous occasion, I decided to tell them about it. Much to my surprise, both Papa and Mother took the afternoon off from work. It would be the first time since leaving Prague that my parents would see me compete in any sport. Now the pressure was really on!

Governor Meyner looked much younger than I had expected. As soon as he arrived, he was surrounded by reporters, while I was ignored at the other end of the court. Finally, he broke away and came to the net to shake hands, and we wished one another luck. I did not mean it, and I am sure he did not either. There were no bleachers at the court so, as we warmed up, people who drifted in stood outside the fence. With each arrival, my nervousness ticked up another notch. Soon they were three or four deep surrounding the court, and my knees were shaking.

The Governor won the racket spin and served first. His first service was a lollypop, compared to the rockets I was accustomed to from high school opponents. So, what did I do with it? I returned it into the net. I lost the next three points and then proceeded to double-fault twice and to lose my serve, as well. Down love-two and embarrassed, I looked for my parents in the crowd. Papa gave me a thumbs-up and Mother smiled. I resolved to turn things around. I crossed myself, as I had become accustomed to doing when shooting free throws.

Whether it was heavenly interference or simply getting my act together, I do not know. I do know that I started exploiting Meyner's anemic serve and weak backhand, and I ran off ten straight games to win the match, 6-2, 6-3. At the end, he was gracious and wished me luck in the upcoming rounds. Most important to me, I had made my parents proud.

"Isn't it amazing?" said Papa on the ride home. "A refugee kid beating the governor of New Jersey! We're real Americans!"

Unbeknownst to me, this would be one of only two glorious events of my tennis "career." The first had taken place back in Prague when, on a Saturday morning, I had the privilege of shagging balls for a future Wimbledon champion. I happened to be at the Lawn Tennis Club when Jaroslav Drobný needed a ball boy to assist him while he practiced serving. I jumped at the opportunity and thus became a hero to my friends for having worked for Czechoslovakia's top athlete—not only a tennis star, but also a member of the national hockey team.

Following my victory over Governor Meyner, my competitive tennis went downhill. In college, I was only good enough to play second doubles on the freshman team and failed to make the varsity. Following graduation, I would decide to try the Southern California amateur circuit. That effort lasted all of thirty minutes. That is how long it took a guy who had played number one singles at Valparaiso University to dispatch me, 6-0, 6-0. After that, it would be strictly recreational tennis for me—until rotator cuff issues would force me to give up the game altogether.

Finally, there was baseball. In Morristown, I played for Twirlers A.C., which sponsored a team that played its home games at Ledgewood Field. At the same time, I played for an American Legion team in nearby Rockaway. I was a first baseman for both teams, batted over .300 in each of my seasons with Rockaway and one year finished with a .414 average with Twirlers, earning the team's Most Valuable Player trophy.

"I'm going to be the first player in history to earn a

hundred thousand dollars a year," I told my unbelieving mother. "I'll buy you and Papa the biggest house in town."

Having placed my MVP trophy in the center of a shrine to Larry Doby in a corner of my room, I imagined myself playing alongside my hero in the major leagues. Ego inflated, I accompanied my Rockaway teammate, pitcher Bob Sanders, to a Philadelphia Athletics (today, Oakland A's) try-out camp. There, my dream of instant glory received a setback when Bob was signed to a contract and I was sent home.

"You're a very good hitter," one of the coaches told me. "But you're a singles hitter, and we expect first basemen to hit for power. That's something you don't have right now. Work on strengthening your body and come back next year."

I worked on it, and my long-ball hitting improved. But I had seen enough talented baseball players at the try-out camp to realize that I had too far to go. My ticket to glory and riches was going to be basketball. I would walk on at Oklahoma State and become a star. Following graduation, NBA teams would throw money at me, and I would buy my parents that big house.

Oh, the dreams of an immigrant!

Occasionally, someone would find out that I was a refugee from Czechoslovakia. A teacher or a fellow student would ask me what life had been like during the war. I gave my standard response:

"After the Nazis came, my father escaped and joined the British army. Because they knew he was fighting against them, the Germans put my mother in a slave labor camp, and I was hidden out on a farm."

The conversation would end there. My tone was intended to discourage further probing. I feared that digging deeper would jeopardize my chances of being accepted into the American mainstream. A child of war becomes an adult prematurely. Deprivation, fear, and a constant fight to survive force a kid to mature long before he or she would under normal circumstances. I was such a kid, one who—from the age of four until a few months after my ninth birthday—skipped childhood. Now, I tried to be like my American friends who, unlike the people of post-war Europe, were full of optimism, energy, and humor. I began to realize that I would need these friends, as well as my small family, to help me overcome obstacles—current ones, as well as those yet unforeseen.

Perhaps because I was surprised by Americans' lack of knowledge about the war, I was determined to learn as much about it as I could. The ladies at the Morristown public library smiled when I walked out with five or six books every two weeks, most of them memoirs and novels of the war, particularly about the Holocaust. Reading them under the dim light of my bedside lamp, I became a character in each book—most often a concentration camp prisoner. Frequently, I awoke in a cold sweat, facing death at the hands of a German. Daylight brought a return to my life of a make-believe typical American high school kid, one who did not share his nightmare experiences with anyone.

CHAPTER SIX

BEWITCHED

In my first two years of high school, sports occupied so much of my time that I did not have time for something as mundane as dating girls. Then, late in the summer between my sophomore and junior years, fortune turned the tables on me. My friend Eddie Tarrant was invited by our classmates, Pete Hartdegen and Robert Gray, for a swim at Mount Kemble Lake, a small body of water surrounded by a private, upscale community located between Morristown and Bernardsville, New Jersey. Eddie asked me to come along.

When I climbed out of Eddie's sister's Plymouth in the small parking lot above the beach, I was dazzled by the bucolic scene. The water was calm, its glasslike surface disturbed only by the wake of a canoe and the splashing of a few children. The opposite shore was dotted with small sailboats tied to docks and with kayaks and canoes resting upside down and perfectly perpendicular to the water's edge. Atop steep, wooded banks stood beautiful homes with terraces providing their residents with magnificent views of the body of water known simply as "The Lake." It was a far cry from my middle-class neighborhood, with its modest homes on small lots, with views of automobile traffic on busy Mill Road.

Directly below us was a grassy bank that led down to a small sandy beach and a wooden dock with a diving board. I recognized several kids I had seen in school sitting on towels, some engaged in conversations, others reading and some simply working on their tans. In addition to Pete and Robert, I spotted brothers Art and Chuck Jenkins, Peggy Graessle, Carolyn Eible, Deirdre Dunn, Bobby and Midge Gray.

On that fateful day, I spotted a beautiful, tall, shapely, dark-haired girl wearing a blue one-piece bathing suit with white trim. She was sitting alone, applying baby oil to her tanned arms and legs. The previous week, I had seen a movie called *Million Dollar Mermaid*, in which the gorgeous swimmer/actress, Esther Williams, portrayed a swimming and diving star.

Wow! I thought as I stared at the girl sitting on the towel. *She's Esther Williams!* I fought to overcome my shyness and approached.

"Hi, my name is Charlie Heller," I said. "I've seen you in high school."

"Yes, hi, I've seen you too. My name is Sue Holsten."

"What are you reading?" I asked, using the book laying on her towel as an excuse to continue the conversation. I do not remember the answer. I recall only that I was smitten on the spot. I discovered that her full name was Susan Elizabeth Holsten. She was going into her sophomore year at Morristown High and lived within a five-minute walk of the beach with her parents, Edward and Viola.

I was taken in by her shy smile, its perfection disrupted only by a slightly crooked front tooth. Most of the girls I had met in high school were gregarious and talkative—in the jargon of the period, "cheerleader-types." They did not interest me. Sue, on the other hand, seemed quiet, introspective, and reserved. I was convinced that she was "my type." I could not stop thinking about her after Eddie and I left The Lake that day.

However, I was too busy with sports and too shy to ask her for a date. Until then, I had had only one date in my entire life: in eighth grade, I had taken one of my classmates, a girl named Marcia Silk, to a movie on a Saturday afternoon. With Sue, it took me nearly a year to overcome my timidity and finally to ask her to go out with me. She accepted.

Despite the fact that they lived in an upscale community, the Holstens were as poor as we were, and Sue had to work in order to have a little spending money. Her jobs consisted of babysitting for families at The Lake and nearby Jockey Hollow, where George Washington's troops had once wintered, now an enclave of expensive homes. I was impressed by the fact that this pretty girl was a fine athlete. She played baseball with the neighborhood boys, tennis on the local clay court, basketball at school, enjoyed target-shooting, skated on The Lake in the winter, and was one of the strongest swimmers there in the summer. Like me, she was a sports fan. On a subsequent date, she reached into her handbag, pulled out her wallet, and showed me a photo she carried of her favorite baseball player: Yogi Berra.

One of our earliest dates was on Sadie Hawkins Day—an annual pseudo-holiday with its origins in Al Capp's Li'l Abner comic strip. Observed on the Saturday that followed November 6, it was a day of gender role-reversal: a girl inviting a boy out on a date, typically a dance. Sue invited me to the Sadie Hawkins dance at the Mount Kemble Lake clubhouse. She informed me that she would dress as a Morristown High football player, and I would come as a cheerleader. I had no problem with dressing like a girl, wearing a wig, and even putting rouge on my cheeks and lipstick on my lips. However, I was frightened by the fact that Sue would discover something about me that, until then, had been my secret. I did not know how to dance. In fact, as much as I loved to listen to music, I hated dancing. I considered it a stupid waste of time.

When we arrived at the clubhouse on the dreaded evening, I had a pronounced limp.

"I sprained my ankle in basketball practice," I lied, hoping to be excused from dancing.

"That's okay," said Sue. "We'll just dance the slow ones."

It was useless to argue, so I agreed. Then I had a brilliant idea.

"Hey, you're the big football player and I'm the cheer-leader," I said when we got out on the floor. "You lead."

It seemed to work. Wherever Sue's feet moved, mine followed. We had a good time, and I even learned to do the Bunny Hop, a line dance during which I forgot about my faux sprained ankle and kicked up a storm.

A few dates later, Sue and I were "going steady," a 1950s term for a commitment not to date anyone else. For reasons that escape me now, I began calling her "Sammy," an affectionate name that stuck. She agreed to be my girlfriend despite the fact that I finally confessed as to my inability to dance.

Because of Sammy's frequent babysitting gigs, we did not have many opportunities to go to the movies or to attend parties. But we had something better. She would inform me where and what time she would be babysitting. I would wait a half hour after the parents left home before joining her inside. After she put the kids to bed, we talked for a while, but then we began to "make out," as kids of that era referred to the act of kissing and beyond. I liked nothing better than "helping" with babysitting. Sue was paid in cash; I was compensated with something better.

From the time I began visiting the Holsten home, I found immediate rapport with Sue's father Ed, a tall, handsome gentleman with black hair and dark mustache. He was a self-made man with minimal education, but with skills I envied. As a career bus garage supervisor for Public Service of New Jersey, he knew everything about cars. Eventually, when I would drive my own cars and they needed a tune-up, a new fuel pump, a valve job, or a U-joint replacement, we did it in Mr. Holsten's large garage, with him not only supervising, but performing most of the work. He was an expert gardener, too, and spent endless hours in his greenhouse, working with his plants while listening to his beloved New York Yankees' games on the radio. He was handy with all types of tools and could repair anything, from neighbors' lawnmowers to broken plumbing. Sue was proud of him because he worked two additional jobs—as a part-time police officer and as a clubhouse bartender—in order to be able to afford to live in their ritzy community.

Ed was born on a farm near Dayton, New Jersey, in 1904, the middle child of nine kids born to his father, Charles Herman Holsten, a German immigrant known as "Pop." Ed's mother, Minnie, was Pop's third wife, and the three oldest boys—Harry, Herman, and William—were Ed's half-brothers. Pop and Minnie had five boys—Charles, Ed, John, Fred, and Irving—before finally giving birth to a girl, Adeline, in 1920.

My relationship with Sue's mother, Viola, took a little longer to develop. In part, this was because I had much more in common with her father—interest in baseball and cars. But there was another reason. When we decided to go steady, I knew from hints Sue dropped from time to time that her mother had a problem with my religion and worried that her daughter might someday marry outside her faith. An old-fashioned, church-going Methodist, Vi Holsten came from a generation of Protestants who considered Catholics ritualistic heathens.

Had Vi known the whole truth about my complex religious history—one that I did not comprehend fully at the time—she may have thrown me out the door before my first date with her only child.

Born Viola Ruth Quick in Blairstown, New Jersey, in 1905, Sue's mother was the youngest child of John Quick and Sarah Elizabeth Ruth. Her sisters were Mamie and Sadie. After graduating from high school, Vi moved to Newark, where she went to work for Prudential Insurance. She and Ed met in 1928 and were married a year later. Living frugally through the Great Depression, they saved enough money to buy a cottage they called their "Little House" at Mount Kemble Lake in 1932. When Sue was born, their home consisted of a single bedroom, one bath, a small kitchen, and a combination living room/dining room.

"When I was seven years old," Sue told me, "we moved to a bigger house just down the street. For the first time, I was able to have my own room!" This was the home in which I would spend many hours while courting her and trying to win over her parents. The house was constructed of logs, stained dark brown both outside and in. Consequently, the rooms were quite dark, and the entire house had a unique aroma: that of freshly-cut wood mixed with the smell of paint pigment. I loved the smell and, when Sue and I were apart and I would think about her, it would penetrate my nostrils, as if by magic.

I discovered that Sue was born on October 25, 1936—exactly, to the day, nine months after I came into the world. It was quite a coincidence that our birth dates, when written numerically—1-25-1936 and 10-25-1936—differed only by a zero. *That must be a sign of some sort*, I thought. In future years, I would joke to friends that Sue was conceived on the day I was born.

Although an only child like me, Sue had a huge extended family, particularly on her paternal side. When I joined their Fourth of July picnics, Holstens easily made up two full softball teams, with plenty of adults and children left over as pinch-hitters and spectators. Having lost all relatives except my parents in the Holocaust, I was an oddity with no grandparents, uncles, aunts or cousins. I was somewhat befuddled and a bit intimidated as a fringe player in this huge family.

As the end of my senior year in high school approached, it was time for Sue and me to make a decision of great consequence. What would be our relationship while I was fifteen hundred miles away in Oklahoma and she remained in Morristown for her senior year of high school? Both of us professed our love for one another and considered it a given that we would get married someday. However, we disagreed on the form of our near-term status.

"I think both of us should date others, and then we'll be together again whenever you come for Christmas and summer vacations," Sue would say.

"No, we're going steady, and we should keep it that way," I would counter. "It'll only be a few months between my visits home, and we'll both have plenty of things to keep us busy in the meantime—school, sports, and other stuff. We won't need to date anybody."

After perhaps a hundred conversations along the same lines throughout the spring of 1954, with neither of us backing down, I declared a stand-off.

"Okay, go ahead and date others," I declared. "But I won't be dating anybody in college. As far as I'm concerned, we'll still be going steady."

I hoped that my pledge would shame Sue into making the same commitment. Instead, she simply answered: OK.

My four years at Morristown High School were over. I had achieved decent grades, learned a great deal, made many friends and only a few enemies, fell in love, and—very important to me—having attained this small degree of success and thus gaining others' respect, I "felt American." When I graduated in June 1954, the inscription next to my photo in the yearbook read:

Here is a popular senior who comes to us from Morris Township. "Chuck" has been at MHS for four years, and his ambition is to become an engineer at Oklahoma A&M. All sports rate high on the list with this athlete, and one of his few dislikes is the music of Guy Lombardo.

Surely, I must have disliked something other than the mellow music of Mr. Lombardo, and I wished they had not called me Chuck, but it did not matter. Most significant to me at the time was the fact that I was considered simply AN ATHLETE FROM MORRIS TOWNSHIP! No mention of my being a refugee and an immigrant, despite the fact that I was not yet a US citizen. (Immigration laws required a five-year waiting period, and I had a few more months to wait.) My classmates already accepted me as one of them.

Life was good. I had my own car, a 1940 Hudson coupe I purchased from my friend Pete Sheldrick for seventy-five dollars. I had a summer job waiting for me as a junior draftsman at Bell Telephone Laboratories, thanks to our family friend and neighbor, Jack Geils. Although she wanted to date others while I would be away at college, Sue was in love with me, and I was in love with her. And I had not only been accepted to Oklahoma State University, but one of the most revered coaches in America, Mr. Henry Iba, promised to give me the opportunity to walk on to the basketball team and attempt to earn a scholarship. So far at least, I was managing to swim in America.

CHAPTER SEVEN

COWBOY FROM PRAGUE

The week before Labor Day 1954, my parents drove me to New York's Penn Station, where I boarded a train bound for Chicago. When the train began to roll out of the station and I saw Mother and Papa waving to me from the platform, it suddenly dawned on me that this was the beginning of a new chapter in my life. Except for holiday vacations, 47 Mill Road would never be my home again. I was eighteen years old, I was alone, and I was scared. I thought about Sue. She would be entering her senior year of high school in Morristown, New Jersey, and I would be in Stillwater, Oklahoma, fifteen hundred miles away. I was madly in love with her, and she said she loved me. Still, I wondered if our relationship would survive the separation.

As the train headed west, I began to wonder if I should have accepted that basketball scholarship offer from Rutgers. I would have been in New Brunswick, less than an hour from my parents and Sue. Now it was too late. Once again, my father's instructions to overcome all difficulties echoed in my head.

In Chicago, I changed to a southbound train headed for Oklahoma's second largest city, Tulsa. As the train sped through miles and miles of farm country of Illinois, Indiana, and Missouri, I realized, for the first time, how vast my adopted nation is. In Czechoslovakia, a less than a day's ride on a train had taken us from Prague to the Slovak capital, Bratislava. Now, on my second day since leaving New York, I had not even reached what I had been told is the east-west dividing line of the United States, the Mississippi River.

When I arrived in Tulsa, I was met by our family's friends, Professor Jan and Hana Tuma. As we rolled along toward Stillwater in their silver Packard, we were surrounded by an infinite nothingness. Thousands of acres of flat land covered with scrub brush and scorched grass were only occasionally interrupted by a boulder, a tree, a fence, a house, a barn, and the ever-present tower with a whirling propeller providing electrical power to a water pump. Except for the oil wells that resembled giant dogs nodding their heads and popping up in the most unlikely places, the Oklahoma countryside reminded me of the Indian territory about which I had read in Karl May westerns as a hidden child in World War II Europe. At any moment, I expected a band of Indians to appear over the horizon, chased by a cavalry led by a dashing young officer with flowing blond hair and a sword at his side.

I had given up the opportunity for a free education elsewhere by turning down three basketball scholarships and opting to take my chances as a "walk-on" at Oklahoma State. This meant that, without a scholarship, I could not afford to live on campus. I would move in with the Tumas.

My decision to come to OSU had been driven by more than basketball. As a high school senior, following my father's orders to become an engineer, I had determined that the most interesting engineering discipline would be designing buildings and bridges. From Professor Tuma, I learned that OSU's School of Civil Engineering was on the rise as one of the nation's best in his personal specialty—the analysis and design of structures. Moreover, I had learned in high school that there was a major difference between most universities in the East and those in the Mid- and Southwest. The former—particularly those in the Ivy League—were similar to institutions of higher learning in Europe. They were elitist, catering primarily to students from well-to-do families. Those in the center of the country, by contrast, were built on a democratic principle, one I considered emblematic of America: that education should be affordable and attainable for anyone who was intelligent and hard-working. With semester tuition of $66 and an out-of-state fee of $120, Oklahoma State University certainly was one of these low-cost, low-barrier-to-entry institutions.

Upon arriving in Stillwater, I deposited my two small suitcases in a small room in the Tumas' apartment near campus. Their first permanent home in America—a ranch house north of the campus—was still under construction, and Professor Tuma proudly showed me the plans he had drawn for it.

Jan Tuma had completed the equivalent of a Master's degree in structural mechanics in Prague, prior to going into exile with Hana a few weeks after my own family's escape. The Tumas' sponsor in America had been Edith Hamilton, a writer of mythology. Born in Germany, Miss Hamilton came to the United States at a young age and became world-famous for her books, *The Greek Way* and *The Roman Way*. My parents and I visited the Tumas often in Miss Hamilton's guest house on the banks of the Connecticut River and met the great lady. While living there, Jan worked as a structural engineer, but his ultimate goal was to teach and do research at an American university. Since US academia gave him credit for his Czech education only as the equivalent of a bachelor's degree, he needed to attain a graduate degree in order to secure a teaching position.

Through a Czech-American organization, he was given a scholarship to Oklahoma State, where he completed his Master's degree and several requirements toward a doctorate in one year. Vernon Parcher, then the head of the School of Civil Engineering, would write of Tuma a few years later: "His brilliant and creative work as a Master's candidate in structures led to his appointment to the rank of associate professor in 1952. Within two years, he was a full professor." Tuma was climbing up the academic ladder and, during my time there, would become head of the school and build its structures program into one of the top five in the nation, alongside MIT, Columbia, Illinois, and California-Berkeley.

After unpacking that first day, I walked to the campus. The centerpiece was the Library, which stood at the head of a large, grassy, flower-filled mall, crisscrossed by sidewalks leading in various directions. At the foot of the mall, bordering College Avenue, was Theta Pond, the campus' romantic spot surrounded by benches scattered among huge willows. Seeing couples on the benches, holding hands, made my heart ache. I held back tears when I thought of Sue, the distance separating us, and the fact that I would not see her for more than three months.

The campus buildings were constructed of red brick, in the Georgian architecture style. Next to the Library was the Engineering Building, slightly south of it was the Classroom Building, and even farther south was the Student Union, second only to the Library in size. In addition to Gallagher Hall (today, Gallagher-Iba Arena) and dorms, I would spend the majority of my five-and-a-half years at OSU inside these buildings. "The Union" was hailed as the finest and most modern in the nation, and it was the center of student life at the University.

After my self-guided tour of the campus, I was due to attend a freshman "smoker," a social event held on the terrace behind the Union, with the stated purpose of letting new students get to know one another. It was anything but that for me. Most of my classmates came from Oklahoma high schools and many knew one another. They gathered in small clusters, drinking Cokes, smoking, laughing, and gossiping. They had no interest in including a scared kid from Prague by way of New Jersey. I felt very much alone as I trudged back to the Tumas' apartment.

But, there was little time for reflection or feeling sorry for myself. Classes started the next day. For me, it began with Engineering Orientation, where a couple hundred of us crowded into a stuffy auditorium. The professor began his lecture with a prediction:

"Look at the person on your right; look at the person on your left. Only one of you will graduate."

I do not remember who was on my left, but the guy who sat to the right of me was Johnny Wright, a football player. We introduced ourselves, and I was happy to discover that there was at least one other jock studying engineering. We went our separate ways after that, but I would find out years later that Johnny and I had defied the professor's odds. Both of us would graduate, and—by amazing coincidence—Johnny and his family would live less than a quarter mile from us in Severna Park, Maryland, in the late 1960s.

Oklahoma State is a land-grant school, and, by federal law in those days, all male students at such colleges were required to take two years of ROTC (Reserve Officers Training Corps). At OSU, we had both Army and Air Force ROTC. I chose Army, mainly because of my father's illustrious career in the Czechoslovak Brigade of the British army during World War II. On the second day of classes, we were issued pre-war uniforms, and I went to my first class. We were seated in alphabetical order, and I was assigned a seat next to a tall, skinny, bespectacled guy named Don Gafford. We spoke to each other in class, never suspecting that we would become best friends in the future.

During the first weeks of classes, I was busy making the transition to college student and working hard at converting myself from a Yankee to a "good guy" (in Oklahoma, the two were not synonymous, and my New Jersey accent gave me away, just as my Czech accent had done five years earlier). At the same time, I was undergoing my second culture shock in five years.

Having survived the transition from European customs to those of the eastern United States, I was now faced with learning those of the Great Southwest. On the positive side, I found Oklahomans considerably more outgoing and friendly than folks back east. But I was shocked and saddened to find among these friendly people an atmosphere of ugly racial prejudice—against Negroes (as African Americans were called in polite circles) and against American Indians. I wondered if they held the same bias toward immigrants and remained silent about my history. I feared that prevailing biases would cause me great difficulties going forward.

On a less serious, but not trivial, note: I missed pizza. I found it amazing that Oklahomans had never even heard of this Italian delicacy, which I had discovered and grown to love in New Jersey. It would take four years of craving before the first pizza parlor would open in Stillwater. In the meantime, I had to learn to eat such novel foods as chicken-fried steak and fried okra.

My first personal experience with racial prejudice in Oklahoma came on the first day of basketball practice. A major reason for my coming to OSU was a desire to play for one of the most famous coaches in the nation, Mr. Henry P. Iba. In those days, freshmen were not permitted to play varsity sports, so my hope of gaining a scholarship rested on my ability to make the freshman team, coached by Sam Aubrey.

Surrounded by great athletes, I was so frightened that my

knees practically buckled when I stepped on the hallowed floor of one of the most famous arenas in the country.

Oh, man! Why didn't I go to Rutgers? I thought at that moment. But, the feeling did not last long. The coaches put us to work.

We ran the steps in the stands and went through passing drills. We had been told that the highlight—some players described it as the lowlight—of every practice session, freshman and varsity, was a two-on-two, full-court drill. Two players would start with the ball at one end of the floor and the defensive pair would pick them up at mid-court. Of course, the objectives were for the offensive guys to score and for the defensive players to stop them from scoring. We were informed that this was the most critical daily drill in terms of being evaluated by the coaching staff. Then came the bombshell: a rumor spread that Mr. Iba himself would be in the arena to watch the two-on-two. The word was that this was tradition. Each year, he attended the first freshman team practice to observe the newly arrived talent.

My dream, or nightmare, would soon come true. The man I had worshipped for so long, yet had never met or even seen in person, would see me play! Soon he arrived. The tall, stately, imposing man walked in alone and sat down about ten rows up from the floor, at center court; the coaching staff took this as a signal to begin the two-on-two drills. I was paired with a scholarship player named Chuck.

"You bring it up. Pass it to me after you cross center court. I'll dribble to the left of the key. That'll be your signal to take off down the right side. I'll hit you with a pass, and you'll lay it in," said Chuck.

Yeah, right. Nothing to it, I thought to myself, wondering if my jangled nerves would allow me to pull it off.

I hit him with a chest pass. He dribbled to the left side of the foul lane, and I took off down the right side toward the basket. But Chuck's man covered him closely, and he had trouble getting off his pass in time. Finally, he threw the ball to me and took off for the basket in order to be there for a rebound in case I missed. The ball hit my hands perfectly, chest-high, and hard. But it came too late. I was in the air and too far under the basket to shoot. Using my New Jersey, playground-learned reflex and skill, I pulled the ball away from my defensive man, and whipped it around my body, a perfect behind-the-back pass to Chuck, who laid it in for a score.

I raised my arms in triumph, thinking I had just shown everyone in the building, and especially Mr. Iba, that I was a rising star and future OSU Cowboy. As I trotted away feeling on top of the world, that world came crashing down around me.

The silence of the arena was broken by a deep, guttural groan that seemed to come from the sky, but really came from the man sitting in Row 10—

"Stop playing like a goddamn nigger!"

For a few moments, there was dead silence. Then things returned to normal—for the other players. I had heard the n-word many times since coming to America, usually uttered by white kids telling racist jokes. Perhaps because I had experienced bigotry and racism under the Nazis, I was sensitive to such language. I found it disgusting and offensive. Now I heard the word called out in public, aimed at me, and by a man whom I had worshipped from afar. They say that you should never meet your heroes; maybe this was proof. My initial reaction was to walk out of the arena, pack my belongings, and head east and as far away from racist Oklahoma as I could.

In New Jersey, racial discrimination had been covert. Negroes lived in separate communities, often under horrid conditions. When I had visited one of my few Black friends in Morristown's ghetto—The Hollow—I was horrified by the overcrowding, noise, and lack of sanitation.

I live in a beautiful little house on a quiet street, I thought at the time. *I'm an immigrant. These people were born here. What did they do to deserve this? How can they ever escape from it?*

In Oklahoma, racism was considered normal. I nearly choked the first time I saw rest rooms marked "white" and "colored" inside the State Capitol. It took me back to a day in the early days of the war when Mother pointed out a bench in a Prague park with a sign, "Jews forbidden." I was further astonished when I learned what Americans had done to Indians, several of whom would become my friends at Oklahoma State University.

How could they have sent native people of 560 different nations to reservations? Did Americans, and not the Nazis, invent concentration camps?

Now, stunned by Mr. Iba's racist rebuke, I was dealing with my own issues. I managed to make it through that first practice with my mind processing a thousand scenarios. When I returned to the Tumas' apartment, I recalled my father's words while lying on my bed:

Put your head down, and go do it! And, no matter what you do, don't ever give up!

How disappointed my parents would be if I quit! It was simply out of the question. I had to succeed—not just at basketball, but at acquiring an education and a degree. And it would have to be at Oklahoma State University. Anything else would constitute breaking my parents' trust.

On the academic front, I was doing reasonably well, although I was not setting any records. At the beginning, I experienced some difficulties in the classroom because of terrible study habits. I had coasted through high school without studying a great deal. Wartime secret private tutoring followed by two-and-a-half years of formal education in Czechoslovakia, home schooling in refugee camps, and later math mentoring via correspondence by Professor Tuma, surprisingly put me so far ahead of my American schoolmates in grades eight through twelve that I seldom cracked a book after school and sports practice. But now I was in college, taking my first engineering and advanced mathematics courses, and the days of coasting and faking it were over. Having to complete long assignments and pulling all-nighters in preparation for tests was a new and challenging experience for me at Oklahoma State.

By December of my freshman year, I received my partial basketball scholarship and moved into the "jock dorm," which was not a separate dorm at all, but a wing of Bennett Hall, a huge men's dormitory located across the street from the fieldhouse and football stadium. There, I met a burly blond senior named Jim Fisher, a New Jersey native who played tackle on the football team. In those days, unlike today, college students generally received two weeks' vacation over the Christmas holidays, came back to school in time to prepare for final exams, took the exams, and then got another week off before the start of the spring semester. OSU was no exception. I caught a ride home for Christmas with Fisher and a couple of his friends.

While I was happy to be with my parents and to spend every evening with Sue, the highlight of this vacation occurred in a courthouse in Newark, New Jersey. There, on December 20, 1954, I was sworn in as a citizen of the United States of America, but not before I received a scare. After a short wait, I was called into a small office, where a very serious, dour little man in a dark uniform sat behind a desk.

"I'm going to ask you a few questions," he said. "You must answer all of them correctly; otherwise, you won't get your citizenship."

Piece of cake, I thought. *Hell, I'm a college student who has taken history and civics classes, and I read newspapers. There's nothing this guy can throw at me that I won't know.*

"What is the name of the President of the United States?"

he asked, and I wanted to say, *You must be kidding!* Instead, I replied:

"Dwight D. Eisenhower."

"Correct. Who is the Secretary of State?"

"John Foster Dulles."

And so it went, and I thought I was home free.

"One last question," he said finally. "What kind of a government do we have in the United States of America?"

"A democracy," I replied confidently.

"Wrong!" he said sternly. "Try again."

Oh my God, I thought. *I just flunked the test. My parents got their citizenship a few months ago, and I'm going to be stateless. What the hell is the right answer?*

"Should I have said 'a republic'?" I asked after a long delay.

"Yes, you should. OK, you passed."

I was too shocked to celebrate until I arrived back in Morris Plains, and my parents opened a bottle of champagne for the occasion. A few days later, I returned to Stillwater, from where I had departed a Czech and now returned an American.

When I first arrived at OSU, I had no car. Soon, I discovered that being in the middle of the prairie without personal transportation was equivalent to imprisonment. During the fall semester, I had walked everywhere and, on the rare occasion that I got to visit one of the two big cities—Tulsa or Oklahoma City—I depended on schoolmates or the Tumas to let me tag along.

The biggest problem arose when the semester ended in mid-January. We had a week off from classes, and, since we had no games scheduled, Coach Aubrey gave the team a week off from practice. Although I had been gone from home only three weeks, I was homesick and lovesick, determined to go to back New Jersey.

On the way back to Stillwater from Christmas break, Jim Fisher had informed us that he and his girlfriend had gotten engaged over the holidays and that they would be getting married during the semester break. We laughed and joked about our suspicion that this must be a shotgun wedding due to the apparent urgency. I saw it as an opportunity to see Sue again.

Having decided that a visit with her was worth a three-thousand-mile round trip, with nearly four days on the road and only three days at home, I asked Jim if I could ride with him when he returned for his wedding. He agreed, and we traveled east again together. About thirty hours into our trip to New Jersey, I asked Jim when he would like me to be ready for the ride back to Stillwater.

"What? You're kidding!" he laughed. "You really think you're going to tag along on our honeymoon?"

Oh, my God! I thought. *Why the hell didn't he tell me this before we left?*

"Oh, yeah, sure. I wasn't thinking," was all I could say.

For the moment, I was dumbfounded. I did not have enough money to take a bus or a train, much less to fly, nor did I know anyone else with whom I could catch a ride. I was not about to ask my parents for money, so I would have to hitchhike back. While I had thumbed rides nearly every day in high school, I had never tried hitchhiking fifteen hundred miles. After contemplating the task in front of me for a few minutes, I came to the conclusion that it would not be all that bad, and that it would be a small price to pay for a few days with my girlfriend. However, I knew that my parents would be concerned about my safety, so I did not tell them.

After spending three wonderful days with Sue, meeting her each day after high school let out and spending evenings at her house, it was time to return to Stillwater. Early one morning, I had a friend pick me up. I said goodbye to my parents who were under the impression that I was going to rendezvous with Fisher, and we drove to the New Jersey Turnpike. There, I stuck out my thumb and caught a ride to the Pennsylvania Turnpike, where a truck driver took me west toward Pittsburgh. Several cars and many hours later, I was standing near a Greyhound station south of St. Louis, trying to catch a ride for the final leg of my trip. It was midnight, and it was freezing. When I left OSU, the weather had been unseasonably warm, and I had ridden with Fisher in a pair of khaki pants, a sweatshirt and a light windbreaker. Wanting to travel light for such a short trip, I had left my winter clothes in the dorm room closet. Now, as I stood there in the cold, with light snow falling, my face, hands, and feet freezing, I yearned for a warm coat, a hat, and long underwear.

Very few cars passed through at that time of night, and those that did were not stopping to pick up a hitchhiker. Every few minutes, I saw a pair of headlights come up over the rise and reflect from the gently falling snowflakes. I stuck out my arm and, with thumb extended, hoped and prayed that the car would slow down and eventually stop for me. No such luck. Whenever the biting cold became unbearable, I went inside the station restaurant to warm up and to get a cup of coffee. Around four o'clock in the morning, I walked into the small terminal and checked the bus schedule. A Greyhound bus for Tulsa would be leaving in about half an hour. The clerk informed me that the fare would be eighteen dollars. I had twenty bucks in my pocket, and so, in desperation, I bought a ticket.

Once on the bus, I made a major decision. In the future, I would no longer be dependent on friends, buses, trains or the kindness of strangers for my transportation. I would buy a car. But it was one thing to decide to buy a car and another to pay for one. Much to my surprise, my father agreed to lend me four hundred dollars toward the purchase.

A couple of weeks later, my friend Bob Graham drove me to Oklahoma City to make the rounds of used car lots. We came upon a wide boulevard lined with automobile dealers on both sides, as far as the eye could see. I had never seen anything like it in the East, and certainly not in Europe. Noting that I would have choices, I told Bob I would like to find a Studebaker dealer. My father's first car in America had been a 1949 Studebaker Champion, and I was partial to the brand. Besides, as a budding engineer, I admired the fact that Studebaker cars were known for their advanced technological features, and I liked their unique appearance. Studebakers were nearly totally symmetrical: their fronts and rears were almost identical.

We found a dealership a few blocks down the street, made our way to the used car lot, and—lo and behold—there it was! A powder-blue 1949 Studebaker Champion in all its glory, with a huge number, "$350," written on its windshield in red.

"Bob, I think I've died and gone to heaven," I said. "If this car runs, I'm buying it. No need to look any further."

The salesman came out and let me drive around the block. The six-year-old automobile performed perfectly. I looked under the hood in order to appear knowledgeable.

"I'll take it," I told the startled salesman, who no doubt expected me to negotiate the price or at least look at other vehicles on the lot. He filled out the papers and attached an Oklahoma license plate, I handed over the cash, and I was on my way back to Stillwater feeling liberated and exhilarated. Despite the fact that the Studebaker's slipping clutch would cause me many a problem and embarrassment in the future, life was good. Eventually, I would discover that the clutch did not slip in reverse gear. Since the car was essentially symmetrical in its profile—it looked the same going forward or backward—I would climb many a hill with the headlights pointing in the wrong direction. But I could live with that. The Studey gave me independence!

Like most college freshmen, I had to learn to manage my time. With classes, studying, and basketball, I had no social life. In February, the basketball season ended. I had put in many hours of work on the practice court, and, in retrospect, the season had been a mixed experience. I was unhappy about the fact that I had become a member of a group that called itself the "20-20-20 Squad." We joked that we got into games when we were either twenty points up, or twenty points down, with twenty seconds left in the game. While we laughed about our status, all of us had had much higher expectations for ourselves. But at the same time that I lamented being primarily a practice player, I was both shocked and elated when Coach Aubrey handed me a letter signed by Mr. Iba—God himself—stating that I had earned a half scholarship. Not only was this a huge ego boost, but it would practically guarantee that I could afford to graduate with an engineering degree. All I had to do was work my butt off, studying and staying on the team.

When I finished reading the letter, my first thoughts turned to Morristown High School. I thought back on old Mac, the coach who had played me out of position, where I had been unable to show my talent. But mostly, I thought of the football coach, Bill Flynn. I sent a copy of my scholarship letter to the *Morristown Daily Record*, with only one thing in mind.

I hope that son-of-a-bitch Flynn reads about the goddamn immigrant freak!

By spring, I had several friends with whom I hung out. I went out for tennis and made the freshman squad, playing on the second doubles team. The freshman coach resigned just before the start of the season, and a varsity tennis player took over the coaching duties. He was Myron Roderick, an All-American wrestler and three-time national wrestling champion, who would later become an Olympian and, eventually, OSU's athletic director.

Sue reiterated during my visit home that we should not be "tied down" and that both of us should date others, "except in the summer." I was unhappy, but after some time I decided to try dating. My friend Bob Graham had a cousin named Harriette Hayman, a freshman home economics major from

Oklahoma City. He introduced us, we dated a few times and had a fun time. Harriette was a very nice person, from a refined and, by my standards, wealthy family. However, I considered her more a friend than a lover.

Toward the end of the school year, she expressed the hope that we could enter into an exclusive relationship. I disappointed her by saying that I could not promise anything until I returned to New Jersey and gauged my standing with Sue. Without realizing what an ass I must have appeared to be, I told Harriette that I would not be able to give her my decision until I came back to school next September. Little did I know at that time that "next September" would become September of the following year, and that I would never see Harriette again.

The semester came to an end, and I felt good about myself. I had done reasonably well in the classroom, finishing with a 2.8 grade-point average, equivalent to a B-minus. Despite the fact that I had not achieved the playing time I had hoped for, I had earned a partial basketball scholarship. I gained many friends and became extremely fond of Oklahoma State University. I had been on my own for nearly a year and considered myself a young man—no longer a kid. Now I was excited about going home to spend the summer with my parents and with Sue.

CHAPTER EIGHT

DUMB AND DUMBER

In June 1955, I decided that my 1949 Studebaker would look sexier if I could change its color from light blue to black. Not one to be deterred by past failure—unsuccessfully having painted my 1940 Hudson with a brush—I elected to try again. After all, I had learned my lesson and was now a proven automobile artist.

When I finished, I stood back and admired my masterpiece. The car stood in the driveway, with the wet paint glistening in the sunshine. It was beautiful! I was proud of myself and anxious to show it off to my parents and Sue. I popped open a can of Ballentine beer and celebrated. Then I went inside and took a shower.

I came back outside to regard my work once again. Disaster! The paint had dried. Where it had been shiny only a half hour before, it was now dull and lackluster. The sun no longer reflected off it. Instead, its rays revealed hundreds of brush strokes and several rivulets that ran vertically from the windows to the bottoms of the doors. My Studey was downright ugly, and there was no way to undo the damage. I would have to live with it. Fortunately, not for long because Mother had seen and heard enough about my perils of driving backward up hills.

"I don't want you spending any more money on that ugly black thing," she declared. She talked Papa into lending me money to buy a better, safer car. Persuading my father was not easy, but she succeeded. Convincing me required no effort at all.

All summer, I had been eyeing a jewel in the used-car lot of a dealership in nearby Bernardsville. It was a two-door 1953 Studebaker Champion, red with a cream-colored top, white-wall tires, and faux leather upholstery. It showed less than 20,000 miles on the odometer and was in cherry condition. It was the most beautiful vehicle I had ever seen.

My parents accompanied me to the dealership on the day of the purchase. After we completed the necessary paperwork, the salesman removed the license plates from the car that had by now become known as the "Black Sheep" and attached them to the bumpers of my new love. Finally, I was ready to get behind the wheel and to take my first drive as the owner of this red-and-cream beauty. As I prepared to do so, Mother grabbed my arm and looked me in the eye.

"We want you to make us a promise," she laughed. "That you'll never, ever paint this car."

"I promise," I said with a smile, and I lived up to my pledge.

By now, my parents had settled into American middle-class life on Mill Road. Papa had received several promotions at McGregor Sportswear, where he had started as the lowest-level pattern-cutter. Mother, who had begun life in America as a cleaning lady and later "graduated" to a better job as a seamstress at Maidenform Bra, became a lab technician at the Warner-Lambert pharmaceutical firm. I marveled at my parents' ability to have come so far after starting from nothing only six years earlier.

Although they remained thrifty, they permitted themselves a single indulgence: they bought a boat. It was a fourteen-footer—a pretty runabout with a mahogany deck and Mother's name, "Ilona," inscribed on the transom. They surprised me by also purchasing a pair of water skis. Sue and I worked summer jobs—she as a counter person at Morey LaRue Laundry in Morristown and I as a junior draftsman at Bell Labs in Whippany. But we spent most weekends with my parents, boating and skiing on nearby Lake Hopatcong. And we began a summer tradition of vacationing with the boat at Lake George in upstate New York, always staying at a small, cozy resort called Alpine Village. The Heller family was now totally Americanized.

In New Jersey that summer, I saw Sue nearly every evening after work as well as on weekends. Our relationship was strong again, following the rocky year during which she had insisted that each of us date others while we were apart.

"So, how many dates did you have with Jack Holmes last year?" I asked one evening, knowing that she had gone out several times with her high school classmate and fellow band member while I was in Oklahoma. I really did not want to know but could not resist asking.

"Oh, three or four," Sue replied.

"Is he going to college?" I asked.

"Yes, he'll be going to Trenton State."

Oh, my God! I thought and felt the blood rush to my face. *They'll be on the same campus!*

The prospect of my girlfriend and my rival going to the same school occupied my thoughts nearly every waking moment for the remainder of summer. I fought to control my jealous streak but failed miserably.

As I prepared to leave for OSU in late August, I made the sudden—and ultimately incredibly stupid—decision not to return because I could not stand the thought of being fifteen hundred miles away while Sue might be dating this guy. Unbeknownst to my parents, I drove to New Brunswick, home of Rutgers University, and met with Coach Don White who, a year and half earlier, had tried to recruit me to play basketball at his school.

"You've got to be joking," said the coach when I asked him if his offer was still good. "Don't you know the NCAA rules? I can't waste a scholarship on a guy who will be ineligible for a year as a transfer student." With that, he dismissed me.

After a half hour of inner turmoil, I took my transcript to the registrar's office, where I enrolled as a regular student. Then came the hard part. It was time to tell my parents, who would not only have to approve my transfer, but also would have to pay for the majority of my tuition and room and board. This, after I had earned a partial free ride that included room and board as a basketball player at Oklahoma State.

"Absolutely not!" was my father's initial reaction.

I had a very close and loving relationship with my parents. They were shocked and listed all the reasons I should return to OSU: I had done well there during my freshman year, I had many friends, I could not abandon my teammates and coaches, and I could not disappoint our family friend and my mentor—Professor Jan Tuma.

I continued to persist into the following day, and even challenged Mother and Papa with "Don't you want me to be closer, so that we can see each other more often?" Reluctantly, my parents eventually gave in. But they were not ready for my next surprise.

"I'm going to change my major from engineering to journalism," I announced.

"No, you're not!" my father replied and banged the table with his fist. "Engineering is hard, and you're looking for an easy way to earn a degree. We will not permit it. You'd graduate and either have no job or you'd find a job that pays next to nothing."

"But, Father..."

"No buts. You're going to work hard and become an engineer. You have to think of the future. This conversation is over!"

There was no way I could convince my father that I loved to write and wanted to make writing, rather than engineering, my career. One does not argue with a traditional European father, so I gave up. However, there were other ways to deal with him. I would show him up. Until that moment, the hardships I had encountered in my young life—hiding from murdering Nazis, being forced to escape Communism, starving in refugee camps—had been inflicted on me by others. This time, I would "shoot myself in the foot" of my own volition. This time, *I* would be the hardship.

Because the semester was about to begin, there was no room for me in the dorms or in off-campus housing in New Brunswick. The first couple of weeks, I made the daily forty-five-minute commute by car. Then Anthony Lucia, a high-school classmate who was a member of Pi Kappa Alpha, invited me to pledge his fraternity and move into the PiKA house. I took this path of least resistance and became a pledge of a fraternity known on the Rutgers campus for partying and academic nonperformance (although Anthony himself was an excellent student).

In order to convince my parents to change their minds about allowing me to switch majors, I decided not to buy books that semester. Predictably, I flunked test after test. Because I registered late, some of the required courses in civil engineering were closed. I did find one course that had room for me—City and Regional Planning—expecting it to be another boring technology class. To my amazement, I found it fascinating and made an exception of it. I actually bought the textbook, read it, and did the homework. At the end of the semester, the course would stand out on my transcript: a "B" among a sea of "Ds" and "Fs."

Although I enjoyed being less than an hour up the road from Sue, and thus being able to see her at least once a week, I hated Rutgers from day one. It was not friendly, warm, and welcoming like OSU had been. From the beginning, I knew I had made a mistake. I realized that I was an Oklahoma State Cowboy, through and through. Moreover, Rutgers was a men's school. There was something depressing about seeing nothing but unshaven, unkempt, guys day in and day out in classes and on campus. The pretty girls of Stillwater were but a clear and enticing memory.

Like OSU, Rutgers was a land-grant school and, by law, required all male students to take at least two years of ROTC. At OSU, all engineering majors in Army ROTC automatically became members of the Society of American Military Engineers and were given a ribbon to wear on their uniforms. I had kept my ribbon. Rutgers had no SAME chapter, but I pinned the ribbon onto my chest as a conversation piece. One afternoon, a general came down from Fort Dix to inspect the troops. As squad leader, I stood in front of my guys at port arms when he and his contingent came to check us out.

"What's the ribbon for, Cadet?" the general asked me.

"African campaign, sir!" I shouted out without hesitation.

I could hear the bolts rattling in my squad members' M-1 rifles as they tried to contain their laughter. The general's face and ears turned beet red from anger.

"Dock this man!" he ordered the cadet commander as he walked away.

I was given sixty demerits, an all-time Rutgers record. A demerit was worth one point off the ROTC course grade, although each point could be worked off by cleaning rifles at the armory for thirty minutes. I put in one hour, brought up my grade by two points, and gave up. I was not about to waste my time wiping oil and dirt from M-1s. Bottom line: I flunked ROTC. It turned out that I was the second person in Rutgers' history to do so. That really hurt! It was difficult to fail something as easy as ROTC, but I had thought that at least I had been a pioneer. But who remembers the *second* person to fly across the Atlantic or the *second* person to scale Mount Everest? My "achievement," too, would be forgotten.

Sue's "military career" at Rutgers was considerably more successful than mine. In the spring, I nominated her for the title of Military Ball Queen. She was selected as one of six finalists from a field of nearly fifty beautiful young ladies and, as a member of the Queen's Court, reviewed the Rutgers Army and Air Force ROTC troops at the school's annual field day, riding in the back of an open Jeep. She was terribly nervous, but proud of her achievement. That evening, she did me the favor of allowing me—an ROTC screw-up—to escort her to the Military Ball.

When the fall term ended in January 1956, I had flunked all but two courses, so to say that the spring semester at Rutgers began with me behind the eight-ball would be a terrible understatement. Over the first couple of weeks, I came to the painful conclusion that I had not really shown up my parents and that they were not going to let me switch majors just because I had done poorly. The only thing I had managed to do was to dig a deep hole and jump into it. Now I would have to climb out or, otherwise, I might find myself working construction for the rest of my life. I moved out of the frat house, bought textbooks and hit them hard. Much to my parents' surprise, I completed the term with passing grades.

As a civil engineering major, I was required to attend summer surveying camp near the campus. I made an "A" in the course, the first such grade I earned since leaving Oklahoma State. With the summer session completed, we celebrated with a picnic in Johnson Park. I was pitching in a faculty vs. students softball game when a courier drove his Chevy close to the infield, and, after the third baseman pointed me out to him, he ran to the mound.

"Dean Easton wants to see you," he said.

"Now?" I asked.

"Yes, now!"

I walked off the field and hopped into the kid's car, wearing blue jeans, a sweatshirt, and baseball spikes. When we got to the engineering building, I walked down the hall in my socks, carrying my shoes and hat. I entered the Dean's office expecting to be feted with the "most improved student" award. Instead, the Dean of Engineering hit me with a thunderbolt.

"You just can't overcome your first-semester performance," Easton told me. "My academic review committee has given me no choice but to ask you to leave."

I walked out of his office in a daze. I was being thrown out of school! The Dean's assistant drove me back to surveying camp on the other side of the Raritan River, and I attempted to figure out what to do next. The last thing I wanted to do was face my parents. I had violated my father's dictum: to persevere in America, no matter what.

I got into my car and started to drive, without knowing the destination. In my confusion, I decided that I would go to Florida, where I would find a job. There, no one would know me, and I could hide my shame.

I passed only two or three exits on the New Jersey Turnpike before my head began to clear. I realized that I had to confront my parents and to tell Sue.

I had done this. I had to take responsibility and to face the consequences.

When I arrived at home to face the music, my father shocked me.

"Listen to me. We beat the Nazis, and we beat the Communists," he told me in a gentle voice. "We'll beat this together, too."

I would hear this refrain from Papa several more times in the future, whenever I came to him with a seemingly insurmountable problem. Every time I needed his help or his calming influence, he was there to provide it.

This time, he picked up the phone and called Jan Tuma in Stillwater, Oklahoma. In the next two days, an incredible series of events took place. OSU took me back. By this time, Professor Tuma's star had risen at the university, and he not only talked the registrar's office into accepting me back, but into doing so without transferring my "Ds" and "Fs" from Rutgers. Miraculously, Tuma convinced the administration to accept the few "Bs" and "Cs," and one "A," but to banish forever from history the courses I had failed or come close to failing. How he did this, I never found out, and I was not about to ask questions. Without this "act of God," it would have been extremely difficult for me to overcome the effect of my disastrous Rutgers record on my grade point average, eventual chances to get into graduate school and to find a decent job. Instead, I was starting over as a sophomore with advanced standing and with a new lease on life.

Oklahoma State's generosity was even more shocking than my dismissal from Rutgers. I was amazed and grateful beyond words: not only did I love OSU, but OSU loved me back. The fact that so many people had stepped up to save me from my bad choices was astounding, and it drove home to me the importance of forming strong, steadfast relationships. I realized that the pressure was on me to perform in order to prove deserving of this magnanimity and love.

As it turned out, my imbecilic year at Rutgers brought about a change in my life, and Dean Easton's stunning dismissal became one of my great motivators for the next several years. As a footnote, the next time I saw Easton was eleven years later, in the summer of 1968, at an American Society for Engineering Education conference at Dartmouth College, barely two weeks after I received my doctorate in engineering.

"Dean Easton," I said as I approached him at a reception.

"My name is Charlie Heller. Do you remember me?"

"I'm sorry. I don't," he replied.

"I came to your office in my softball gear, and you informed me that I'd been dismissed from Rutgers." I waited for a sign of recognition, anxious to tell him that I was now *Doctor* Heller.

"Gosh," he said. "I'm very sorry, but I don't recall the incident. But it's nice to see you."

With that, he turned to the bartender and asked for a glass of wine. Amazing how one person's seminal moment can be another's totally forgettable one!

In the 1950s, the United States had a compulsory draft of eligible males. Satisfactory standing as a college student provided a deferral. Consequently, I had become concerned about my draft status after flunking ROTC and other courses. So, while still at Rutgers, I decided to join the Army Reserves. I became a private in the New Brunswick unit. One of the obligations of a Reservist was to attend a two-week camp each summer. Two guys in my company, Rutgers students Walt Duka and Hank Holtzman, and I were ordered to Camp Drum (today, Fort Drum) in upstate New York for basic training. We were placed under the guiding hand of Drill Sergeant Fugere, a five-foot-six-inch loudmouth with a strong southern accent and an even stronger little-man complex.

"OK, you volunteers, get your asses out of bed!" he screamed each morning at 3:30, as he burst through the barracks door. He seemed to have a special interest in our derrières because, whenever we were ordered to police an area on the base, he walked around yelling:

"I wanna see nothin' but asses and elbows!"

Toward the end of basic training, we participated in maneuvers. My artillery company was to fire live rounds from a 4.2-inch mortar at a concrete target surrounded by woods about a quarter mile away. Holtzman and I were singled out by Sergeant Fugere.

"OK, college boys," he sneered. "You know this math shit and can use the aiming circle. You'll be forward observers and will call in fire on the pillbox."

Hank and I made our way through the woods until we could spot the target. Hiding among trees, we made our computations and radioed back to our company with range and coordinates. We heard the command to commence firing over the radio and then heard the explosions—"Pop! Pop! Pop!"—as three mortar rounds landed. Somewhere other than on or near our target. From the sound, we knew that the impact zone was somewhere beyond the woods, far to the right of the concrete pillbox.

We made our way back to our unit, just as Sergeant Fugere and a couple of soldiers set out to reconnoiter the effect of the firing. When they returned twenty minutes later, I knew from the expression on Fugere's face that we were in trouble.

"Congratulations, college boys," he said with a wicked grin on his thin face. "You destroyed New York State property."

It turned out that we had called in fire on the state highway that ran just outside the fence defining the Camp Drum boundary. One of the two lanes had three craters that would have to be repaired by the Corps of Engineers. Fortunately, the road had been closed to traffic during maneuvers. Holtzman and I were assigned to the supply room for the remaining few days of summer camp, and I was happy that we did not have to pay for the damage. I was even happier that I would not be returning to my New Brunswick unit in September, where the story of our episode would be a source of great entertainment for the troops. Fortunately, I would be out of range and on my way to resuming my life at Oklahoma State University.

CHAPTER NINE

BLEEDING ORANGE

I returned to Stillwater in September 1956 with a new determination, dedication, and resolve to pay back all the people who still believed in me: my parents, Sue, Jan Tuma, and all the beautiful people at Oklahoma State University. I knew I would "bleed orange" for the rest of my life. I felt most indebted to Professor Tuma. I had disappointed him, but he had not lost faith in me. He had stuck out his neck for me at the risk of his own reputation with the university's faculty and administration. There was no way I would fail him this time. And Mr. Iba? He granted back to me the half-scholarship I had earned during my freshman year. How could I possibly disappoint him?

The single blip on my happiness upon returning to OSU was the fact that, once again, I would be half the country away from Sue. Moreover, she insisted again that we date others while in school, despite the fact that this time both of us were certain that we would marry as soon as she would receive her degree in elementary education from Trenton State College and I would get mine in civil engineering from OSU. In the meantime, she declared that "we should both enjoy college life."

At OSU, I opted to stay away from the jock dorm and was assigned a corner room on the third floor of Cordell Hall, where I was greeted by a roommate with whom I had nothing in common. Bob Black was an agriculture major from the small farming town of Darrouzett, in the Texas Panhandle. He seemed to have no interests beyond country music. Bob played a guitar and listened to records cut by singers of whom I had never heard. One of them, to whom he listened constantly, struck me as particularly obnoxious. His name was Elvis Presley; it turned out that no one else on our floor had ever heard of him either. It would be several years before Elvis would be crowned King.

My first day back, I became reacquainted with a guy who would become one of my best friends for life. I was on my way to class in the Engineering Building (today known as Engineering South). Walking in the same direction were hundreds of other students eager to check out their professors and courses. Most of the guys were dressed in the engineer's uniform of the period: khaki pants, blue oxford shirt, brown loafers, and the inevitable slide rule hanging from the belt.

On a sidewalk that crossed the campus diagonally and eventually merged with ours, one figure stood out. He was about six feet four, weighed about 180 pounds, and looked and walked like a cowboy straight out of a movie. He was tall and lean, wore low-slung jeans, leather boots, a black Stetson hat, and a belt buckle that I could see from a hundred yards away. He was different, and I was impressed.

I found my classroom and settled into my seat. Lo and behold, the cowboy—now with his hat off—entered the same room and sat down next to me. He extended his hand.

"Hey, Charlie. Remember me? I'm Don Gafford," he said.

I recognized him immediately as the guy who had sat next to me in ROTC class our freshman year. Close up, I saw that, unlike Hollywood cowboys, Don wore thick horn-rim glasses and clothes that looked as if they had been used to do real work on a farm. Later, I would find out that, not only could Gafford not rope, ride or shoot, but there were much deeper reasons he was not a typical cowpoke, let alone a John Wayne type.

Determined to get off to a good start, I studied hard. My roommate seldom opened a book, and I found it difficult to work to the accompaniment of Elvis, Hank Williams, Hank Snow, and others. So, I spent most of my evenings in the library, often leaving only when it closed for the night. One night, I woke up in an easy chair in the library's Browsing Room, a reference room furnished with comfortable chairs and sofas. The entire building was dark. I looked at the glowing dial of my watch; it was 2:30 a.m. I stumbled down the main stairs to the front door. It was locked—no fire doors in those days. I considered finding a phone and calling the campus police and requesting to be let out, but I was too embarrassed. Instead, I groped my way back to the Browsing Room and spent the night there, sleeping on a sofa. In the morning, I waited until students began to file in and casually walked out into the sunshine.

"Where were you last night when the tornado came through?" a fellow student asked me as soon as I sat down in my first class. It seems that I had managed to stay asleep while a twister roared over the campus and touched down a couple of miles outside Stillwater, cutting a swath through several farms.

Despite our differences, Bob Black and I became friends, and he invited me to come home with him for Thanksgiving. With a couple of days off from basketball practice and eager for the chance to see Texas and to have a turkey dinner with Bob's family, I accepted. Near the halfway point of the 180-mile drive west, we heard on the radio that a dust storm was raging in the panhandles of Texas and Oklahoma. Sure enough, an hour later, we were in the middle of something similar to storms I had only experienced on our family's European ski vacations—a white-out. Except that the particles which filled the air were brown, and not white, and they were dust pellets, rather than snowflakes. It was amazing! Bob slowed to a crawl and eventually stopped on the side of the road. We waited nearly an hour before the storm subsided. I could not believe what I saw in the aftermath: huge mounds of dirt, similar to snowdrifts, piled up alongside the road, against trees and around telephone poles. Bob's Chevy had turned an ugly brown.

"I've got to get the car cleaned up before we drive out to the ranch," Bob said. "The engine is probably loaded with dust."

The wind was still howling when we drove into a small town in the Texas Panhandle. There, we pulled into a Chevrolet dealer to get the car serviced. While they were cleaning under the hood and washing the outside, I asked a salesman if I could use the men's room.

"Oh, we don't have rest rooms inside," he said. "We use the public outhouse across the street."

I ran there and quickly shut the door behind me. I dropped my pants and sat down. Just as I began to relieve myself, a huge gust of wind shook the four-holer. Suddenly, wham! Two of the walls came crashing down. There I was, in the middle of a Texas town, with my bare butt hanging out! Quickly, I pulled up my pants and casually strolled back to the dealership. No one said anything, but to this day, I have a feeling that some good folks in that town remember the day a kid from Prague by way of Stillwater and New Jersey mooned them.

I enjoyed meeting Bob's family, and we spent a very pleasant Thanksgiving on the Blacks' large ranch outside of Darrouzett. But when we returned, Bob found an academic warning waiting for him. If he did not pull up his grades, he was in danger of being thrown out of school. This did not seem to faze him, and he continued to enjoy college life without bothering to hit the books. Sadly, he flunked out at the end of the fall semester, and we never touched base again. When he departed, he told me he would try to enroll at Abilene Christian College. I hope he succeeded.

When I came home for the Christmas holidays in 1956, I found my parents angry at President Eisenhower—again! As commander of the Allied forces in Europe, Ike had stopped General Patton, to whose division my soldier father had been assigned, from liberating Prague. The resulting "liberation" of the capital by the Red Army was a major cause of the country's having become a Soviet puppet state from which we escaped in 1948. My parents never forgave Ike for his role in turning the country Communist. Now, Dwight D. Eisenhower was President of the United States. In October, Hungarians had revolted against their Stalinist government. They had been encouraged to do so by the United States and consequently assumed that America would come to their aid. However, our country did nothing. The Communist government, backed by Soviet troops, put down the revolution, killing 2,500 patriots and causing another 200,000 to flee the country.

Out of a feeling of guilt, the US government suspended its immigration laws and flew several thousand of the Hungarian refugees out of Europe. They were interned temporarily at Camp Kilmer, located just a few miles from the Rutgers surveying camp I had attended until the day of my dismissal from the school. My parents were incensed by the lax immigration policy because, when we and thousands of other Czechoslovaks had escaped Communism, we had to wait for many months in refugee camps while a sponsor found the head of the family a job, a home, and arranged for a visa, whereas the Hungarians got a free pass.

At OSU, Don Gafford and I became friends. Don had entered Oklahoma State an introvert who lacked confidence in himself because of his small-town background. The guy who looked like a super-confident cowboy was overwhelmed by his new surroundings. But soon he discovered that he could not only handle the academic work, but that his fellow students accepted him and showed him respect because he was one of the brightest guys in every class. No one really cared that he had come from a village in rural Oklahoma. Years later, the President of the United States would not care either, when he would place the Presidential Medal of Freedom around Don's neck for having saved the crew of the Apollo 13 spacecraft.

Like me, Gafford had been absent from Stillwater the past year. Unlike me, he had done it for a valid reason: he had to work for Chance-Vought aircraft company in Fort Worth in order to make enough money to continue his schooling.

When I returned to Stillwater from Christmas break, I discovered that Don had decided to pledge a fraternity, Kappa Sigma. Our mutual friend, Bob Graham, was president, and he promised him that he would not be subjected to hazing and other childish frat tricks and pranks. But during initiation, the brothers ordered Gafford to duck-walk and to perform other demeaning acts. They did not know my independent friend very well if they expected him to comply. He quit on the spot.

On that day, Don sat next to me in class. He told me that he was moving out of the fraternity and needed a place to live. The timing was fortuitous, since Bob Black had moved out only a short time before, and I needed a roommate. After class, we went to the Kappa Sigma house, gathered Don's belongings, moved them to Room 301 in Cordell Hall, and became roommates for the year and friends for life.

Unlike most of my engineering classmates, I took my free electives not in technical subjects, but in the English department. In a creative writing class, I came under the influence of a wonderful professor named Cecil B. Williams, a well-known author and recipient of the Friends of Literature Award. Dr. Williams reinforced my love for books and helped me find joy in writing. I confided to him my secret desire to become a writer, rather than an engineer. He was sympathetic with my situation but explained that my father's concern about my economic well-being was prudent.

"You can always be a full-time engineer and a part-time writer," he said. "But you'll never be able to be a full-time writer and a part-time engineer." That made sense to me, and I intended to follow his advice. If I could have seen into the future, I would have been shocked to discover that one day, after years of entrepreneurial terror in the world of high tech, I would finally make writing my profession.

The other thing I did not know at the time—and would not know until many years later—was that Don Gafford, too, was a reluctant engineer. But, while my area-of-study decision was made by my father in the best old European tradition, Don decided for himself.

"I wanted to major in history or English," he informed me years later when we were in our seventies. "But I knew that engineers didn't have to look for jobs. All my decisions have always been along the path of least resistance." This statement was typical of my friend's self-deprecating style.

Don was born in 1936 and grew up in the tiny town of Idabel, population four thousand, in the most poverty-stricken county in Oklahoma. That part of the state was known as "Little Dixie," and young Don did not find out until his early teens that there were places in the world which did not have segregated schools, water fountains, rest rooms, and other public facilities. He attended a one-room school in Hayworth, population two hundred, and graduated from Hayworth High School in a class of twenty-one.

His mother, Viola, was one of eleven children and, according to her son, "had no interest in anything but the family. Nothing existed for her outside the bubble she lived in." His father, Charles "Curly" Gafford, was an outstanding basketball player, but he cut his sports career short when he and Viola married immediately after graduating from high school. Although Curly would undergo a transformation later in life, during Don's childhood years at home, his father was "a bigot like all the others in that part of the country," as Don recalled much later. I have always marveled at the fact that one of the most intelligent, insightful, anti-racist, and fair-minded people I have met in my lifetime came from such an environment.

After high school, Don enrolled at both the University of Oklahoma and Oklahoma State University. He chose OSU "because its classes started a week later, and I was working on the pipeline and could make more money by working an extra week." Lucky for me that he did not become a hated Sooner!

CHAPTER TEN

GODDAMN IMMIGRANT—ENCORE

Watching Stillwater shrink in my rear-view mirror on a cold morning in January 1957, I felt good about myself. My smugness grew as the countryside changed from flat, endless prairie of Oklahoma to the rolling hills of the Midwest and, eventually, to the urban sprawl of the East. I would be able to tell my parents that I had righted the ship and that my first semester back at OSU had been a success. Although I would not know my final grades until I returned from mid-year break, I expected exceptional results. I had worked hard throughout the semester and done well on final exams. I was back on the Cowboy basketball team and on scholarship. Most importantly, I had returned to a nurturing environment, where I felt welcomed and respected. Thus, I was totally unprepared for the surprise awaiting me in Stillwater following a week with Mother, Papa, and Sue at home in New Jersey.

One of my favorite courses that fall had been second-year physics, taught by Professor Perkins. Dr. Perkins was something of a celebrity on campus for a couple of reasons:

one, he had been a prominent member of the Manhattan Project, the super-secret operation that developed the atom bomb that ended World War II in the Pacific. Two, he was rather quirky—or, by most students' accounts, weird.

His quirkiness provided us with great entertainment. We had been warned about his obsession with neatness and order. His former students told us that, prior to beginning each lecture, Dr. Perkins would inspect the classroom. Are the desks perfectly aligned? Are framed photos on the walls squared off? Is his desk free of clutter? Are the blackboards clean? Naturally, his neurosis presented an opportunity a group of undergraduates could not pass up.

In the hallway outside the classroom stood a Coke machine. The first student to arrive for our one-o'clock class was tasked with buying a Coke, drinking it, and then placing the empty bottle in the center of Dr. Perkins' desk.

Every class—three times a week throughout the semester—began with an identical ritual. Perkins arrived precisely five minutes after one, stopped in the doorway, and surveyed the room for imperfections. The 360-degree inspection ended at his desk. As he walked toward it, he switched the clipboard containing his class notes from his left hand to his right. Once he reached the desk, he stopped and took a Ruthian swat at the Coke bottle with the clipboard. The bottle flew through the air like a crazed bird—sometimes landing on a student's desk, at other times smashing against a wall and breaking into pieces, and occasionally rolling harmlessly on the floor. Whatever the result, Perkins said: "Clean it up!" to the student nearest the bottle or its remnants. Then calmly, as if nothing happened, he began to lecture.

On occasion, we extended the entertainment and short-ened the lecture. On a classroom wall hung a giant slide rule, used to teach freshmen how to use this tool indispensable to engineering and science majors of the 1950s. A slide rule consists of two fixed horizontal scales, a sliding scale between them, and a clear plastic slide with a hairline used to align numbers among the three scales. To Dr. Perkins' exacting eye, the zeroes on the three scales had to be aligned perfectly, with the hairline on the plastic scale passing through them. Of course, we could not resist the opportunity to disrupt perfection—ever-so-slightly—thus driving Perkins into an alignment frenzy, as we labored to repress our laughter.

Despite the comedy—or perhaps because of it—I enjoyed the physics class and did very well in it. I scored "A's" on tests and earned a number of "well done" comments on weekly quizzes and homework assignments.

"See me after class, Heller," Dr. Perkins said one day.

Soon after I sat down in his office, the man we teased in class was transformed into a demigod. I stared in awe at the photographs on the walls: Perkins with President Truman, Perkins with Dr. Robert Oppenheimer, Perkins with the crew of the 'Enola Gay,' the airplane that dropped the atom bomb on Hiroshima.

"Charles," he said, dropping the formality of the classroom, "why don't you change your major to physics?"

I was speechless for a few moments. "Sir, that has never occurred to me," I replied finally.

"You're the best student in that class. You could accomplish great things as a physicist."

"Thank you, sir."

"Well, what do you say?" he asked.

"I'll have to give it some thought."

"Do that, and let me know soon."

I did give it some thought—perhaps thirty seconds. By now, I was determined to become a structural engineer, one who would design spectacular buildings and bridges. I had no interest in spending my life in some laboratory, chasing after atoms, molecules, and electrons.

"So, what did you decide?" asked Dr. Perkins two or three weeks later.

"I'm going to do it, sir," I lied, planning to tell him the truth once the semester ended, and I received an "A" in the course.

Now I was back on campus from mid-year break, anxious to find out how I had done in my fall courses. In those days—long before the enactment of privacy laws—grades were posted outside professors' offices.

Feeling confident, I marched into Gunderson Hall and headed for Dr. Perkins' office. Taped to the wall was a typed sheet of grades. Midway down the page was the only line I cared about:

CHARLES O. HELLER   C

Stunned, I stood riveted to the floor. I ran my finger along the line with my name, making sure that I had not read someone else's grade. I had not. *This can't be right,* I told myself. *I had a strong 'A' going in, and I think I aced the final. Some clerk must have screwed up.*

I knocked on Professor Perkins' door. No response. I knocked again.

"All right. Come in," growled the professor.

"Oh, Heller," he said, as I stood in the doorway. "What do you want?"

"Sir, I think somebody made a mistake with my final grade."

"Nobody made a mistake," he said without looking up from the paper in front of him.

"But I had an 'A' for the semester, and I thought I did well on the final."

"You did well," he said, and I held my breath, waiting for the shoe to drop. "But you lied to me. You've proven to be just another goddamn immigrant liar. Now, get the hell out of my office!"

When I related the story to my friends, they urged me to file a grievance. I considered it but did nothing. The "C" grade would be a setback in my comeback effort as a student, but what could I do? After all, I was a goddamn immigrant—and immigrants do not make waves. Once again, my past affected my present: Czech kids did not question authority.

"If you want to make friends," I was often told, "there are two subjects you want to avoid discussing in polite society: politics and religion."

I was not out to make enemies, but, as part of my maturation, I became more and more interested in, and inquisitive about, both of those taboo subjects. As I formed opinions and unshakable beliefs, I was not shy about expressing them to friends and strangers alike.

Oklahomans were a conservative lot, their views on race in the 1950s being closer to those of denizens of the Deep South than those of most of the folks I had left behind in New Jersey. Back when I made my first visit to OSU as a high school student, I had been taken on a tour of the State Capitol in Oklahoma City. There, at the seat of power, I was stunned to find rest rooms and water fountains marked by "white" and "colored" signs. It affected me deeply and brought back memories of my childhood and "Jews forbidden" signs in German and Czech on park benches and public rest rooms.

As a high school student planning to attend OSU, I had been even more shocked when I read about an event that became known as "The Johnny Bright Incident." Bright was a star running back—and preseason favorite to win the Heisman Trophy—when Drake University came to Stillwater to play Missouri Valley Conference rival Oklahoma State on October 20, 1951. Before the first quarter was half over, Bright was knocked unconscious three times by the same OSU player, a defensive tackle named Wilbanks Smith. The last blow broke Bright's jaw and eventually forced him to leave the game.

The incident received national attention not only because

it curtailed the career of a great player, but because of its racial implications.

"Get that nigger!" hundreds of spectators heard a coach and several players shout prior to each tackle.

I had been unaware of the episode until a couple of years later, at which point I had already selected, and committed to, Oklahoma State University. My father and I were at the Morristown Public Library. He was thumbing through old copies of *Life* magazine while I was searching for a book in the stacks. When I returned, Papa opened a two-year-old issue of the periodical to a page with a sequence of photos that illustrated Smith's obscene attack on Bright.

"Do you really want to go to that school?" he asked.

I failed to answer and wavered for many days. Eventually, my desire to play basketball for Mr. Henry Iba and to study under Professor Jan Tuma won out. *The country is changing,* I rationalized. *Surely, Oklahoma is changing for the better, too.*

When I arrived in Stillwater in September 1954, it did not take me long to discover that I had been fooling myself. Oklahoma's traditions remained deeply rooted in those of the segregationist South. Out of some ten thousand students at OSU, there were perhaps ten African Americans. There was not a single Black man on our basketball team; in fact, the first and only Black athlete in the history of OSU was Orlando Hazley, a world-class sprinter on the track team. When Coach Iba screamed at me to "stop playing like a nigger!" during our first practice, I had become thoroughly conflicted. Do I stay or do I head back East? Many sleepless nights followed while I went back and forth.

Once again, I managed to rationalize my way out of the dilemma. My father had taught me to stay the course, no matter what. "Never quit!" he insisted. I had to follow his dictum. Moreover, I convinced myself that if I stayed, I might have the opportunity to change some minds. I stayed, but whether or not I changed minds is questionable.

Despite my liberal political leanings, my philosophy was still in its formative stages, and I tried to keep my mind open to others' ideas. With respect to both politics and religion, I tested the waters at the extremes, as well as the center, while entering this new and exciting world full of choices and possibilities.

A friend attending rival University of Oklahoma introduced me to the writings of Ayn Rand. I devoured her *Atlas Shrugged, We the Living,* and other novels that praised individuality over the collective good. For a few weeks, I was taken in by this me-first philosophy and began to believe that each person should be responsible only to, and for, himself or herself.

We came to the US with absolutely nothing, I rationalized as I analogized myself to Rand's heroes. *My parents slaved to buy a modest house and to put food on the table, while I had to work construction and earn a scholarship in order to attend college. So, why can't the Negroes who have lived here for many more years pull themselves up by their own bootstraps, and why should the government have to help poor people, black or white?*

Fortunately, my reading did not end with Ayn Rand. I had been brought up on the teachings of the founding father and first president of Czechoslovakia, Tomáš Garrigue Masaryk. I had brought an English translation of his best-known book to school with me. While still in my "Ayn Rand mode," I forced myself to take *Ideals of Humanity* off the shelf and to read it from cover to cover. Masaryk's words were more powerful than any uttered by Rand's fictional characters. It took only that single reading to resurrect my humanitarian philosophy and to realize that all of us are, above all else, members of the human race. As such, we have responsibilities that go far beyond our personal well-being and the gathering of personal wealth.

The 1950s were years of relative disengagement of college

students from politics. Don Gafford and I, and our closest friends, were oddballs of sorts. Our engineering classmates considered us strange because we read books for enjoyment or edification, and not just because they were assigned by professors. Moreover, we were very vocal activists on behalf of equal rights for all races. As an editorial board member of the *Oklahoma State Engineer* magazine, I wrote a strongly worded story, advocating the rights of Black people to the same education as whites. This made me something of a controversial figure. Civil Engineering Professor Ed Witt—known by his students as "Half-Wit"—wrote a scathing letter to the editor of the local paper, the *Stillwater Daily News-Press*, denouncing me as a Communist and pointing out the facts that I was a Yankee and that I had been "born in a foreign country." He, too, considered me a damned immigrant freak. No wonder I had such un-American ideas!

CHAPTER ELEVEN

FAREWELL, MY LOVE

Although I was eligible to play college basketball again, my role was primarily that of a practice player and bench-sitter. Today, ours would be known as the scout team. Back then, my peers and I called ourselves the "dogmeat squad" because our usual role amounted to emulating players on the next opponent's team in scrimmages against the front-liners. Actually, while it was frustrating to play in front of empty stands, it was also fun. As a guard, I got to "be" players like Oscar Robertson (in my view today, the greatest player of the twentieth century), who played for the University of Cincinnati and later starred in the NBA.

One cold February day, I walked into the fieldhouse at 3:15 p.m. sharp, as always on non-game weekdays during the season. I changed into my practice uniform and ran into the gym. As I began to warm up with my teammates, one of the student assistants came over.

"Mr. Iba wants to see you after practice," he said.

"Why?" I asked, as I nearly fainted from shock and fear.

"How should I know?" replied the short, fat kid, obviously

pleased that he had just scared the hell out of a varsity player.

Henry Iba was strictly old-school: a hard driver whose word was never questioned, a strict disciplinarian who tolerated nothing less than all-out effort, total obedience, and good manners on and off the court. In today's world of college sports, coaches must be a combination of mentor, psychologist, and parent figure. God help them if they utter a disparaging word or, horrors, lay a hand on one of the coddled darlings they had recruited into their program. They would find themselves on the carpet in the university president's office and with a player considering entrance into the so-called transfer portal.

Mr. Iba would find it impossible to coach a twenty-first-century basketball team. Like the great majority of coaches in the 1950s, he was the undisputed boss of the basketball program. We may not have liked it, but we expected to be screamed at when we threw an errant pass and had our hands smacked with a stick when we took a forbidden drink from a water fountain during practice. We had no interactions with Mr. Iba outside the court and locker room—no parties at his home, no private sessions to discuss our personal problems, nothing but basketball.

Very few of us had the opportunity to see another side of a man who seemed one-dimensional but was, in fact, a complex, sensitive human being.

Mr. Iba insisted that his players not only attend classes, but that they maintain grades above the campus average. Like everyone else, I was terrified of this ramrod-straight man with a booming voice hoarse from years of screaming at players and referees—the same voice that had traumatized me with the "n-word" at my first practice. Now I had to go for a one-on-one session with the man we called "God" behind his back. I had nearly three hours to wonder why he wanted to see me, although I suspected that it might have to do with my performance in the classroom, which had not been great of late, particularly in one engineering course.

I had made the mistake of signing up for what I had been told was an "easy-A" engineering elective course in metallurgy. Taught by crusty old Professor Sodestrom, it consisted of segments in forging, foundry, heat treatment, and welding. Twice a week, we met in a dingy building that smelled like my godfather's blacksmith shop back in Czechoslovakia. For the first thirty minutes, we sat in steel bleachers while Sodestrom lectured. This was followed by a short quiz, and then came the hands-on portion in which we learned to make sand molds, to weld, solder, and otherwise work with metals. For some reason, my brain had a difficult time absorbing the theoretical parts: the intricacies of molecular bonds and other esoteric concepts.

Soderstrom's weekly quizzes always consisted of ten multiple-choice questions, and he awarded a positive point for each correct answer and a negative point for each wrong answer. His unique right-minus-wrong system was my undoing.

When Mr. Iba sent for me, my average in Professor Soderstrom's class was *minus* two—twenty percent below zero! Knowing that Mr. Iba tracked his players' academic progress, I had a feeling he was aware of this situation as I entered his office. There, behind an old wooden desk sat the tall, distinguished man who parted his hair in the middle like someone from a 1920s photo.

"Sit down, Heller," he said sternly, as he examined some papers on his desk.

"Thank you, sir."

"I see that your grade-point average is slipping."

"Yes sir, it is. But it's mainly because of one course, and I'm really trying to bring all my grades up," I replied meekly.

Mr. Iba looked at me over his horn-rimmed glasses.

"I realize that you're in a tough major. Most players take easy courses. But I still can't tolerate lousy performance in your classes."

"I understand, sir."

"And I have to tell you that this is the first time I've ever seen a *negative* grade!" I thought I detected a slight smile, but I did not respond.

"Do you think you'll ever play professional basketball?" he asked, and I wondered why he would ask such a ridiculous question of a practice player.

"No, sir."

"Then why the hell don't you quit basketball and concentrate on becoming an engineer?"

His words hit me like an exploding grenade. Despite my status, I still harbored hopes of a breakout practice, substantive game minutes, and subsequent stardom. Now the dream was about to be shattered. He was dismissing me from the team!

What would my parents say? As recent immigrants, we were so poor that I had not even been able to afford to make a single phone call home from college (long-distance calls were expensive in those days), and, during the off-seasons at OSU, when not eating at the training table, I had subsisted on Cokes, Hershey bars, and rice. How could I afford to finish school without a scholarship that paid half of my tuition, out-of-state fee, books, and room and board?

"I know your background," said Mr. Iba, seeming to read my mind. "I admire you and your family, and I know that you'd have a hard time affording school without basketball."

"Yes sir," I said meekly, astounded that he knew my history.

"So, I've decided to let you keep your half-scholarship until you graduate. At the end of next year, I want to see you on the platform in cap and gown."

"Sir, I don't know what to say," I stammered, grateful to Mr. Iba, but devastated by the fact that he had just brought an end to my love affair with basketball.

"Don't say anything. Now, get the hell out of here and go to work! And don't forget us. Come by during practice every now and then."

When I walked outside into the cold air, it hit me. I knew deep inside that I was not good enough to be a starter at the Division-I level. Moreover, the man had just told me he was giving up an invaluable half-scholarship slot just to see me graduate. The NCAA limits the number of scholarships a school can offer, so this was truly a magnanimous gift. *He did this for an immigrant?* In an instant, I became one of an army of his former players who worshiped and honored the man they had feared while playing for him.

I came to practice a few times and dished balls to my former teammates. More often, I sat alone and anonymous in the darkness, high up in the stands and watched—dreaming of what might have been. I attended games as a fan with my friends for the rest of my time at OSU. I was happy when Mr. Iba brought in our first Black players and felt gratified when the guys told me he treated the African Americans like his own sons, protecting them from hostile opponents and fans. His racist outburst from my first practice faded into history.

The next time I met Mr. Iba was in 1972, twelve years after graduating from OSU with a Master's degree. He was head coach of the US Olympic basketball team, and I was living in Annapolis, Maryland. His team was in Baltimore to play the NBA's Bullets as part of a nationwide tour of exhibition games intended to raise travel money and to train his squad against top competition. I came to the Civic Center early, hoping to have a chance to say "hello" to him. I took my seat a few rows above the US team's bench, just as the players came out for their warm-ups. When the coaches arrived, I walked down slowly, hoping to catch Mr. Iba's eye. I saw a well-known local TV sportscaster and his cameraman grab him for an interview, and I hung back. They were on the side of the court talking, with the camera shooting, and I stood a respectable distance from them, awaiting my chance. Suddenly, in the middle of the interview, I saw Mr. Iba's eyes avert the cameraman's bright light and look over at me.

"Excuse me," Mr. Iba said to the startled reporter. "But, there's one of my former players."

With that, he walked away from the interview and approached me with hand outstretched. He gave me a hug.

"Great to see you! What are you doing here?" he asked. I could see that he did not recall my name, but I was amazed that he had remembered my face and startled by the fact that he would stand up Channel 13 for a guy who had once been a member of his "dogmeat squad."

Proudly, I told him that I had received my PhD degree in engineering four years earlier and that I was CEO of a software company. I expressed my gratitude to him and to Oklahoma State for giving me a second chance in life. It was the first time I ever saw Mr. Iba smile.

"I'm so proud of you!" he said and hugged me again. That wonderful moment became engraved in my memory.

Sadly, Mr. Iba was not smiling a couple of months later in Munich. In those days, the US national team was made up of amateur college players, and this one was the youngest in history, dubbed "Iba's Kiddie Corps" by the press. Players such as Tom McMillen of Maryland, Doug Collins of Illinois State, and Tom Burleson of North Carolina State, were less than twenty-one years old, while Iron Curtain country teams fielded squads of rugged veterans of international play. Nevertheless, the team sailed through its preliminary rounds. The United States was 63-0 since the inception of Olympic basketball competition as it entered the finals against the Soviet Union.

The game was a difficult defensive struggle, but the Americans won it, 50-49. Or so it seemed. After the final buzzer, an Olympic official in the stands, with no connection to the game, ordered the scorer to reset the clock at three seconds and to give the Russians another chance to score. Mr. Iba protested—to no avail. The Soviets got the ball but failed to score. Once again, the buzzer sounded, with our team ahead. This time, the referee determined that the scorer had reset the clock improperly, and the Soviets were given yet another chance. Due to the pandemonium on the court, the Americans had no chance to set up their defense. The Soviets passed the ball to a player named Belov, who charged into two US defenders, and scored on a lay-up. No charging call—game over. This time, the score was final, 51-50 USSR. How unfair that Henry Iba became the first American coach in history to lose a game in the Olympics! The whole world knew that he did not really *lose*, but who will remember?

After my unhappy experience with a fraternity at Rutgers, one would think that I might have sworn off Greek life. But no, a year after Don Gafford and I became roommates, I was persuaded to pledge Acacia, the nation's only fraternity named after a tree. I had met a senior named Gene Allen in one of my classes. He was a caring guy, a Korean War veteran from nearby Cushing, and he began to recruit me for his fraternity. Gene was very persuasive and, when he introduced me to some of the Acacia brothers, I was impressed. Unlike the partying Pi Kappa Alpha guys at Rutgers, these men seemed mature, serious about their studies, and genuinely interested in me. Their logo was a right triangle because their role model was the Greek mathematician and philosopher, Pythagoras, a man who believed that all things could be predicted and measured using mathematics. How could I go wrong?

In September 1957, my junior year, I moved into the Acacia house on College Avenue. Don Gafford rented a tiny house a few blocks away on Hester Street, along with an Argentinean student with an American-sounding name, Ted Harris. Unlike Don's experience as a pledge, mine was relatively easy. I had left the OSU varsity basketball team, but I was captain of the university's club soccer team and played on a very competitive AAU volleyball team. In addition, I was one of the best players on Acacia's intramural teams in basketball and softball. So, partly due to my jock status, and partly because I was a couple of years older than the other pledges, the brothers seldom bothered me with demeaning or silly tasks.

However, I still found life in the fraternity house difficult. I lived in a large dorm room with about thirty other guys. We slept in two-tiered bunk beds. A light sleeper, I had difficulty with guys coming in at all hours of the night, creaking springs, snores coming from all corners of the room, and the stereophonic sound and acrid smell of farts bombarding me through the night. Worst of all, during sleepless nights, I was reminded of the refugee camps, where my parents and I had endured living in the same room with twenty-some strangers.

At the Acacia house, we had a common study area with small individual desks, but the distractions there were such that I found myself more and more going to study at the library or in the houses or dorm rooms of various classmates.

Gafford was having difficulties of his own. His roommate turned out to be a Latin lover whose goal seemed to be to bed every co-ed at the University. He informed Don he was implementing a system that would indicate whether or not Don could enter their tiny house at night. The outside light turned on signaled that Harris and a girlfriend-of-the-day were together in his bedroom, and Gafford was forbidden to enter the house. If the light was off, Don was allowed to come home. This irked my friend to no end, but he was stuck with a year-long lease and no way to get rid of Harris.

One evening, Don and I had been working at the *Oklahoma State Engineer* magazine office, preparing the next issue. When we finished, we decided to stop at his house for a beer. However, as we pulled into the driveway in Don's white 1957 MGA, we saw that the outside light was on. So, instead of having a beer at the house, we drove into town and stopped in a bar. An hour later, we returned, but the light was still on. Obviously, Harris was having a good evening. We drove away and stopped for another beer. Once again, we hopped into Don's car and drove to his house. Lo and behold, the light was still on. By now, it was well past midnight, and both of us had early morning classes.

"Let's go in," I said to Don.

"I'm not sure that's a good idea."

"He can't keep doing this to you. This is unfair. Let's go."

Don unlocked the front door and we walked in. He opened the refrigerator, looking for something to eat, when Harris burst through his bedroom door.

"What the hell are you doing here? Didn't you see the light?"

"Look, you son of a bitch," I yelled back. "We've been riding around all night, waiting to get in here. This is Don's house, too, and he has every right to be here."

Harris, wearing only a pair of underpants, lunged at me. Standing next to Don, I reached into the refrigerator and grabbed a raw egg. Just as Ted reached for me, I smashed the egg on his forehead. He stood there stunned, as the white and yellow goo spread over his face and chest. He turned and rushed to the bathroom. Don and I looked at each other, wondering what would come next. I had enough beers in me to be in a fighting mood and ready to take on Harris. But soon, the Latin lover and *l'amour du jour* emerged from the bedroom, fully dressed and, without another word, left the house.

A couple of days later, Don pulled me aside after class.

"Harris told me to tell you that he's going to shoot you at St. Pat's Ball. I think he means it, and I know he has a gun."

St. Patrick is the patron saint of engineers. The social event of the year for engineering students at OSU, culminating Engineers' Week, was St. Pat's Ball, held in the Student Union ballroom. As a run-up to the ball, an election of St. Pat's Queen was held. The winner was always one of the best-looking girls on campus. Tradition dictated that the editor of the *Oklahoma State Engineer* escort the queen to the ball. Bob Graham was the editor, but since he could not attend, he asked me to take his place. I was already scared stiff because of my inability to dance, and I wondered how I was going to perform the solo fox-trot which officially opened the ceremonies. Now, I had to worry about being assassinated, too.

Although I did not really believe that Harris would go through with his threat, I could not get it out of my mind. I got through the first dance without stepping on Gayle Powell's feet, but throughout the evening, I kept stealing glances at the balcony which surrounded the ballroom.

"Are you looking for somebody?" Gayle finally asked me.

"Gayle, I probably should have warned you, but a guy threatened to shoot me tonight because I hit him with an egg."

She laughed and asked: "You don't really believe that, do you?"

"I don't, but I can't get it out of my mind."

"Don't worry about it. This isn't the wild west anymore. Let's have a good time," she replied, smiling, seemingly relaxed about the situation. She was right. I did manage to have a good time, and I lived to walk Gayle home at the end of the evening.

During that school year, 1957-58, the *Oklahoma State Engineer* magazine became my passion, replacing basketball as my major extracurricular activity. The previous year, I had been Assistant Story Editor, while Bob Graham was Story Editor. Now, Bob was the head man, and I followed him as Story Editor. I recruited Gafford to be Feature Editor and a fellow Czech immigrant, Lad Svoboda, to head the photography department. For my story staff, I brought in several of my fraternity brothers who were engineering majors—Bill Adams, Russ Joyner, Bill "Magoo" Foster, Tom

Gillespie—and Ann Brous, one of the few girls I dated while at OSU. We were a strong team producing a quality magazine that began to receive national notice.

The following year, Don Gafford and I came back together. He left Harris and the little house, and I moved out of Acacia, although I remained a member. We moved into a room in North Murray Hall, a former women's dormitory just west of Theta Pond.

"Hey, my name is Gary Lei. I live next door," said an Asian guy who walked into our room one evening, interrupting a poker game that was taking place on Gafford's bed.

Lei, whose full name was Teh-Ling Lei, was short and brown, and spoke with a strange accent—a mixture of Chinese and English with a definite New York/New Jersey tone—and he called everyone "Babe." His demeanor was that of a person Oklahomans referred to as a "typical Yankee"—glib and arrogant. At least, that is how he came across upon our first meeting. Over time, we found out that he was not like that at all, as our frequent taunts brought out a new humility in him.

Lei was born in mainland China, the son of prominent parents. His father, Lei Chen, was a professor at the National Central University and later assistant secretary-general of the People's Political Council in the Chinese government. When the Communists came to power, their opponents, the Nationalists, retreated to the island of Taiwan, where they established a separate nation headed by President Chiang Kai-shek. Lei Chen and his family, including the young Teh-Ling Lei, fled to Taiwan in 1949. There, Lei Chen launched *Ziyou zhongguo* (*Free China Fortnightly*), a magazine that, for the next eleven years, represented the voice of democratic liberalism. When Don and I met his son, Lei Chen was trying to organize a political party opposing the corrupt government of Chiang Kai-shek.

In 1960, the Taiwanese president had him tried for sedition and accused him unjustly of spreading Communist propaganda. Lei Chen was pronounced guilty and imprisoned for the next ten years. After his father's death, Teh-Ling Lei's mother would spend many years working to have her husband's name cleared and to cause this injustice to be officially recognized. Ultimately, she was successful, and she was named Senator-for-Life in Taiwan.

Teh-Ling Lei had followed his sister to the United States, where he entered Mount St. Mary's College in Emmitsburg, Maryland. After graduating in 1957 with a degree in social science, he decided to prolong his stay in the country and to pursue a degree which would lead to a well-paying job. He wrote to a number of universities with good civil engineering programs. OSU offered a scholarship, and he accepted. At Mount St. Mary's, in the long tradition of Asians in America, he had adopted an American nickname, Gary. He wanted us to call him Gary, but much to his displeasure, we decided that a new name would be more fitting. We christened him "Lei-babe," in honor of his favorite name for everyone he met. The name stuck and nearly all his friends at OSU called him that, although, after graduation, we would drop the suffix and simply call him "Lei."

Don, Lei, and I became inseparable, and we decided to room together during Don's and my senior year. We found a second-floor apartment on Ramsey Street, just a short walk from the south portion of campus. Lei's sister lived in New Jersey, and he rode with me whenever I returned home on vacation. On our return trips to Stillwater, Lei carried plastic containers of Chinese food prepared for the road by his sister. I found the smell of seaweed, raw fish, and Lei's other delicacies insufferable and opted for my mother's salami sandwiches as we sped west with the windows open, even in the dead of winter.

One of the many things that bonded Don, Lei and me was poverty. We pooled our money for food. Once a week, we purchased several packages of rice, which Lei boiled on

Sunday night in a large pot provided by my mother. Throughout the week, Lei and I treated ourselves to a variety of dishes: rice with cut-up hot dogs, rice with chicken and okra, rice with hamburger meat. For dessert, we enjoyed rice with butter, sugar and cinnamon. Don refused to eat rice in any shape or form and ran his own gourmet kitchen.

"I am a product of the Great Southwest," he explained years later. "I did not eat rice then, do not eat rice now, and never will eat rice. I get my carbohydrates from fried potatoes and my proteins from pinto beans and fried bologna at almost every meal except breakfast."

We obtained a used black-and-white TV, which we placed in the corner of our tiny living room near the front door. The first thing a visitor saw in our home were rolled-up pieces of aluminum foil, emanating from the TV, and snaking up the wall in every direction. One of the initial engineering designs for all of us, this constituted an antenna that pulled in, with accompanying snow, one channel from Oklahoma City and another from Tulsa.

I had been brought up to be neat. Everything had to have its place, my bed had to be made before I left the house in the morning, and my room had to be spotless. I carried this habit with me to college. Don lived at the other extreme. When he got up in the morning, his bed stayed unmade, and he spent minutes searching for his clothes that were scattered on the floor of his bedroom and under his bed. He rolled his socks into balls that seemed to attract the dust that collected along the edges of the room. Lei was somewhere between the two extremes—not a neatness freak like me, nor a slob like Don. Tidiness was one of the few things on which Gafford and I disagreed, but it was seldom a major issue since he kept his mess on his side of the room. Ten years later, when Neil Simon's play, "The Odd Couple," became a hit, Sue and I laughed about the similarity. Don Gafford was Walter Matthau to my Jack Lemmon.

During the spring semester of our senior year, Don began dating a local girl named Kay from nearby Perkins. As he began to spend more and more time with her, Lei and I, and some of our friends, often frequented the local dives without him.

About that time, I met a new friend, James D. Cobb, with whom I had a number of classes. Jim was a veteran of the Korean war, married, and considerably more mature and serious than I was. His influence on my life was truly profound. After my Rutgers debacle, I had come back to OSU with a new determination to do well academically. However, while my improvement was titanic, this was only on a relative scale. I was more serious than I had been, and I worked much harder than I had in the past. But compared to the high achievers in the classroom, I was still a bit of a slacker.

Along came Jim with a work ethic I could only envy. He was kind enough to let me—no, actually, force me—to study with him nearly every weekday evening. He and his wife LaVerna lived in a little house with a small shed in the back, one that Jim converted into an office. It was just big enough for the two of us to sit side-by-side, night after night, solving structural analysis and mathematics problems. Jim's Monroe calculator became our best friend.

The Cobb effect on me did not end with forced studying. I had been subsisting on the rice dishes I shared with Lei plus Hershey bars, Cokes, and coffee I bought at the Student Union on the way to class in the morning. After leaving the basketball program and its nutritious training table, my diet became a disaster. This is where LaVerna Cobb stepped in. My one or two decent meals a week came at the Cobbs' dinner table. I learned to love chicken-fried steak, fried okra, and other Oklahoma delicacies, as well as LaVerna's wonderful pasta dishes.

The only "A" grade I had transferred from Rutgers was in surveying. OSU's requirements were more stringent than those of Rutgers, and I needed three more credit hours of summer surveying camp. So in the summer of 1958, to fulfill graduation requirements, I registered for the latter portion of camp. Unlike Rutgers, which taught surveying across the river from its main campus, Oklahoma State ran its camp in the rugged mountains of Colorado.

My fellow students had been at the camp for four weeks already when I landed at Denver's airport on a Saturday afternoon to join them for the second course of the summer. I had written Jim Cobb, who had his car at the camp, asking him to meet my flight. I got off the airplane, picked up my bag, and began to look for Jim.

It turned out that he had misread my letter and thought I was coming in the next day. Following a frightful night in a fleabag hotel, one where the majority of guests were prostitutes, their customers, and drug users, Jim came for me. We rode for about two hours to Buena Vista, the closest town to the camp. The last twenty-five miles passed through the San Isabel National Forest, surrounded by snowcapped mountains of the University range, until we reached Camp Webster Lance Benham, named after the father of David Benham, a distinguished and successful owner of one of Oklahoma's largest consulting firms. I was greeted by many old friends and classmates as I moved my gear into a primitive log cabin. I thought I was beginning a three-week vacation in the spectacular Rockies.

The next morning, I found out that surveying camp was no vacation. It was mostly hard labor. After morning lectures, we worked in four-man teams, running surveys up and down rugged mountain slopes, and in valleys and meadows. A couple of evenings each week, we were required to watch movies dealing with mind-numbing technical subjects. The other three weekday nights, we drove twenty-five miles to a bar in Buena Vista, where we drank Coors beer with the local population of Native Americans and Mexican farm workers.

One day, we were running levels in a particularly desolate area and came upon a small shack. We broke in and discovered that it had been the home of a goldminer. Amazingly, it appeared that no one had entered the shack since the miner abandoned it some forty years earlier. We found his correspondence from friends and relatives in Philadelphia, indicating that he had come out to Colorado soon after the turn of the century in search of gold. After several unsuccessful years, he turned to mining for copper. The last dispatch was dated 1915. As I read the messages to him from his family, I could not help but admire the miner for his persistence despite overwhelming odds. I gathered the stack of letters and brought it back to camp, hoping to sell the historical records when I returned home. No such luck. I showed my discovery to Professor Roger Flanders, who confiscated it and turned it over to a local historical society.

After two weeks, we were given the weekend off. We had heard that the town of Estes Park was a haven for college students working in various Colorado resorts. On Friday night, Jim Cobb, Corky Chitwood, Bernie Babb, and I hopped into Jim's Ford wagon and headed for a night on the town in Denver, prior to proceeding to Estes Park the following day. On Saturday, we arrived in the resort town and discovered that the rumors were true. The place was crawling with boys and girls of college age, and it was obvious that they had begun partying early in the day. We stopped at a motel to secure a room for the night but had no luck. It was fully booked. We proceeded to try several others, with the same result.

As we continued driving through town, desperately looking for a "vacancy" sign, we saw an overhead banner, announcing a talent show that evening at a local hotel. Someone in our group came up with a brilliant plan. Before implementing it, we stopped in a couple of bars in order to bolster our courage and to work on a strategy. Finally, feeling no pain, we drove to the hotel, walked in and asked for the person in charge of the talent program.

"We saw your sign about a talent show," I told him. "Actually, we're the Four Lads, and we're just passing through. There seems to be a shortage of vacant rooms in town, and we'd be glad to sing for you tonight in exchange for a room."

The Four Lads were one of the country's most popular singing groups of the day. The man stared at us incredulously. Our bravado must have made us believable because he bought the story and agreed to our deal. Laughing and slapping one another on our backs, we left the hotel in search of more refreshments. In back of a dark bar stinking of stale beer, we rehearsed "Moments to Remember," a current Four Lads hit. We had enough to drink to convince ourselves that we would pass the test in front of an audience.

A couple of hours later, we walked back to the hotel. It seemed that every young person in Estes Park was heading there, as well. When we arrived in the large hall in which the talent show would be held, every seat was filled, people were standing on the sides and in the back, and some kids had even climbed onto the wooden roof trusses above the hall. We were getting nervous as we sat down to wait for the show to start. The buzz from the day's many beers began to wear off as we listened to some of the amateur acts that opened the show.

God, I thought, as I listened to them, *they're a hell of a lot better than we are, and we're pretending to be big-time stars?* Then, suddenly, it was our turn.

We walked out on the stage. The master of ceremonies— the same guy with whom we had struck our deal earlier— reached for the microphone to introduce the Four Lads. Then, just as a hush came over the audience and we had our mouths open and ready to sing, a loud voice came from the rafters:

"Hey, Heller, what the hell are you doing down there?" it boomed.

Startled, I looked in the direction of its origin. There, sitting on one of the rafters with his feet hanging down and laughing like a maniac, was Ed Blackley, one of my Acacia fraternity brothers from OSU! Our cover was blown. We looked at each other, briskly walked off the stage, and slinked out of the hotel as quietly as we could.

We spent that cold Rocky Mountain night in Jim's station wagon. As I lay on my side, with my body wrapped around a wheel well—stone sober now—I wondered how I was going to explain the Four Lads incident when I returned to the frat house in the fall. But the next morning we paid a visit to the Coors brewery in Golden, and the embarrassment of the previous night was quickly forgotten. A week later, Jim dropped me off at the airport in Denver, and I flew home to New Jersey, while he drove back to Stillwater.

CHAPTER TWELVE

HONOR AND OBEY

Upon my return home from surveying camp in the summer of 1958, I went back to Bell Labs in nearby Whippany, New Jersey, now as an experienced junior draftsman, creating drawings of printed circuits for Nike Zeus missiles. My mentor, Jack Geils, had been promoted and now was vice president of the Labs' parent company, AT&T, living and working in New York City. But, having proven myself to my superiors, I no longer needed Jack's support.

I saw Sue nearly every night and on weekends. One of my favorite dates was at a drive-in theater—not so much for the movies, but for "making out," which was facilitated by the bench seat of my Studebaker. One night at the drive-in, there was no smooching. I do not recall the name of the movie. I remember only a graphic scene from a concentration camp, depicting Nazi doctor Josef Mengele, known as the "Angel of Death," selecting Jews for sadistic medical experiments or for murder in the gas chamber at Auschwitz. Suddenly, the memories that I had worked so hard to suppress—and hide from Sue—came flooding back. I saw my six-year-old self, standing on the platform with *Dĕdeček*, my beloved great-grandfather, and saying goodbye to him before the train took him away toward his ultimate murder at the Treblinka death camp.

Sue felt my body stiffen, and soon she saw tears streaming down my cheeks. For the first time in a very long time, the little pilot light inside me, the one that kept my old memories alive, burned brightly. And for the first time, I told Sue part of my story. However, I stopped short of revealing the entire tale, that of the Jewish side of my family. I fell back on the party line that Mother had used during the war to explain to me the reason for our suffering and deprivation.

"We were persecuted because my father was fighting against the Nazis with the British army," I explained. Fear of jeopardizing our relationship prevented me from disclosing the complete truth to Sue.

Later that summer, prior to returning to school for my last semester of undergraduate study, I decided that it was time to formally propose and ask Sue to marry me. Now I knew I had no choice but to confront the issue of my ethnicity. Sue's parents and I had become fond of each other, and my Catholicism seemed to have dissipated as an issue for her mother. Now I would hit the Holsten family with a new bombshell? Should I? Would I? For the remainder of the summer, I lay awake at night trying to decide what to do.

How will Sue react when she finds out that I am not just Catholic, but that I am also part-Jewish? Is her love for me stronger than the prejudices that have surrounded her at home and in her native country throughout her life, or will I blow everything by revealing my secret? If I don't tell her now, she's bound to find out someday, and what will happen then? If I do tell her now, will she turn her back on me? Will her mother forbid her to marry me?

I went back and forth. One day I was prepared to tell her. The next day my fear of the consequences scared me off.

Finally, after weeks of agonizing, I decided that I would confess. With my return to OSU rapidly approaching, I had to do it soon.

I brought Sue home from a date and, while sitting in my Studebaker in her driveway, I finally I got up the courage to come clean.

"Sammy, I love you very much, and I want to spend the rest of my life with you," I said.

"I know," she whispered.

"But there's something I have to tell you."

"What's that?"

"My father is Jewish," I blurted out and held my breath, consumed with fear as I waited for her reaction.

She smiled, wiped away my tears, kissed me, and whispered:

"That's nice. I like your father. And I love you very much."

While my memory fails me when it comes to the details of that evening, I do know that it was one of the happiest of my life. But of course, the total story of my ethnicity was even more complex than I realized—or, at least, admitted to myself—at that time. Intellectually, I might have been aware of it, but I was not prepared to confront it emotionally. I had not told Sue the entire truth: that I once had three Jewish grandparents and thus was classified a Jew by the Nazis and that this was the *real* reason I had to be hidden from them. Looking back now, I do not think the deception was deliberate. Upon my father's orders, I had attempted to erase these memories and thus had not probed deeply into our family history. After all, I knew what I was: a native Czech, a proud American immigrant, and a Catholic.

I asked Sue to marry me in August 1958, while we were sitting on a bench in Burnham Park in Morristown. She said "yes" without hesitation, and we talked about a June 1959 wedding, immediately after her graduation from Trenton State College.

In the fall of 1958, I returned for my last semester of undergraduate work. At the same time, Jim Cobb and I were getting a head start by taking a couple of graduate-level courses because Professor Jan Tuma had convinced us to stay on for our Master's degrees after fulfilling our BS requirements.

Then something remarkable happened. I completed all the courses for my Bachelor's degree in January 1959 and, at the end of the academic year, the civil engineering faculty selected me as the recipient of their highest award—that of "Outstanding Graduate." Really?! The goddamn immigrant who had flunked out of Rutgers—wow!

Jim and I continued to study together, as we became fully immersed in our joint pursuit of Master's degrees. Both of us became graduate assistants, with adjacent offices in the bowels of the Engineering Building. My officemate was a brilliant fellow named John Tinsley Oden—known as "Tin" or "J. T."—who had received his undergraduate degree from Louisiana State University. Tin would stay on for his doctorate and eventually end up at the University of Texas at Austin, where he would carve out a distinguished career as a researcher and teacher. He would be the first-ever winner of the Lohmann Medal, the highest honor conferred by OSU's College of Engineering, Architecture and Technology (one that would be bestowed on me a few years later).

During my time at OSU, Jan Tuma became an academic superstar. He put the College of Engineering on the map by creating one of the highest-ranked structural engineering programs in the country. His designs—which included the terminal building at St. Louis' Lambert Field, the beautiful Vinita arch over the Oklahoma Turnpike, and the ultramodern hyperbolic paraboloid shell of the First Baptist Church in Oklahoma City—gained him international recognition. As a result, he was named Head of the School of Civil Engineering at OSU.

Tuma was writing and publishing many papers on his "Carry-Over Moment" numerical method in structural analysis, and those of us working on our theses under his tutelage were applying the technique to various types of structures. In addition to attending classes, Jim's and my theses dovetailed, and Tuma intended for us to get them published in the American Society of Civil Engineers (ASCE) Journal. One thing both Jim and I knew: we were determined to finish our MS degrees by the end of January of 1960, and no one, including the persuasive Jan Tuma, was going to convince either of us to stay on for our doctorates or for any other purpose. We needed to get out and earn some real money, to be free of the constant demands of school, and to have some fun.

There had been no graduation ceremony at the end of the fall semester in January 1959 when we completed our undergraduate work, so Jim and I waited to receive our BS diplomas officially in May, while already in graduate school. My parents flew to Oklahoma from the east coast for this very special day, no doubt to make certain that I was not making all of this up. It had been a hard road, with many bumps along the way, primarily placed there by my own hands. But I made it. Mother cried, and Papa could not stop hugging me. The three of us, along with the Cobbs, celebrated with a party at the Stillwater home of Jan and Hana Tuma.

After the celebration, Mother, Papa, and I piled into my Studebaker and headed east. I had never seen my father as happy as he was those three days on the road. While I drove, he laughed, sang, told jokes, and recalled humorous stories from Czechoslovakia and the war. I was elated because, finally, I had earned his pride and brought him happiness. After all the disappointments, I had graduated from college, with honors no less! A bit late perhaps, but I had managed to live up to his long-standing challenge: *Don't ever let anyone tell you that you're not capable of doing something. Put your head down, and go do it! And, no matter what you do, don't ever give up!* I was proud of myself and looked forward to the future, one which I would spend with Sue Holsten, who would become my bride in just a few days.

Sue graduated from Trenton State College (today, College of New Jersey) on the first day of June 1959. Two days later, we were married at the United Methodist Church in Morristown. My roommate and best friend, Don Gafford, drove his white MGA fifteen hundred miles from Oklahoma to be my best man. Sue's maid of honor was her college roommate, Ginny Sands. The wedding was relatively small, with less than fifty people attending the church ceremony and, for economic reasons, there was no reception other than an intimate dinner at the Hampshire House with our four parents and Don and Ginny.

Even before our celebration concluded, it became obvious that our relationship with my father had undergone a transformation. I had introduced Sue to my parents early in our courtship, and she and Mother found immediate rapport. Things had not gone as well with Papa.

"I like your father, but I'm scared of him," she admitted following an early visit to our home.

I had been afraid of that reaction and understood completely. In those initial years in the United States, Papa was different from the fathers of my friends. His manner was formal, almost aristocratic, when compared to that of casual, informal Americans. To new acquaintances—and certainly to Sue—he appeared cold and unfriendly. At the same time, he was strict with me and did not hesitate to whack me when I misbehaved. The last whipping I received from him came during my sophomore year in college. I had said something to Mother that Papa considered inappropriate. Despite the fact that, by then, I enjoyed a five-inch height advantage, I stood defenseless as I absorbed his blows.

But now, following our marriage, Papa had transformed

himself from a stiff European to a friendly American. He became more trusting of strangers; his manner was less formal; he smiled and laughed more often. With Sue, he became warm and funny. He began to treat me less like a boy and more like an equal. His true self came to the forefront: he was generous, loving, and tender.

Mark Twain's words best described the change in our relationship. "When I was a boy of seventeen, my father was so ignorant I could hardly stand to have the old man around. But when I got to be twenty-one, I was astonished at how much he had learned in four years." When Sue and I reached twenty-three, Papa had "learned" and became our loving friend.

Our "honeymoon" consisted of our Studebaker pulling a small U-haul trailer that carried all our possessions west on the Pennsylvania Turnpike and down Route 66 toward Oklahoma State University. I had made reservations for our wedding night at a nice motel along the way. When we arrived there near eleven o'clock at night, flushed with anticipation, we were turned away by a sleepy, surly manager who told us that we were too late and he had given away our room. We drove on until, around midnight, we spotted a "vacancy" sign. The motel turned out to be a fleabag, but it had a bed—and that's what mattered that night.

We arrived in Stillwater just in time to stand up for Don and Kay Gafford at their wedding, a simple civil ceremony at the county courthouse in Stillwater. Don was commissioned in the US Army by virtue of having completed Advanced ROTC at OSU. Now, he was off to serve two years of active duty while I stayed on to finish my Master's.

I had already missed a couple of days of summer school classes, so I had no choice but to become immersed in my studies immediately. Our first home as a married couple was a furnished apartment in a one-story cinderblock structure in the style of a small motel. It was located in the back of the Dairy Queen parking lot, not far from the OSU campus. A coffee table we purchased for five dollars, a fan we bought for twenty bucks, a card table with four folding chairs that we got by redeeming our parents' Green Stamps, two used lounge chairs we bought for two dollars each, and a twelve-inch black-and-white TV we received as a wedding gift were our sole possessions, besides our car, books and clothes. Yet, as Ella Fitzgerald sang in those days, we felt "as rich as Rockefeller."

As soon as summer school ended, I had to depart for Army Reserve duty at Fort Chaffee, Arkansas. Sue and I had not had a real honeymoon, and we had not spent much time together because of my heavy study load and her job as a professor's secretary. Now I had to leave her for two weeks. Both of us felt the pain. During my first week at camp, I befriended a fellow student Reservist from the University of Oklahoma named Mike McConnell. When I informed Mike how much I missed my wife, he came up with a brilliant idea.

"Why don't you go back and get her when we get our weekend twenty-four-hour pass?" he asked.

"What good would that do?" I countered. "We're not allowed off base during the week."

McConnell had a solution. Both of us were working at Division headquarters. The next day, Mike typed an official-looking letter, constituting an automobile pass. I stole a 95th Division decal used on helmet liners and pasted it on top of the page. At the bottom of the letter Mike typed the words, "Authorized by:" and scribbled an illegible signature above the words: "Commanding General."

Armed with the letter, and having made reservations at a motel outside the camp gate, I hitchhiked some two hundred miles to Stillwater. Sue packed a bag, and we drove our Studebaker back to Fort Smith, where we checked into the motel. The next morning at 4:30, one hour before reveille, I left the motel and drove through the gate, where I got a salute from the MP when he saw my "permit." I sneaked into the barracks and got into my bunk. A half hour later, I got up with the troops and went through the day's routine until the evening meal. After dinner, I drove out through the gate and walked into the arms of my waiting bride at the motel. And so it went all week until it was time to break camp and return home.

Now what? I was supposed to return to Stillwater the way I had come to camp, via a deuce-and-a-half-ton Army truck. But I had my car, and Sue and I wanted to go on a mini-vacation, instead.

Mike McConnell to the rescue once more. Mike's unit had come by Army bus from Oklahoma City. On the departure date, I arrived early as usual, stood formation with my company and answered roll call. Then, as the troops made their way to the barracks to pick up their duffel bags, I drove out through the gate and to the motel. Sue and I checked out and headed for the Lake of the Ozarks in Missouri. We would finally have our honeymoon.

Meanwhile, on the bus bound for Oklahoma City, Mike waited an hour before he removed his name tag from his uniform and replaced it with mine. He walked to the front of the bus where he found the senior officer:

"Sir, my name is Heller. Is this bus going to Stillwater?"

"No, son," said the officer. "We're headed for Oklahoma City."

"Oh, God," lamented Mike. "I got on this bus instead of the truck to Stillwater."

Upon arriving in the city, the concerned officer called the Stillwater Reserve unit to assure everyone that I was all right. He gave my stand-in five dollars out of his pocket for bus fare to Stillwater. Mike sent me my name tag and wrote that he considered the five bucks his payment for helping me go

AWOL. I thought he had been grossly underpaid, but I was in no position to remedy that.

Upon returning to Stillwater from our brief belated honeymoon, Sue and I resumed our lives as married graduate students. Sue was taking a couple of education courses while working full-time as a secretary at OSU. I threw myself into completing my Master's thesis by the end of the fall semester. Both of us were anxious to get out of town as quickly as possible and to begin a life that held out the promise of something beyond work and study.

CHAPTER THIRTEEN

GOLDEN STATE

Jim Cobb and I received our Master's degrees together in January 1960, having taken the same courses, studied together, and written our theses on the same topic under the guidance of Professor Jan Tuma. A week before graduation, the Cobbs and we bought our first-ever new cars—1960 VW Beetles—for $1,850 each. Ours was light blue; theirs was green.

Sue and I paid cash for our car using money we had saved from wedding gifts, our respective summer jobs, my graduate assistantship, and Sue's salary as secretary to my old nemesis, Professor "Half-wit," the man who had called me a Communist because I believed in federal aid to education.

Unlike college students of today—many of whom are saddled with student loans so large that they affect their ability to live comfortably after graduation—I owed a mere $3,500 after earning two degrees from OSU. My "banker" was my father, and the loan was interest-free. Our agreement was that, once I would begin full-time work, I would pay him back at the rate of $150 per month. I lived up to the agreement.

What I did not know was that Papa would deposit all my payments into a special savings account. On Christmas Eve following the last installment, he and Mother would present us with a savings account book, titled in our names, and valued at nearly $4,000. My parents, who had arrived in this country with no material possessions, continued to teach me about prudence, thrift, generosity, and love.

Jim and LaVerna Cobb returned to Jim's hometown of Oklahoma City, where he went to work at Cobb Engineering Company, a civil engineering consulting firm founded in 1921 by his father, Fred. Jim was one of four employees when he started. In 1971, he would buy the company outright and build it into one of the largest in the region, with more than a hundred engineers and other professionals designing and supervising the construction of highways, bridges, and various municipal projects. Jim and LaVerna went on to have four children—Dan, David, Dena, and Diana—all of whom graduated from OSU. In 1965, Jim came up with the concept of a club to raise money for Cowboy athletics. The organization, which became known as OSU Posse, eventually grew to more than six thousand members. The Cobbs' generosity toward our alma mater knew no bounds and was recognized through many awards, culminating in Jim's election to the Oklahoma State University Hall of Fame in 2008.

The last part of my college career at OSU coincided with the start of the space race, which began in 1957 when the Soviet Union launched the first satellite, Sputnik. A year later, the United States answered by launching its first orbiter, Explorer I. Then, during my senior year, the USSR shocked the world by crashing the Luna 2 probe onto the moon's surface. The race was on, and Americans were energized. I was no exception. Instead of applying my recently-learned skills to designing traditional civil engineering structures such as bridges and buildings, I was drawn toward the excitement, glamour—and, I must admit, money—of space.

My OSU fraternity brother, Bob Larkin, and his wife Peggy lived in Long Beach, California, where Bob worked as a structural engineer in the airplane division of Douglas Aircraft Company. I informed Bob that, following an interview trip to another company in the state, I had fallen in love with Southern California and convinced Sue that we should try to move there. When I also told Bob that I wished to get involved in the space program, he informed me about Douglas' Missiles and Space Division located in Santa Monica.

"Lark," I said to Bob. "You can't imagine what a dream come true this would be! A lot of times in school, while you guys were studying, I was sitting in my room reading Isaac Asimov, Arthur C. Clarke, and Alfred Bester, imagining myself traveling through space to another planet. Now, I could be designing those spaceships, and to do it in a beautiful place like Santa Monica! That would be like dying and going to heaven."

Bob gave me the name of Adrain O'Neal, the guy in charge of all structural analysis on the space side of Douglas (and yes, that is the correct spelling of his first name, pronounced "ey-dren"). I wrote him a letter, enclosed my resume, and requested a job interview. His response was a surprise—instead of an invitation to visit, he sent me a job offer. At $660 per month, it was less money than I had been offered by Boeing, but Boeing was in Wichita, Kansas, and not in God's country. I accepted without hesitation.

When the semester ended at the end of January 1960, and I had completed my Master's degree requirements, we packed all our belongings into our VW Beetle and headed west. Along the way, we celebrated the start of our new life by sightseeing in New Mexico and Arizona, stopping at the Grand Canyon, the Meteor Crater, and Indian cave dwellings. Finally, we reached the western terminus of Route 66, where the famous highway dead-ends at the most beautiful street in the world, Ocean Avenue in Santa Monica.

The next day, we found our new home—in a two-story, tan house surrounded by immaculately-kept flowerbeds resplendent with red blossoms—a fully furnished, one-bedroom apartment, for $125 per month, on the ground floor of 220 San Vicente Boulevard. The rent included all utilities and the use of a carport. We were thrilled. Most of what little money we had, we put up as advance rent payment and moved in. Being down to our last few dollars would be no problem because I would start work the next day, and I knew from Bob Larkin that every Friday was payday at Douglas.

The next morning, after arriving at the company, adjacent to Santa Monica's municipal airport, I was put through the normal drill of a first-day employee. I filled out a variety of forms, applied for a security clearance, and had my photo taken.

"No smiles; no profiles," instructed the crabby woman who took pictures for the company badge.

Finally, in the late morning, I submitted all my completed paperwork to the personnel department, and I was anxious to meet my boss and co-workers.

"I see that you're a naturalized citizen," said the woman behind the desk.

"Yes, ma'am."

"May I see your naturalization papers, please?" she asked.

I explained to her that my naturalization certificate was in a safe deposit box in a New Jersey bank, and that no one had told me I would need it at Douglas. I asked if I could begin work while the certificate was *en route* to me from my parents.

"Absolutely not," she hissed. "You can't work in the space program without at least a temporary Confidential security clearance, and we can't give it to you till we have a copy of your naturalization certificate on file."

Once again kicked in the butt for being a goddamn immigrant, I was devastated. We were broke. There was no FedEx or UPS in 1960, and fax machines had not yet been invented. I would have to call my parents, who would need to go to the bank in Morristown and then air-mail the paper to me. We were looking at a delay of four or five days. Sue and I had twenty dollars to our name. The first credit card had only recently been introduced, but we did not qualify for one. Besides, I had been taught at home that debt is bad, and thus there was no way that I would ever buy anything on credit.

The thrill of having arrived in paradise ended, and the waiting began. In the meantime, we ate bread and little Vienna sausages out of a can, and we got ourselves invited to a couple of dinners by the Larkins. It took a week for my papers to travel from the east coast to the west and, finally, I began work as an aerospace engineer.

Sue could not find a teaching position, so she became a teller at a Bank of America branch on Wilshire Boulevard, where several of her customers were movie stars. With her good looks and Southern California tan, she became a popular teller. When I waited for her on Friday evenings, the line at her window was always at least twice as long as the other queues. Proud to be the husband of such a beautiful young lady, jokingly I accused her of giving away cash and kissing her male customers.

At Douglas, I discovered why I was offered a job so quickly, without an interview. In 1960, advanced technical degrees were rare, and the company was trying to make itself more competitive by hiring as many engineers with Master's degrees as it could find. In the Strength (structural analysis) section to which I was assigned, I was one of only two people out of nearly a hundred with an advanced degree. The other was the Section Chief, Adrain O'Neil, a graduate of Mississippi State University. Yet, despite my glorified academic standing, I was given tedious, incredibly boring, assignments. My initial work consisted of checking the calculations of others. Whenever I found an error, I marked it with a red circle. When the calculation was correct, I placed a red dot above the result.

So much for the glamour of designing spaceships. The only excitement each day at the office was a lunchtime game of hearts. I was bored to death.

But outside of work, life was good. Almost overnight, it felt as if I had been released after a long prison sentence. Suddenly, there were no tests for which to study, no all-nighters to complete a report, no classes to attend. Sue and I had nights and weekends free for reading, watching TV, socializing with new friends, sightseeing, or just enjoying each other's company. We had money in our pockets, and we were in Southern California—paradise on earth. For $325, I bought a red 1952 MG-TD roadster. Finally, after years of dreaming, I owned my own sports car!

With the top down (actually, the car had no top), we tooled all over the Southland, visiting the sights from La Jolla to Santa Barbara, from Disneyland to the LaBrea Tar Pits, from Hollywood to Newport Beach, often with Bob and Peggy Larkin following in their car. We had our favorite haunts: The Broken Drum (motto: "You Can't Beat It!") restaurant, where we discovered beef stroganoff; Zucky's, a fabulous Jewish deli with three-inch-thick pastrami sandwiches; and the Surf Rider, where we were introduced to exotic Hawaiian drinks. We spent endless hours reading on the beach.

I got hooked on bodysurfing and, with a fellow enthusiast, Fernando Oaxaca, searched for the biggest waves from Malibu to Newport Beach. Proudly, I sported an always-fresh scab on my nose, a trademark of Southern California bodysurfers who rode the big waves and often crash-landed, nose-first, on sandy bottoms.

The idea of living in paradise was enhanced by the beautiful people who seemed to surround us. In a restaurant around the corner, we spotted the glamorous Hollywood couple, Esther Williams and Fernando Lamas. Hoagy Carmichael waved to us from his Rolls Royce convertible as we passed him in our MG. Joel McRae, a Hollywood cowboy star, lived in the house behind us, and a former Dead End Kid, now a film producer, resided in the apartment above us. (The Dead End Kids were a group of young actors who starred in a series of films, mostly comedies, for more than twenty years.) One night, in a drunken stupor, the former Kid threw most of his furniture out the window and onto the lawn. Such was life in La-La Land.

Sue and I made many friends, mostly through my job at Douglas. All of us seemed to be in the same mode: young, newly married, athletic, and party-loving. There were Phil and Jackie Handleman. Phil was a graduate of UCLA and Jackie of USC—an unlikely mix—and Phil's cousin was Ron Mix, an All-American football player who would eventually make it into the NFL Hall of Fame. The American Football League was formed that year, and we attended many Los Angeles (later, San Diego and now again, Los Angeles) Chargers games to root for Ronnie and our new hometown team, surrounded by thousands of empty chairs in the 100,000-seat Los Angeles Coliseum.

There were Wendy and Joan Allen, our good friends from Texas. They were tournament bridge players who taught us to play the game, though at a much lower level. Both loved horse-racing, and the four of us spent many Saturdays playing the ponies and losing money at Hollywood Park and Santa Anita.

We befriended Bill and Bettina Loomis. Bill was from Ohio and a graduate of MIT. Bettina was an immigrant from Germany. They began dating when we first met them, and I helped to convince Bill that he should marry Bettina. He did, and they would be married happily for nearly as many years as Sue and I.

Then there were Don and Sue Griffin, both Alabama natives and graduates of the University of Alabama. Don and Sue became our closest friends. They had a baby boy named Clayton, to whom we became Uncle Charlie and Aunt Sue. Don explained to me that he wanted me to be Clayton's godfather, but that his wife, a devout Catholic, had been instructed by her priest that they needed someone who was a practicing member of the Church; I no longer qualified. We and the Griffins got together for bridge and drinks nearly every weekend, and Don and I spent our breaks at Douglas together. Like my Sue, Sue Griffin was a teacher. Although both were products of the Deep South, the Griffins abhorred racism and shared our liberal philosophy. Regrettably, many years later, our friendship would end on a terribly sad note, and even worse tragedies would strike the Griffin family.

In November 1960, I became eligible to vote for the first time. Sue and I had watched the dynamic, young Jack Kennedy destroy the dour Richard Nixon in the first-ever televised presidential debate on our twelve-inch black-and-white TV and became devoted fans of JFK. I was inspired by his youth and his message of hope for America. Like many young people, I was ready to follow him to the barricades.

Neither Bill Loomis nor I satisfied California's residency requirements because we had not lived in the state for a sufficiently long period. Thus we could not vote the standard ballot that included candidates for state and local offices. For people like us, those who could vote only for the office of President of the United States, there was a single polling location in the entire Los Angeles metro area. It was in downtown L.A. Bill came from a long line of Midwestern conservative Republicans, and he was going to vote for Nixon. Of course, I was going to vote for Kennedy. Despite the fact that we knew that we would cancel one another's vote, we wandered around L.A. in Bill's green and white Chevy looking for the polling place for two hours before we found it. Each of us thought he could change the other's mind by the time we arrived. It did not happen. Yet, neither of us considered it a wasted afternoon because it was a historic occasion for both. For me, a recent immigrant, it was particularly significant. Of course, the best news was that John F. Kennedy won the election and was inaugurated in January 1961. And I, an immigrant, had helped to put him in the White House!

That year, Sue left the bank and finally began her teaching career with a second grade class at Madrona School in Torrance. She had a relatively long commute. The San Diego Freeway ended in Culver City, so she had to travel along Lincoln Boulevard, with its many signal lights and much traffic. I was much luckier. Even after Douglas moved our Missiles and Space Division from Santa Monica south to Culver City, I had only a quarter-hour ride to work, and Bill Loomis and I took turns driving.

In order to continue to fulfill my military obligation, I transferred from the Army Reserve unit in Stillwater to one in Santa Monica. While my Oklahoma unit had consisted mainly of college students and a few faculty members, my new outfit was quite eclectic. The company commander, who became a good friend, was Ted Fio Rito, Jr., son of the famous bandleader, pianist, and composer of the same name. By now, I was a staff sergeant and serving under me in my squad was a private named Westbrook. One morning, a few months after I joined the Reserve unit, I picked up *The Los Angeles Times* and saw Private Westbrook's photo in the lower-left corner of the front page. He just turned eighteen and received a million dollars from his late father's trust. The article went on to explain that he would receive the other forty-nine million when he reached the age of twenty-one. These were 1960s dollars, and he was one of the dogfaces under my command! I found it difficult to believe that I, not long ago an impoverished newcomer to America, was hobnobbing with the rich and famous. What a country!

My Reserve obligation included attendance at a two-week camp each summer. In 1960, Douglas had sent a letter to the Department of the Army, stating that my services were "essential to the nation's space program," and thus I could not be spared for two weeks. I was excused from camp. When

Douglas submitted a similar request in 1961, the Army turned it down. I had to go. Our battalion took a train to Paso Robles in central California, and from there we were driven to Camp Roberts. My only problem was that, just before leaving, Professor Tuma had called from Oklahoma to inform me that he and Hana would be driving west to Laguna Beach in a couple of days, so that they could have their new baby, Jan Peter, baptized there. They were bringing him to California because they wanted me to be his godfather. I felt honored, but I explained that I would be at Reserve camp, some 250 miles north of Laguna Beach. But my debt to the Tumas was such that I had to figure out a way to get there.

We were due a twenty-four-hour pass on Sunday after the first week of camp. I informed Ted Fio Rito about the situation, and he arranged to extend my leave to forty-eight hours. On Saturday morning, I hitchhiked a hundred and seventy-five miles home to Santa Monica. On Sunday morning, Sue and I drove to Laguna Beach where I participated in Jan Peter's baptism. After lunch, we drove back to Santa Monica, I put on my Army uniform, Sue dropped me off on the side of the Pacific Coast Highway, I stuck out my thumb and hitchhiked back to Camp Roberts. I arrived in the barracks early the next morning, exhausted, but feeling good about the fact that I had done something for the Tumas, who had played such a huge role in my education at Oklahoma State University. I was proud to be their only son's godfather.

The initial exhilaration of working in the space program at the height of the race with the Soviet Union wore off quickly. It was exciting to tell family and friends that I was part of the small team that designed the engine section of the Delta rocket, which over the years would carry more satellites into outer space than any other booster. And I was proud to tell them that I had been in charge of the design and manufacture of the canister that contained the Echo balloon, a communications satellite orbiting the earth. But in reality, the work was routine and boring. I was looking for a greater challenge. After some cajoling, I managed to convince my bosses that I could make a more meaningful contribution elsewhere in the company. My timing was good.

Under the management of a superb leader named Ray Zaller, a small structures research group was being formed. At the outset, it consisted of its director, Howard Levy, and me. I was energized, as Howard and I began to apply pioneering computer techniques to the analysis and design of aerospace structures, while everyone else was still using slide rules. I was learning a great deal, but often found that my knowledge was inadequate to tackle the complexities of structures in space. I had never before been faced with having to analyze the effects of metal fatigue, of dynamic loads during launch, of thermal stresses upon re-entry, and other incredibly complicated issues. After weeks of being overqualified for the mundane work of the Strength section, I was in over my head. Desperate to learn, I began to think about returning to school for a doctorate.

Sue and I loved Southern California. The informal lifestyle, the weather, the energy of a youthful population all suited us. We had many good friends, we lived a couple of minutes from the beach, and we had money to spend on ourselves for the first time in our lives. Nevertheless, although neither of us had any desire to return to New Jersey, we missed our parents. Moreover, both of us felt guilty. We were only children, and we would be three thousand miles away if our parents needed us.

My father must have sensed this when he and Mother visited us in 1961. Late that year, Papa spoke with our friend and former neighbor, Jack Geils, about it. When we came east for the Christmas holidays, Jack—now Vice President of AT&T—asked if I would be interested in coming back to work at Bell Labs, where I had been a junior draftsman during college summer vacations.

"Jack, I hope you can understand, but Sue and I really don't want to live in New Jersey," I said. "I guess we've been spoiled by Southern California."

"Where do you want to go, and what do you want to do?" he asked.

"We want to be on the East Coast, so that we'll be within a day's drive of our parents. And whatever job I take, I intend to start working on my doctorate part-time."

Thus ended the conversation, and I assumed that any path back to Bell Labs was closed.

I gained an appointment as a part-time Lecturer at UCLA, where I was teaching a course in Space Structures. I found teaching exciting and satisfying and began to toy with the idea of going into academia full-time. I interviewed at Sacramento State College (today, California State University, Sacramento) and was offered a position as Assistant Professor. I was intrigued, but this would not take us closer to our parents nor would it help me toward getting the next degree because Sac State did not have a doctorate program.

Then, seemingly out of the blue, I received a letter which appeared to solve both of these problems, courtesy of my friend and mentor, Jack Geils. It came from Bell Labs and, without so much as an interview, I was offered a choice of any one of three jobs: two in New Jersey—at Murray Hill and Holmdel—and a third at a field laboratory in Baltimore, Maryland. All of them would be part of a special program, wherein I would be allowed to attend classes toward a doctorate up to three half-days per week. Sue and I eliminated Murray Hill and Holmdel. Not only were both in New Jersey, but the only school with an appropriate program for me would be Columbia University. There was no way I was going to commute to New York, a city of which I was not particularly fond.

Baltimore sounded interesting, and I quickly learned that the University of Maryland had a doctoral program that would suit me. Neither of us had ever been in Baltimore, except for each having once passed through on the way to Washington. My parents volunteered to drive to Maryland and check it out for us. Perhaps we should have considered it a bad omen that they had an accident in thick fog on their return trip up the New Jersey Turnpike. Mother and Papa sent us a package that included photos of the city, of various garden apartment complexes, and of some landmarks. On the floor of our living room, we opened the enclosed map of the city of Baltimore.

"This is fantastic," I said to Sue. "Look at all that water!"

Everywhere we looked, there were areas in blue: Patapsco River, Middle Branch, Northwest Harbor, Curtis Bay. On paper, Baltimore looked similar to our neighborhood: Santa Monica, Pacific Palisades, Malibu. Even the place where I would work was on the water, on Colgate Creek. I accepted the job, and we prepared to leave sunny Southern California behind.

Having lived in a fully-equipped apartment, we had no furniture of our own. We had accumulated only a few possessions, so we packed them into two boxes, put the boxes in the cockpit of my MG, and drove the sports car to the train station in downtown Los Angeles. The MG was on its way to Baltimore by rail. We placed the rest of our belongings in our Volkswagen Beetle, said goodbye to our friends, and headed east.

On the way, we stopped in Oklahoma City, where we stayed with Jim and LaVerna Cobb, and we visited the OSU campus and the Tumas in Stillwater. Two days later, we arrived in Maryland. It was June 1962, on the day of the official ribbon-cutting ceremony marking the opening of the Beltway, a freeway ringing the city of Baltimore.

CHAPTER FOURTEEN

"BAWLMER, MERLYN"

We had spent nearly three years living in Paradise. Suddenly, following a three-thousand-mile trek across the country, we were transported into Hell. At least, that is how it affected us. Actually, it was called Baltimore—or, as we would find out when the natives pronounced it, "Bawlmer." Missing were palm trees, movie-star mansions, gaily-colored stucco buildings, and cheerful flowers. Even on this warm, sunny, June day, the predominant color was gray.

We set out in search of that blue water we had admired on the map stretched out on the floor of our Santa Monica apartment and discovered another surprise. The blue water had been some cartographer's dream. In reality, the water too was gray, with occasional disruptions provided by multicolored flotsam bobbing up and down near the seawall: papers, rotten fruit, old tires, and dead fish with their white bellies exposed to the stinking air.

Disgusted and distraught, we drove away to find the school Sue would be assigned to teach once the fall academic year began, Westport Elementary. It did not take us long to find it. When we did, Sue gasped.

"My God!"

We were staring at broken windows and filthy graffiti sprayed on the walls.

"You're not going to teach here," I said without hesitation.

"Thank you," she replied and kissed me lightly on the cheek. I could feel her tears on my skin. Without hesitation, I stepped on the accelerator in order to get the hell out of the area as quickly as possible. We would check out my new place of work—Bell Telephone Laboratories—in a Baltimore suburb called Dundalk.

On Broening Highway, we came upon the biggest factory I had ever seen. Beyond the large building with a "Western Electric" sign, what seemed like hundreds of smaller buildings were scattered in every direction. Someplace in there would be the Bell Labs field laboratory with my office. Workers were scurrying around on bicycles and on foot, dodging fork-lift trucks, each seeming to be going in a different direction. Across the street, a huge parking lot filled to capacity seemed to spread toward infinity. It, too, was surrounded by a fence more suited to a federal penitentiary. I noticed that the two electrically-controlled gates were locked in the middle of the workday, as if to keep the prisoner-workers from escaping.

"So, this is why I earned two engineering degrees and am about to start work on my doctorate? To work in a goddamn prison?"

We sat there in our little VW for a long time, each lost in our own private thoughts.

Finally, Sue spoke up. "Maybe things won't be all that bad. I'll find another teaching job, and you'll make friends in your job. We'll make the best of the situation."

We moved our meager belongings into a two-bedroom garden apartment on the west side of Baltimore, on Crimea Road across from Leakin Park. The second-floor unit was nearly new and comfortable. We met several neighbors who seemed friendly and hospitable. The apartment complex had a large pool, and the huge public park across the road promised opportunity for hiking and playing ball. Things began to look up.

Bell Labs' Baltimore field laboratory was devoted solely to the design and operation of the transatlantic telephone cable, manufactured by Western Electric. To my surprise, the work I was assigned proved interesting. I was the sole structures specialist, analyzing cable connections to repeaters, stresses in the complex multi-material anatomy of the cable, and assisting in the design of the ship-mounted cable-laying equipment. While not nearly as glamorous as working on spacecraft and satellites, the actual engineering associated with undersea cable was challenging.

Our small group was made up of smart, interesting people. The most memorable was a guy named Bob Langmack. Bob joined the Labs a month after I started and immediately made enemies of most of his co-workers. With pitch-black hair and a thin mustache, he looked like a young Clark Gable, and he acted the part. During our lunch-hour bull sessions, it seemed that whatever subject came up, Bob claimed he had been there and done it. After a few weeks of this, I had enough. In order to try to put an end to his bluster, I took it on myself to prove that his boasts were lies. Amazingly, whenever I challenged him, he brought in photos or documents the next day to prove that he had been telling us the truth.

One weekend in late summer, Sue and I visited my parents in New Jersey. On Saturday, we drove to New York, where we walked around Greenwich Village. We stopped at various street stands where vendors were selling used books. At one, I spotted a thin book with an intriguing title, *God and the Universe, Unity of Science and Religion*. I bought it for a quarter. The following week at work, I took advantage of a warm summer day by walking across the street to the parking lot and spending my lunch hour sitting in my topless car and reading while catching some rays. I was struggling trying to understand the author's attempted mathematical proof of the existence of God.

"Hey, I see you're reading my father's book," said a man's voice. It belonged to Bob Langmack, who was walking by.

This is too much, I thought. *Even for Langmack! What the hell does he mean by "my father's book?"*

"You didn't know that?" he persisted.

"Know what?"

"Well, look at the author's name."

Incredibly, the name on the cover was that of Holger Christian Langmack. I was dumbstruck and could not wait to get back to the office to inform my fellow doubters that, once again, Bob's name-dropping had withstood a test.

A few days later, the coffee-break conversation in the office turned to politics and a friend of President Kennedy, Joseph Tydings, who was running for the office of US Senator from Maryland.

"Joe is a good friend of mine," announced Langmack. "He and I ran track at the University of Maryland and roomed together on the road."

The resulting collective groan made his audience's reaction obvious: another crazy boast. I read in a newspaper that there would be a reception for the candidate at the Democratic Party headquarters in Annapolis and decided to put Bob to another test. Sue and I drove to the state capital, and there we munched on finger food while we listened to the speeches of several dignitaries, including the impressive, youthful Joe Tydings. When he finished, we joined a reception line of the faithful who came to shake his hand. Now I stood in front of the Senatorial candidate, with my prepared test question.

"Hello, Mr. Tydings, my name is Charlie Heller," I said, while shaking his hand. "I understand we have a mutual friend, Bob Langmack." I expected a blank expression on his face and a limp handshake. Instead, his face lit up into a big smile as his hand gripped mine.

"Really?" he said. "Bob was one of my best friends in school. We roomed together when we were on the track team at Maryland. Please say hello to him and ask him to call me. Here is my card."

After that, I never doubted the Clark Gable lookalike again, and we became friends.

In September 1962, I started course-work toward my PhD at the University of Maryland. With Bell Labs allowing me up to three afternoons per week, I had to fit my classes into those afternoons. When I had selected Maryland from three thousand miles away, I had not realized that it, unlike most urban universities, failed to cater to part-time students like me and that it would be extremely difficult to design class schedules to dovetail with my work.

It did not take me long to discover that the electric gates of the Western Electric parking lot really *were* there to keep Western's blue-collar workers from escaping during the workday. Even as a professional, I had to have written permission to leave early in order to go to class. The second time I left early, I pulled up to the gate, expecting the guard to open it for me; after all, I had presented my permission slip, showing that I would be leaving at midday every Tuesday and Thursday, only two days before.

The guard informed me that "even a smart-ass college boy" had to have a new permission slip each time he left the lot early and ordered me to go back across the street to get one. The smirking face and the tone of the guard's voice brought my blood to a boil. I came charging out of my car toward the booth. The door opened and a huge, fat, blue-uniformed slob confronted me. His double chin quivered as he swore at me and called me "asshole." I responded by grabbing his blue necktie at the knot, pushing him up against the barbed-wire fence, all the while calling him every filthy name I had learned in my thirteen years in America.

Suddenly, I looked down and noticed that he had a holstered gun strapped to his size 50 belt. I let go, expecting the worst. But the guard just stood there, and I saw fear in his eyes. He walked away from me and into the guard house. Without a word, he opened the gate. As I drove away toward College Park, I feared the consequences that would be awaiting me when I came to work the next day.

Half the morning passed, and no one said anything. There were no phone calls, no summons to the boss's office. Finally, I could no longer stand the suspense and knocked on the door of Bob Reilly, the head of Bell Labs' Baltimore office. I asked Bob if he had heard about my confrontation in the parking lot. He had not. I proceeded to tell him the whole story.

"So you tangled with Driftwood," he said, smiling, when I finished.

"Driftwood?"

"That's the nickname of the big, stupid, son of a bitch who likes to intimidate people. I'm glad you called him out. Not many people do. He's a coward. I've been trying to get Western to fire the bastard for years."

With that, Bob dismissed the situation and told me not to worry. From then on, he assured me, I could leave the parking lot anytime I wanted without the need for a written permission slip. He was true to his word.

Reilly did not keep my fight with the guard a secret. By afternoon, everyone seemed to know what had happened, and I received compliments even from people I had never met. I found out the origin of the name Driftwood. During World War II, when people were paying high prices for scrap metal, the guard was stealing copper and steel from Western Electric. His superiors suspected him but had no proof and could not figure out how he was removing it from the plant despite tight wartime security. Then one night, a crudely constructed raft was found adrift in Colgate Creek, which flowed by the plant. The raft was loaded with metal sheets and coils of cable; the captain was a big man in a guard's uniform. Following his arrest and eventual release, no one knew the guard with whom I would tangle years later by any name other than Driftwood.

My long commutes to the University convinced me that my topless, heaterless, Southern California sports car was not ideal for cold weather, nor was it made for long, high-speed, commutes. As winter approached, it became more and more obvious that I would have to sell my beloved little red MG. I advertised it in the *Baltimore Sun* on a Saturday morning for $800, hoping to get $500. I sold it less than two hours after the paper came out for my asking price, and phone calls kept coming in all day. Obviously, I had left money on the table. I replaced it with another used British sports car—a white Triumph TR-3. It had a top, a tonneau cover, and a heater.

There was one benefit to being co-located at work with Western Electric. I was able to take advantage of some of the big company's numerous recreational programs. I discovered that Western was forming a basketball team to play in a high-level industrial league against such opponents as Bethlehem Steel, Black & Decker, and Westinghouse. I had not touched a ball in nearly four years and was anxious to get back on the hardwood. Together with a fellow named Tom Flynn, I signed up for a try-out. Tom, who worked with me at Bell Labs, had played at Iona College, where he had been a prolific scorer. Both of us made the Western team, the only guys on the team who had played Division-I college ball.

In the middle of the season, Tom informed me that he was going home to New York City to play in the annual alumni game against the varsity of his high school alma mater, Power Memorial High. On Monday morning following his trip, he sat down next to my desk.

"How was the game?" I asked, expecting him to tell me that he had poured in thirty-some points against a bunch of high school kids.

"I scored six, all but two from the foul line," he answered.

"You're kidding!"

"I'm not. I spent the whole night being guarded by this kid who was so big that I was at eye level with 'Power Memorial' on his shirt. Remember this kid's name because you're going to hear about him: Lew Alcindor!"

I heard about him, all right. Lew Alcindor starred for the undefeated national championship teams at UCLA, and later, as Kareem Abdul Jabaar, became one of the finest players in the history of the National Basketball Association.

After completing my second semester at the University of Maryland in May 1963, I was able to sit back and contemplate my life and my future. Sue was teaching second grade at Woodlawn Elementary School near our home, we had made new friends, and we were happy with our social life. We were particularly close to my co-worker Fred Klappenberger and his fiancée, Fran Wilson, and to a teacher at Sue's school, Eileen Shapiro, and her husband Dave. But we did not particularly enjoy living in Baltimore. We were thinking about having children and began to consider moving to a place more conducive to raising them. The University of Maryland was still making my life difficult when it came to scheduling classes, but otherwise I liked it there and was doing well.

I enjoyed the benefits that came with working at Bell Labs—getting time off to attend school and playing basketball and softball—but I no longer enjoyed my work. After the first few months, it had become monotonous and boring. I recalled how much I had enjoyed teaching as a graduate assistant at Oklahoma State and a lecturer UCLA, and I wondered if life as a college professor might be more gratifying. The problem was that most universities required a doctorate, and I did not have one yet.

Then, out of the blue, a solution arrived from an unexpected source. The Labs hired a fellow who had just gotten out of the Navy, and whose last assignment had been as an instructor at the United States Naval Academy. He informed me that a major change was in the works there.

"They're making a transformation from a trade school to an honest-to-God university," he said. "They're hiring civilian faculty to teach courses in various new majors."

I discovered that USNA would be forming an Aerospace Engineering Committee within the Engineering Department and was granted an interview with the head of Engineering, Captain Wayne Hoof. Subsequently, I was offered a position as Assistant Professor, earning two-thirds of my Bell Labs salary. Without hesitation or negotiation, I accepted. Sue and I fell in love with Annapolis—the beautiful, historic town on the Severn River—and we were anxious to start a new life there.

CHAPTER FIFTEEN

CRABTOWN

The Navy made a momentous decision to transform the United States Naval Academy into a military service university. The magic date for this earth-shaking transition was September 1964, one year after our arrival in Annapolis. Quite a few civilian professors were hired at the same time, and many others would come the following summer in preparation for the "new USNA."

My agreement with administration was that, once we made the transformation, I would be part of the small initial nucleus of the new Aerospace Engineering Committee. For the first year, though, while all midshipmen still took a standard core curriculum, I would be part of the Third-Class Committee. At the service academies, first-year students are known as fourth-classmen, second-year students are third-classmen, and so on. Thus, our faculty group taught the engineering courses taken by all sophomores: Statics and Dynamics, Strength of Materials, and Engineering Materials.

This was fine with me because it would give me a year to become adjusted to life at a service academy. Moreover, I knew the subjects of Statics and Strength cold and thus lecture preparation would be a breeze. This would not only provide me with more time to continue my studies toward a doctorate, but it would also allow me to take advantage of the Academy's fabulous athletic facilities. I played tennis and basketball during breaks and on weekends, and I learned to play squash. I became a volunteer coach with the plebe (freshman) soccer and basketball teams.

The biggest event for the entire family arrived just as I was starting out at Navy—Sue announced that **she was pregnant**! Since both of us were only children, the elder Holstens and Hellers were ecstatic about the prospect of having their first grandchild.

Early in the morning on Thursday, April 9, 1964, Sue woke me up.

"It's time to go," she said calmly.

I dressed quickly and we drove to Anne Arundel General Hospital in downtown Annapolis. I smoked an entire pack of Kent cigarettes as I walked laps around the hospital grounds, regularly popping back into the waiting room to check on progress.

"It's a boy!" a nurse finally informed me after four agonizing hours. When I was allowed in to see Sue, she was asleep and the baby had been taken into a room full of tiny cribs. I was allowed to see my son only through the nursery window and, with his body and most of his head covered by a little white blanket, I could only see his eyes and nose. But I knew that he had to be a beautiful baby—after all, he was *our* baby!

The doctor informed me that it had been a difficult delivery. The baby had turned, and they had to use forceps to extract him. The physician said that, in the process, Sue had suffered some minor injuries which would have to heal before she could go home. He told me there was nothing to worry about; the baby was fine, and Sue would have to stay in the hospital only a few days.

I went home and called Sue's parents to tell them all was well. Then I called my parents to inform them that we had a son named David Arthur Heller, the middle name in honor of Mother's late father, Artur Neumann, my Jewish grandfather whom I had called *Děda* before the Germans murdered him during his attempted escape through Yugoslavia. Mother cried and Papa was ecstatic. I went out, bought a box of cigars, and distributed them among my fellow faculty members in Isherwood Hall. I spent the evening with Sue in her hospital room and went out to the viewing window, but I was unable to see David because his little crib was now far in the back of the nursery.

The following day, after I taught my classes, I returned to the hospital. I rushed to the nursery window, where I found David, now in the front row, surrounded by pinkish white babies. He was different—his color was blue. Something was wrong!

A nurse looked in the window with me, and immediately called the pediatrician on duty. He examined David and came out into the hall.

"Something is definitely wrong. He was bleeding a bit from his scalp where the forceps had cut him, and the bleeding has not stopped since he was born. There must have been some internal bleeding, too. We need to have a laboratory evaluation of his blood. We don't have the capability here, and the best people in this field are at the National Institutes of Health in Bethesda."

In a bizarre series of events that followed, I drove David's blood sample to the NIH, weaving my way through traffic on the Washington Beltway. In a matter of minutes, the doctors at NIH determined that an antibody in David's blood was killing his platelets, the little coin-shaped particles that cause clotting. Without platelets, I was told, he was bleeding, both externally and internally. We had to get him to Johns Hopkins

Hospital in Baltimore for a blood transfusion immediately!

I retraced my steps back to Annapolis and followed an ambulance to Hopkins. By the time I parked my car and filled out a few forms, David was already in the operating room. The wait was excruciating. No one told me so, but I knew that our son's life was hanging in balance on the other side of the stark walls of the waiting room. He was not quite two days old, and already I loved him dearly; I longed to be there holding him while the doctors worked to save his life. After two hours that seemed more like two lifetimes, two men wearing white smocks—one thin, dark-skinned, with jet-black hair, and the other slightly shorter, heavier, and with brown hair—came into the room.

"I'm Doctor Katz," said the shorter one, "and this is Dr. Rodriguez. Your little boy is out of danger now. We made two complete blood exchanges, a last resort in critical cases like this, and they worked. We don't know the cause of his condition or what was killing the platelets, but whatever it was, is gone now. The only remaining question is: how much internal bleeding was there? We don't think it happened, but he may have had some bleeding into his brain. Only time will tell if there was brain damage."

I was relieved, but horrified. David was taken into the children's wing of the hospital, and I was allowed to go in. When I bent down to kiss my son for the first time, I noticed that half his head had been shaved, and several bumps on the hairless portion caused his head to look lopsided. He may have appeared peculiar to others, but he was beautiful in my eyes, even with tubes and hoses attached to his little body.

Now it was time to return to Annapolis and to recount the day's events to Sue. I was under the impression that she was lying in the hospital, unaware of what had taken place. Much to my surprise, she knew and had spent a terrifying afternoon waiting for news of David.

"I never saw David until they told me they were taking him

to Hopkins," she said. "I insisted on seeing him before he left here. When they brought him to me, he was unresponsive and very gray-blue."

After I gave her the good news about the outcome of the Hopkins procedure, I told Sue about my harrowing drives to and from NIH and then from Annapolis to Baltimore.

On the way back, I had decided to give her only the good news and to withhold the fact that there existed the possibility of brain damage. That could wait until she came home. I was totally exhausted when I left her room, and, after calling both sets of David's grandparents, I crashed on our living room sofa.

For the next week, each day consisted of two visits with Sue at Anne Arundel General, teaching my classes, driving to Baltimore for a visit to Hopkins, and, on two of the days, also attending classes at the University of Maryland.

Finally, Sue came home after two weeks in the hospital, and I could tell her about the potential aftereffects of David's near-death experience. I explained that I had learned from Dr. Katz that David's disease was called Neonatal Thrombocyto-penic Purpura, that the cause was unknown to the medical community, and that the chance of total recovery was around seventy-five percent. Dr. Katz also told me that the fact that David's scalp had been cut during delivery had turned out to be a stroke of luck. If the doctor and nurses in Annapolis had not seen that his cut was still bleeding after more than twenty-four hours, they may not have eventually agreed with me that something was wrong. The outcome would have been disas-trous.

After several more days of recuperation from her injury, Sue began to accompany me on visits to the children's wing of Johns Hopkins. Every day brought better news. David was getting stronger and, so far at least, did not exhibit any signs of having suffered brain damage. The key indicator, we were told by those wonderful doctors who had saved his life—

Rodriguez and Katz—was the fact that he was "active." We and the hospital staff were ecstatic each time he kicked his legs, punched the air with his tiny fists, and screamed.

At the end of the first week in May, the big day finally arrived. David came home after a three-week stay at Hopkins. My parents drove down from New Jersey and were there to welcome us when we brought home the little guy with the big lump on his half-shaved head. After the angst of the past month, Sue and I were ready to start a new life as parents.

There would be some serious consequences of David's trauma. He was a late-bloomer in many functions—talking, reading, writing, physical coordination—and doctors and school psychologists kept up their guessing game. They described his difficulties as "perceptual handicaps" or "minimal brain dysfunction" or "dyslexia," depending on their mood or the day of the week. Any and all of these scared the hell out of us. This went on for the first seven years of his life until Mother's closest friend, Dr. Jane Emele, read an article in a medical journal, describing many of David's symptoms and stating that, in many children, they are indicators of *visual* problems. The article went on to discuss an emerging field called "developmental optometry" and its foremost expert, Dr. Morton Davis. Luckily, Dr. Davis was based in Maryland.

We took David to see him, and tests revealed that our seven-year-old son lacked many of the visual, motor, and language-development skills required to complete the visual-verbal matching necessary for learning. David had absolutely no depth perception, no bifocal vision (his eyes could not focus on a single close-up point), and vision in his left eye was suppressed. No wonder the poor kid struggled with learning! And now I understood how difficult it was for him to read, write or to catch a ball.

Dr. Davis, a decorated World War II veteran, became an important part of our lives. He put David on a strict therapy schedule, consisting primarily of eye-muscle training exercises. Our son exhibited immediate improvement. Sue and I took turns driving him twice a week to Davis' office in Columbia, about twenty miles away. After five years, Dr. Davis declared him cured.

Sue and I were only children. At various times in our respective lives, both of us wished we had a sibling or two. We wanted the same for David. We tried. Sadly, a miscarriage and concern that the problems we encountered with our son's birth might be a warning caused us to abandon the idea. As an alternative, we decided that we would adopt a brother or sister for David.

We made an appointment with an adoption agency in Baltimore. A kind lady spent an hour with us, explaining legal issues, the cost of adoption, and requirements of financial stability of the adopting family. Obviously, she was also assessing carefully our personalities, our speech, our maturity, and other characteristics that helped her determine if we would make good parents. Apparently, we passed because she gave each of us a lengthy form to take home to fill out and return.

Anxious to begin what we had been told would be a lengthy process, Sue and I began to fill out the forms as soon as we returned home to Severna Park. For me, all went smoothly until I came to a line that read:

Religion: _____

"Did you answer the question about your religion?" I asked Sue.

"Sure," she replied. "I wrote 'Methodist.'"

"I don't think it's any of their damned business what our religion is," I said.

"We really want this to happen," Sue said. "So, I think we need to give them all the information they ask for."

As a matter of principle, I wanted to leave the question unanswered. At the same time, I wanted to please my wife. Moreover, I recalled an incident from a few years back in

California. I had been recruited for an engineering position at Alcoa in Pittsburgh. During a meeting in Los Angeles, the manager interviewing me asked:

"On your application form, you left blank the part asking your religion. Why?"

"Because that's personal and has nothing to do with my ability to do the job," I responded.

"I'm sorry, but we can't consider you for employment unless you answer the question," he said.

I stood by my principles and left the interview. I was disappointed in the outcome because Sue and I wanted to leave California and move further east in order to be closer to our parents. An OSU fraternity brother was a manager at Alcoa, and I phoned him with my story.

"Don, why do they want to know my religion? What does that have to do with anything?" I asked.

"Oh, they just want to make sure you're not Jewish," he said.

Despite my revulsion as I now recalled this incident, I picked up the adoption agency's application form and filled in the blank:

Roman Catholic.

Two or three weeks went by after we sent in the completed forms, as well as our family balance sheet. Finally, we received a call from the lady who had interviewed us.

"Mr. Heller," she said. "I regret to inform you that we must reject your application because you and Mrs. Heller are of different religions."

Appalled that someone would think that we were unsuitable as parents because one was a Protestant and the other a Catholic, we abandoned the idea of contacting other adoption organizations. David would have to be an only child—just like Sue and I.

CHAPTER SIXTEEN

HIGHEST DEGREE

In 1964, we bought our first house, a pretty rancher in the Oakleigh Forest neighborhood of Severna Park, about eight miles north of Annapolis. Our next-door neighbors, Paul and Sandy Rosswork, had two young sons—Paul (known as P.B.) and Kimber—and the adults and children became the best of friends. We began taking skiing and boating vacations together. We were close to our neighbors across the street, Ron and Jeanne Carpenter, as well. Ron was an adopted son of one of the branches of the DuPont family, while Jeanne came from more modest means and Slavic roots.

After interrupting her career to care for David, Sue became a kindergarten teacher at the Naval Academy Primary School, where she would remain for the next thirty years. Located next to the Navy golf course, across the Severn River from the Academy, NAPS was a school for the children of USNA faculty and military personnel located in the Annapolis area. Because the school was funded entirely by tuition, the teachers were paid considerably less than those in the public-school system. But the low pay was compensated for by an atmosphere of learning, well-behaved pupils, and camaraderie among a small group of highly-motivated teachers. Sue was particularly pleased with the fact that kindergartners attended school only in the morning, which meant that she had weekday afternoons to do whatever she wished.

I continued attending classes at the University of Maryland, but as the number of courses I still needed came down to the last few, I found it impossible to schedule them around my teaching duties at the Naval Academy. The University did not accommodate students who worked full-time, and I saw trouble ahead. Fortunately, I discovered that several of my Navy colleagues were studying for their doctorates at The Catholic University of America in Washington, DC, because CUA catered to working people like us by offering the majority of graduate courses in the evening. I visited, met the man who would become my advisor, Dr. Michael Soteriades, and decided to make the move. It proved to be one of my better decisions.

Catholic University was perfect for me. The classes were small and the professors, some full-time and others adjuncts doing practical work by day, were both knowledgeable and approachable. I thrived in the environment. I completed my course work in January 1967 and passed the language and comprehensive exams. Now it was time to concentrate on completing my dissertation, the subject of which arose from my consulting work for the Navy, in which I had attempted to analyze the structural behavior of complex reinforced aluminum plates used as decking in submarine interiors. By now, I was eligible for sabbatical leave from the Naval Academy—either a full year at half pay or a half-year at full pay. I chose the latter because I could not afford a cut in salary. Then CUA's engineering dean made things even sweeter.

"I have discretionary funds," Dean Marlowe told me. "I'm going to use them to give you the Dean's Scholarship, a free ride for the next six months while you finish your thesis."

With this financial support from both Catholic University and the Naval Academy, I was able to devote all my time to writing, and I completed all requirements for a PhD in engineering in May 1968. On a beautiful, sunny, June day, following a commencement speech by Senator Edward Brooke, and after all the other degrees had been handed out, the University's president announced:

"And now, The Catholic University of America will award the highest of all honors, the doctoral degree."

Sue, dressed in a bright yellow dress, held four-year-old David and stood alongside my parents and hers, as I walked to the podium where I received my diploma inside a leather portfolio. Walking off the platform, I felt the strain of the past few years dissipating. Until that moment, I had been under enormous pressure—to take another step toward the elusive American Dream of success, to overcome another obstacle placed in front of this immigrant, and to gain the prestige and respect I craved. There had been many instances during which I wondered if I had reached my limit. At such times, my father's words of wisdom, imprinted on me when we arrived in America, rang in my ears: *Don't ever let anyone tell you that you're not capable of doing something. Put your head down, and go do it! And, no matter what you do, don't ever give up!* I had done it. I had made my parents proud again!

Sadly, completion of my doctorate was the only positive highlight of that crazy year, 1968. Earlier, the murders of two of my heroes—Martin Luther King and Robert Kennedy—had shaken my esteem for my adopted nation. But, at the same time, there seemed to be hope for my native land. In Czechoslovakia early that year, a phenomenon called the "Prague Spring" emanated seemingly out of nowhere. After twenty years of Communist tyranny, the government of Alexander Dubček gradually began to allow citizens more freedoms. "Socialism with a human face," they called it. Although by now I considered myself that "one-hundred-percent American" my father had ordered me to become nearly twenty years earlier, a tiny spark of Czech patriotism began to glow. For the first time in years, the Czech language returned as my mother tongue, while I listened to broadcasts from Prague on my short-wave radio. I wondered about our relatives, the Hahns, and about the boy who had become my best friend after the war in Prague, Vladimír Svoboda. Perhaps I would be able to see them soon.

But all hopes ended in August, when the Soviets decided that they could not allow their puppet state to deviate from Communist orthodoxy. Red Army tanks, accompanied by soldiers from other Warsaw Pact Communist nations, rolled into Czechoslovakia and enslaved its people once again.

The invasion opened the floodgates of emigration. Thousands of Czechs and Slovaks fled to the West. This generation of refugees, which became known as the "class of 1968" (as opposed to our "class of 1948") arrived in America in relative comfort. They flew in directly via PanAm, whereas our "class" had come on overcrowded Liberty ships, and only after spending many months in refugee camps. There was no love lost between the two classes of Czechoslovak refugees. Members of our class resented the ease with which people who had opted to live under Communist rule for twenty years were able to enter the United States. The newcomers, on the other hand, felt aggrieved.

"We suffered for twenty years while you people enjoyed the good life in America," they said. Jealousy is one unattractive Czech characteristic that lived then and continues to live today.

Regardless of immigrant infighting, the Prague Spring was over, the Iron Curtain was shut tight again, and I was convinced that I would never return to Czechoslovakia.

CHAPTER SEVENTEEN

FOLKS WHO LIVE ON THE HILL

People in academia view the attainment of tenure as the end of the rainbow. It takes hard work, excellence as a teacher, ability to bring research dollars to the institution, publications in refereed journals, and good politics—smooth relationships with the decision-makers—to be granted what amounts to a guaranteed job for life. Thus, I shocked my fellow faculty members by resigning a mere three months after being granted tenure—at thirty-two the youngest person in the history of the Naval Academy to be so honored—in 1968.

I had been supplementing the modest paychecks Sue and I were bringing home by consulting for a number of clients: NASA, Lockheed, Head Ski, the Navy, and others. Not only did these assignments help us financially, but perhaps more importantly, they gave me a taste of running a small business. I did not recognize it at the time, but I had been bitten by the entrepreneurial bug. I was lucky with my timing, having come to the Naval Academy a couple of years prior to the start of a major revolution in the application of computers. We called it "interactive computing"—the use of time-shared computers for real-time communication between man and machine.

This was a quantum leap over traditional "batch computing" of that period, wherein the user wrote a program, punched hundreds of so-called "IBM cards" (each representing one line of code), submitted a box full of the cards to a central computing center, and waited till the next day to receive the results of an overnight run on a huge mainframe computer. The following day, the computer center provided the programmer with a print-out that listed all errors. In a complex program, there might be twenty or more mistakes. After correcting the errors and punching new cards, the programmer submitted a revised program. In the days that followed, the drill was repeated, until one had an error-free program.

By contrast, *interactive* computing allowed a user to perform such runs and corrections almost in real time. Sitting at a terminal and connected to a large mainframe computer at some remote location via a telephone line, one communicated with the machine at the speed of electrons flowing across a copper conductor in the cable. Called "time-sharing," this technology constituted a change that would revolutionize engineering, science, and even manufacturing. With the Naval Academy as one of the world's largest users of time-sharing— four thousand midshipmen and many professors online—I was lucky to be in the right place at the right time. My research, consulting gigs, and doctoral dissertation were unique for the exploitation of this new technology.

I saw an opportunity to capitalize on this experience and to apply interactive computing as a more efficient, accurate, and economical method to design such complex systems as automobiles, airplanes, ships, and buildings. That was my vision. But like many techies before me—and thousands more who would come after me—I was ready to launch a business around a neat idea with no clue of its market acceptability and without a strategy for starting and building a company. I had never worked inside a small company, nor had I taken a business course of any kind. In those days, there were no courses or workshops for entrepreneurs and, in our region, there were no role models or mentors who had "been there and done that" in high-tech ventures. Thus, I knew nothing about marketing, selling or finance. I had only a vision and motivation. Fortunately, I also had friends with similar aspirations.

I will not go into great detail about the agonies and ecstasies of my life as an entrepreneur because they are described at length in my 2017 memoir, *Ready, Fire, Aim! An Immigrant's Tales of Entrepreneurial Terror*. I will say that life as a co-founder and chief executive officer of two high-tech startups suited my personality perfectly. I had been bored while working as an engineer in large companies, and life in academia proved too sedate and secure. Moreover, as an employee, I had little control over matters; I had to live by rules and regulations—often bureaucratic ones—made by others.

I fell in love with entrepreneurship because I thrived on taking risks—not gambles, but calculated risks. I loved building teams and had no qualms about putting in hundred-hour weeks in the office in order to build companies of significance. I took greatest pleasure in having a sense of control over the destiny of a team of overachieving individuals who were the nuclei of each of our companies. The end goal for me was not to become fabulously rich, but to build something of significance and to make a lasting contribution to the human race. And, as with nearly everything I undertook, I was driven by an immigrant's craving for respect. Looking back, I am not able to judge whether or not I succeeded, but those are the things that drove me for many years. The golfer-philosopher, Johnny Miller, must have been thinking of all entrepreneurs when he wrote:

"A person should not be judged by how much he has accomplished; he should be judged by how much he has overcome."

Back in California, Sue and I had dreamed of someday owning our own home. Sitting on the floor of our rented apartment with our arms around each other, we often listened to Peggy Lee singing a song that represented our vision of the future.

> *Someday, we'll build a home on a hilltop high*
> *You and I, shiny and new*
> *Cottage that two can fill.*
> *And we'll be pleased to be called*
> *The folks who live on the hill.*
> *Someday, we may be adding a wing or two*
> *A thing or two.*
> *We will make changes, as any family will.*
> *But we will always be called*
> *The folks who live on the hill.*

[Copyright: Kern, Jerome and Hammerstein, Oscar, "The Folks Who Live On The Hill" (1937). *Vocal Popular Sheet Music Collection.* Score 816. https://digitalcommons.library.umaine.edu/mmb-vp-copyright/816]

By 1971, we had been living in our house in the community of Oakleigh Forest for seven years. Unfortunately, P. B. Rosswork, who lived next door, was David's only friend in the neighborhood. As an only child, David tended to be an introverted loner, and other community children often picked on him. The worst offender was a girl named Katy, the daughter of our other next-door neighbors. Always backed up by her older brother Billy, she tormented David whenever he came outside to play. With Billy standing by to assist if needed, she would step on David's favorite toys—his Tonka trucks— and otherwise make his life miserable.

For Sue and me, the situation became intolerable, and we were despondent over our seven-year-old son's unhappy life. I spent many sleepless nights, beating myself up for not having given David a brother or sister, thus enabling him to team up with a sibling against neighborhood bullies like Katy.

We should have lied about our religion, I often thought when recalling having stood on principle while dealing with an adoption agency. Having been an only child myself, I had not faced the same problems because I fought with my fists whenever confronted by a bully. Now I understood that our son was a gentler soul, and he was paying the price. Sue and I decided that there was only one solution: we would get out of Oakleigh Forest, where David could start a new life.

As CEO of CADCOM—the software company I had co-founded with my colleagues—I was compensated well, and thus we had many choices in the Annapolis area. By now, we were hooked on sailing, so we narrowed our search to waterfront communities.

"A house just came on the market in the most prestigious community in the area," our real estate agent and my frequent tennis partner, Chris Coile, announced on the phone one summer day.

Later that day, we rode through an entrance marked by the sign, "Rugby Hall." Chris made a right turn onto Rugby Road, and soon we were parked on the lower level of a dark brown ranch home located on a corner lot. As Chris led us from room to room, I could tell by Sue's reactions that she was not excited. Following the inspection, Chris took us for a ride around Rugby Hall. We were impressed by the stately homes and made no secret of our enthusiasm when he showed us the community beach and pier on the Severn River. When he dropped us off back in Oakleigh Forest, we told Chris that we would talk things over and get back to him in the morning.

"Well, what did you think?" I asked Sue following Chris' departure.

"I don't know. The interior of the house is so dark, the rooms are small, and I'm not crazy about the layout. Also, I don't like the fact that it's on a corner lot. With two sides of the property exposed to traffic, it might not be a great place for David to play. What did you think?"

"I agree with you completely. I really liked the community, though. The houses are nice, there's a beach and boat slips, and they have access to tennis courts. But the house is not for us."

We informed Chris and he promised to keep looking. Luckily, he did not have to look very long.

"This is incredible!" he almost yelled into the phone a couple of days later. "Houses in Rugby Hall seldom go on the market. Amazingly, the house next door to the one you looked at was just listed. We need to get over there quickly before it sells."

Once again, we passed through the Rugby Hall entrance and took an immediate right. This time, we turned left past the corner house we had inspected earlier and climbed a hill. When we reached the crest, we spotted a beautiful, single-story rancher, with a front of white brick and gray siding. Sitting on a lot of one-and-one-third acres, it overlooked the community from its high perch. The huge back yard was the apparent terminus of what once had been a lane for horse-drawn wagons, marked by a row of mature poplar trees. The rear boundary of the property consisted of a row of closely-spaced, stately, tall pines. A huge willow tree stood at the rear corner of the house.

The inspection of the interior was almost perfunctory. Before entering, I knew that we had found our dream home. Sue was happy with the layout: three bedrooms, a sunroom, a den, two bathrooms, a kitchen, a one-car garage, and a basement that was half finished and divided into a playroom and workshop/utility room. Perfect!

Following a brief negotiation, and the sale of our existing

house, we had become THE FOLKS WHO LIVE ON THE HILL. And for me, it was the fulfillment of another piece of the American Dream—a tiny sliver of the nation that had so kindly taken me in and allowed me a modicum of success and a beautiful, happy family.

We built a swimming pool in our backyard and later added a hot tub. Our little family grew by one when we brought home a Keeshond puppy and named him Sport. Our parents visited as often as they could, and we made frequent trips to New Jersey to see them. My father and mother doted on their only grandchild. They showered David with presents, and Mother usually slipped him a few dollars.

"His allowance is much too small," she told me when I complained.

"But Mother, he's a little kid. What's he going to do with the money?"

"Maybe he'll save it until he's old enough to spend it."

In 1974, I joined the Annapolis Yacht Club, and in 1977, I became a member of the Annapolis Rotary Club. Our immersion into the community was complete. Sue continued teaching at the Naval Academy Primary School, and David—now happy in a neighborhood with friendlier kids—attended NAPS from pre-kindergarten through third grade. For fourth grade, we enrolled him in public school, Jones Elementary, a future Blue Ribbon school not far from our home.

In the fall of 1975, when Sue and I visited the school for a conference, the principal took me aside.

"I heard that you played college basketball," he said, and I wondered where this was leading. "We need to raise some serious money for the school, and I was thinking of putting on an exhibition basketball game."

"What did you have in mind?" I asked.

"The Baltimore Orioles' players have a basketball team that plays during the off-season, usually in fundraisers for charities and other organizations. I'm thinking that we could put together a team of dads of our students and play them. We'd rent a high school gym and raise money through ticket sales."

"That's a great idea," I said. "Do you know if you can get the Orioles to come?"

"Oh, yes. I've already talked to the guy who manages the team. He said they have an open date at the end of January."

"What would you like me to do?" I asked.

"I'd like you to be the player-coach. I'll recruit the dads for you, and you shape them into a team."

The idea appealed to me. In fact, the more I thought about it, the more excited I became about playing one more competitive basketball game—until our first practice.

The seven or eight fellows who showed up were well intentioned, and some of them still retained a few skills they had learned while playing high-school basketball. However, it took only one simple lay-up drill to realize that we had a long way to go before we could go up against a group of elite athletes like the Orioles.

But we practiced two evenings a week through the Holidays and, by mid-January, I thought we had a team that, at least, would not embarrass itself. In the meantime, the principal scheduled the game, arranged for the use of a gym at a nearby high school, and informed us that ticket sales had reached a couple thousand dollars—a sell-out. The game was scheduled for the evening of Tuesday, January 27, 1976.

Why am I writing about this seemingly trivial event? Because two days before the game was my fortieth birthday. My parents drove down from New Jersey to help us celebrate. During my basketball career—high school, New Jersey's recreational and semi-pro leagues, Division-I college—my parents had not even once seen me play. Unlike American parents of today, who cheer for their kids from Little League to high school, European parents of my parents' era considered sports to be the kids' realm, one in which they did not get involved. Now, with the Jones Dads vs. Baltimore Orioles game only two days later, Mother and Papa decided to stay. For the first time ever, they would see me play! At the age of forty, I was not exactly in my prime, but I was thrilled, nonetheless.

We and the Orioles shared a locker room. Their team trainer, Ralph Salvon, was kind enough to tape my ankles, the first time a professional would treat my weak joints since my days as an Oklahoma State Cowboy.

"I hope you're ready for a bit of rough stuff," Ralph said quietly.

"What do you mean?" I asked.

"A couple of the O's couldn't make it tonight, so they asked two Colts to play. Those guys think football rules apply on the basketball court."

It did not take me long to find out that Ralph had not been kidding. I was unlucky enough to be guarded by Mike Curtis, a Pro Bowl linebacker known as "Mad Dog." By halftime, Curtis held me to six points and administered bruises to my arms and body without having drawn a single foul. The referees were as intimidated by Mad Dog as I was. The rest of our team was not bruised, but it had fared even worse than I had. We were down 42-16 as we headed for the locker room.

I gathered the team around me, but I was at a loss for words. We were no match for these major-leaguers, and I could think of no way to prevent further embarrassment before a supportive crowd. Then, a near-miracle took place.

The locker room door opened, and two men entered. I recognized one from photos in the local paper: he was Roger "Pip" Moyer, the mayor of Annapolis. With him was an athletic young guy, about six-and-a-half feet tall.

"Which one of you is Charlie Heller?" Moyer called out from the door. I stood up and walked over to the pair.

"You guys are in trouble. Could you use a little help?" he asked.

"God, yes. What do you have in mind?"

"I want you to meet Kelly Tripucka. He's a high-school All-America from New Jersey."

"Where are you playing in New Jersey?" I asked as I shook the tall kid's hand.

"Bloomfield High."

"I played for Morristown High in the Fifties," I said. "Bloomfield beat the hell out of us a couple of times. You guys always have good teams."

"Would you like Kelly to suit up with you guys for the second half?" Moyer interrupted the New Jersey discourse.

"Are you kidding? Of course."

As if by design, Kelly was wearing a pair of basketball shorts under his trousers. Our team "uniform" was an ordinary white t-shirt, and he was wearing one under a sport shirt. Pip Moyer handed him a pair of sneakers, and our team—plus one—headed out to the floor.

The second half was the reverse of the first. We fed Tripucka, and he scored bucket after bucket. The O's switched to a zone defense, and that got Mad Dog off me. I started hitting jump shots. Between us, Tripucka and I outscored the O's by twenty points. Unfortunately, a twenty-six-point deficit was too much to overcome, and we lost by four.

But it was a blast! Not only that, but we raised much-needed funds for the school without embarrassing ourselves.

The next morning, Papa said to me: "I wish we had seen you play when you were younger." *So do I, Papa,* I wanted to say but did not. I had to be satisfied that my parents had finally seen me on the basketball court.

A postscript for non-basketball fans: Kelly Tripucka would go on to play four years at Notre Dame. He followed up his college career with ten years in the National Basketball Association, two of those as an NBA All-Star.

CHAPTER EIGHTEEN

SEARCH FOR SPEED

I played Division-I college basketball, but I never fulfilled my dream of becoming a star. I played tennis on the Oklahoma State University freshman team and in amateur tournaments, but my game was not strong enough to compete at a national or international level. I was captain of OSU's club soccer team and a member of an AAU volleyball squad, but my play was not of Olympic caliber in either sport. And I did not make good on a promise to my mother to buy her a new house with my major-league baseball signing bonus. Yet sports are in my blood, and I am competitive as hell.

My father had been an outstanding athlete in his youth—a volleyball and soccer player, and co-holder of the European distance record (nearly 800 miles) in a single-person kayak. For me, the drive to emulate him extended to games. When I was young, he had warned me on more than one occasion to concentrate on one or two sports, so that I would not be "a jack of all trades and a master of none." However, he had also instructed me that, as an immigrant, I would have to be better than the natives at everything I undertook. Sports and games were no exception and the urge to compete and to win was simply too strong. I was driven to try them all—well, at least, most—and to work hard to be a winner.

Having reached adulthood and no longer driven by the naïve desire to become a professional athlete, I resigned myself to applying my education as an engineer, combined with my entrepreneurial bent, as a means for supporting my family. One of the reasons I loved entrepreneurship was the competition. But how could I stay active and competitive outside the office? Let me count the ways: there would be tennis, downhill and cross-country skiing, kayaking, hiking, and golf. And, there would even be automobile racing—and eventually, sailboat racing.

My auto racing "career" actually started back in New Jersey, during the summer following high school graduation. For a couple of years, my friends and I had been attending stock car races at Morristown Raceway, a half-mile dirt track next door to the plant that made Mennen deodorants and shaving lotions. By this time, my 1940 Hudson coupe had become a liability. Its habit of stalling each time I stopped at a traffic light made driving hazardous and so embarrassing that Sue and my pals refused to ride with me. One Friday evening, several of us were in the stands at the racetrack, watching a race for novice NASCAR drivers, one that always preceded the major events.

"Hey, Charlie," one of my classmates shouted over the engine noise. "Why don't you take your Hudson out there and race it? You won't have to stop for a stoplight, so it won't stall on you!"

I laughed along with the others. But as the evening wore on and I watched in awe as my hero, Al Keller in car number 88, drifted around corners and blasted down the straight-aways, I imagined myself out there, taking the checkered flag just like Al. The Hudson's days as a street car were numbered, but racing it might be a possibility. The more I thought about it over the weekend, the more I liked the idea. However, there were two major problems. One, the minimum age for obtaining a NASCAR novice license was twenty-one, and I was only eighteen. Two, I knew that my parents would never allow me to participate in a sport they considered dangerous.

Hurdle number one was relatively easy to overcome. I had a summer job as a junior draftsman at Bell Labs in nearby Whippany. One of the secretaries there was well known among young employees as a master counterfeiter who could change a person's date of birth on a draft card without any trace of the crime. In those days, draft cards were the primary means of identification for males and were used to prove that one was old enough to order a drink at a bar. I gave my card to the lady one day, along with a twenty-dollar bill. Presto, the following day, I was three years older.

A NASCAR official accepted the lie and, after I passed a written test, issued me a provisional license that would allow me to race in three novice races, provided that the car would meet safety and other requirements.

My parents were a more difficult stumbling block, so I decided that I had to deceive them, as well. I informed them that the Hudson was no longer safe to drive on the street and that a friend who was twenty-one years old and I would modify it such that *he* could race it at the Speedway. Mother thought the idea was a bit crazy and Papa wondered why I did not just take the car to the junkyard. But they did not object and even agreed to let us work on the car in our driveway.

I purchased a regulation NASCAR helmet and a Nomex fireproof driver suit and stowed both in a box in the attic. Two friends and I then spent evenings and weekends converting the Hudson coupe into a racing machine. We installed a roll-bar and seatbelt; we knocked out the side windows; and we painted a large, white number 14 on both sides of the black car. One day while we were working, it began to rain, so we decided to move the car into the garage. My father had recently acquired a new, green wheelbarrow. It was standing in the middle of the small garage. Since there was no room for it elsewhere, we stowed it inside the trunk of the Hudson while we worked indoors.

A few days later, our work was done, and it was time to go racing. Unlike the professionals, we had no trailer or tow truck. But the Hudson was still licensed to be driven in the street, so we left the license plates on it, and I drove it all the way to the pits at Morristown Raceway, where we removed the tags.

I was a nervous wreck while awaiting the start of the novice race. Finally, on my third visit to the men's room, I heard the announcement to move the cars from the pits onto the track. I ran out, jumped in the car and—with my pit crew patting me on the shoulder—I moved into line entering the track. I gave a quick, cool-guy wave to my friends who were in the stands, seated near the starting line. The race was to begin with a standing start, and I was assigned the inside position of row three.

As I made my practice laps in the middle of the pack of ten or twelve competitors, I kept gaining confidence and began to relax. *I can do this!* I told myself. *I'm gonna kick everybody's ass, and, by the end of summer, I'll be racing in the feature race with the big guys.*

The starter waved a flag, indicating that practice had ended, and it was time to line up for the start. Carefully, I pulled into my slot in the third row, making sure to keep my foot on the accelerator. *I can't let the RPMs drop now and have the engine stall the way it does at traffic lights!* With all cars in place for the start, I continued to rev the engine, both to prevent a stall and to impress my friends in the grandstand: *VROOM! VROOM! VROOM!*

My eyes were on the starter's green flag. Then, suddenly: "BAM!!"

An explosion rocked the car and white smoke billowed

from the hood. *Oh, my God! My car's on fire! I have to get out of here before it explodes!* I snapped my seat belt open, squeezed my body through the side window, and ran as fast as I could to the middle of the infield. As I stood there, horrified and embarrassed, a tow truck screeched to a halt near the Hudson, and a couple of guys with fire extinguishers smothered the smoke. Slowly, I walked back toward the car but, before I arrived, the men hooked up the front end of the Hudson and began towing it toward the pits. I changed direction and, without daring to look up into stands, trudged after the truck.

When I got to our spot in the pits, the hood of the Hudson was open and several men were staring at the engine.

"Look at this!" one shouted at me. "That's the cleanest break I've ever seen." He was pointing at my engine block, which was split into two pieces. "It looks like a piston rod got loose and cut your engine in half. There's still steam coming out of there."

"Hey, man," said another of the onlookers. "Do you own this car?"

"Yes," I replied.

"I own the junk yard down the road," he said. "I'll give you twenty bucks for the battery and five bucks for the car."

My initial reaction was to punch the guy in the mouth. But then I thought more clearly: *I have a useless piece of junk, there's no way I can get it out of here, and I don't have a place to put it.*

"Okay, it's all yours," I said to the man, who handed me five five-dollar bills, pulled up with his truck, loaded the Hudson on a flatbed trailer, and drove away.

I changed my clothes in the men's room and joined my friends in the stands. I expected jokes and smart remarks, but none were forthcoming. Everyone seemed genuinely sorry and interested in hearing what had taken place. We watched the remaining races together, and then I caught a ride home.

A couple of weeks later, while sitting at the dinner table, my father asked:

"Has anyone seen my new wheelbarrow?"

Papa had paid seventy-five dollars for the fancy cart. Along with the Hudson, for which I had received the princely sum of twenty-five bucks, it had been compressed into a small cube of junk steel. Expecting a slap in the face at a minimum, I was amazed to see Papa laugh so hard he nearly fell off his chair when I confessed to him. Of course, I did not tell him that I had been at the wheel of the exploding car.

After the Hudson episode, I swore off American cars. Having attended a few sports car races with Jack, Lynne, and Jay Geils, I became hooked on British automobiles—MGs, Austin Healeys, Triumphs, Morgans. Of course, as a college student, I could not afford any of them and could only admire them from afar. My red and cream 1953 Studebaker Champion was hardly a sports car, but it came close, and I loved and cared for it as if it was one. At OSU, I joined the Aggie Sports Car Club and competed in rallies and gymkhanas with, and against, a number of new friends including George Burrows, Thalia Collins, Alfred Schuler and his future wife Peggy, and Ronnie Sheets, who rode shotgun with me as navigator in rallies.

I joined the Northeast Oklahoma Region of the Sports Car Club of America (SCCA). While at home for Christmas, I dug my concealed NASCAR race suit and helmet out of their hiding place in the attic and brought them with me to Stillwater. I depleted most of my bank account and paid the registration fee to the Carroll Shelby Driving School in Tulsa. Coming in, I was confident that I knew a great deal about racing technique from having observed such luminaries as Phil Hill, Jim Kimberly, and Carroll Shelby himself. Thus, I was surprised to discover that I knew next to nothing. Over three weekends, I learned to shift using the heel-and-toe method, to control understeer and oversteer, to recognize the apex of a corner, and even such rudiments as the proper grip on a steering wheel. On the last day of school, I passed both the written test and a five-lap, all-out run with an instructor in the passenger seat, with flying colors. I received a provisional SCCA license—and this time, I did not even have to present a counterfeited draft card.

There was only one problem: I had no car to race. My Studebaker would not pass for a sports car. But then I got lucky. A fellow member of the OSU sports car club owned a green MG-TD with a roll-bar. When he discovered that I had an SCCA license, he asked me if I would like to drive it in the Eureka Springs Hillclimb. Of course, I jumped at the chance. We drove the car to the hills of western Arkansas, taped the number 14 on both sides, tuned the engine, and I made two timed runs up the steep, winding course. We finished somewhere in the middle of our class, but I felt as if I had just won Le Mans. I was a race driver! After that, I had a couple more opportunities to race other people's cars: an MG-A in Coffeeville, Kansas, and an Austin Healey 100-4 which had been entered by a classmate who was too hung over to drive on the day the SCCA races came to Stillwater airport.

The first sports car I owned was a red 1952 MG-TD I bought after Sue and I moved to California in 1960. But it was strictly a street car, and I could only enjoy the sport vicariously by attending occasional races at Riverside Raceway. My next opportunity to race did not arrive until 1969, soon after I left the Naval Academy faculty and became CEO of CADCOM in Annapolis. It turned out that our marketing director, Ed Grant, was an accomplished race driver. He raced a Porsche at Marlboro Motor Raceway, located off Route 301 in Upper Marlboro, Maryland. Some of the nation's finest drivers— Roger Penske, Phil Hill, Mark Donohue, Sam Posey, Joe

Hauser, and Bob Tullius—got their starts at this unusual venue.

I accompanied Ed to several races, worked in his pit crew and became hooked all over again. Ed petitioned the local SCCA region to reinstate my license, which had lapsed. They refused and informed me that, in order to gain a new permit, I would have to compete in novice races until I proved that I belonged with the big boys. Ed introduced me to Jimmy Harrison, an Annapolis resident who campaigned successfully in a Bugeye Sprite. Jimmy owned another race car, a Triumph Spitfire, which he was willing to rent. When I declared that I could not afford it while our startup company was struggling through its early months, Jimmy brought in his friend Bernie, who was willing to go in 50-50 with me. We would alternate racing the car.

My time came a couple of weeks later, when I entered a novice race at Marlboro. I was doing well, sitting in third place, when I came out of a hairpin turn too fast and spun out. I limped home near the tail end of the group, embarrassed. I would have to enter another novice contest.

In the meantime, members of the CADCOM board of directors discovered that I was racing sports cars.

"Don't you think that car racing is too risky and unfair to our shareholders?" asked Jack Geils, my mentor and friend, at a board meeting. It had been Jack who had gotten me interested in motor sports back when our families were neighbors in New Jersey. The irony seemed to elude him.

"Jack, you know as much about sports car racing as anyone," I replied. "You know how safe it is."

At that point, other directors chimed in and held a conversation in which I decided not to participate. The conclusion: it was really my personal choice, but the Board wanted to go on record as being opposed to my continuing to race. *Thanks, guys*, I said to myself. *I'm going racing.*

Two weeks later, I was back behind the wheel of the

Spitfire. Marlboro was a unique race course. Two-and-a-half miles long, it consisted of a road course with hairpin turns, chicanes (serpentine curves), and straightaways, but a short portion entered and exited an old, banked oval which had once been used by midgets, motorcycles, and stock cars. I was on the sixth lap of a ten-lap race and driving well, in second place behind a Mini Cooper. As we entered the oval, I was two feet off the Mini's rear bumper, drafting it in its slipstream and hoping to pass after leaving the track and entering a chicane. The transition from banked oval to the flat road course created a jump that hurled cars into a high-speed flight as they headed toward the chicane. The lead driver and I went airborne as we exited the oval, with my front bumper nearly touching the Mini's rear end. We were going about ninety miles per hour. Suddenly, I froze.

My god, I screamed at myself. *What the hell are you doing?*

When we touched ground, I backed off and followed the Mini around the course for the next four laps. Ed Grant was in the pits when I finished, and he congratulated me on finishing second and thus probably regaining my license.

"Ed," I said. "I'm done. I have a wife and child at home, and I have a company to run. Back there, when the Mini and I were airborne, I was scared shitless. I decided on the spot that I can't do this anymore."

I really was finished, as was Marlboro Motor Raceway. It closed at the end of that season and was replaced by a new race course in Summit Point, West Virginia. Before the latter opened officially, I made a pilgrimage there with Jimmy Harrison and Sue's father, Ed Holsten. I told Jimmy that Ed was a long-time racing fan who had once attended the Indianapolis 500 and now followed auto racing on TV.

"Why don't you show Ed what it's like to race a sports car?" Jimmy asked when we arrived. "Do a few laps in the Bugeye and take Ed with you."

My father-in-law and I donned helmets and strapped

ourselves into Jimmy's Austin Healey Bugeye Sprite. I relished showing off my ability to downshift, to drift around corners, and to blast out on the straightaways. Ed Holsten's smile indicated that he was enjoying himself. For me, it was an exhilarating, yet melancholy, experience because I knew that it would be my last time behind the wheel of a race car.

Quitting automobile racing created a void in my life. Although I was CEO of a company in the competitive world of high technology, I needed challenges in my recreation as well. That Darwinian gene I inherited from my father was calling out.

I expressed my frustration to my friend and business partner, John Gebhardt, one day while having lunch in a place we referred to as CADCOM's "executive dining room"—in reality a pile of building blocks next to the Dairy Queen on Annapolis' West Street.

"Have you ever thought about racing a sailboat?" John asked.

"No." Sue and I had learned to sail when I taught at the Naval Academy, but racing had never entered our minds.

"I bet you'll find it every bit as exciting as car racing, and our board of directors won't bitch at you for risking your life."

John invited me to come crew on his race boat. I did—and I was hooked.

CHAPTER NINETEEN

WIND AND WATER

I was lying on the quarter-berth of the forty-one-foot sloop, *Motley*, wondering how long it would take for us to die. Racing cars, I risked only one life—mine. Now I had brought my wife, our only son, and three good friends out here into the Atlantic. I would be responsible for their deaths. How could I have done this?

Each time the angry sea rolled the boat, first to starboard and then to port, my body smashed into the sides of the bunk. Whenever the bow slammed down from the top of a wave, I experienced a moment of weightlessness. Monster waves lifted the sailboat up horrific crests, only to drop her into deep troughs. Each ride up slowly compressed my body into the thin cushion under me and then *bang!*—I was released and left airborne as the boat dropped down like a runaway elevator. The hull made oil-canning noises as the fiberglass skin flexed with each explosion. Bulkheads creaked under stresses for which they had not been designed. And I could see the mast, which protruded from the cabin's overhead down to the keel, twisting each time the sloop slammed down. There seemed to be no way the boat could stand up to this pounding much longer. *How long will it take for us to drown once the boat capsizes?* I wondered, realizing that launching the life raft into the enormous waves would be impossible.

Exhausted from my latest turn at the helm, I closed my eyes. My sailing life of the past twenty-five years began to play like a movie in my head.

I recalled how Sue and I had first learned to sail under the watchful eye of a crusty, tough Navy chief in 1965, a couple of years after I began teaching at the Naval Academy. Both of us fell in love with the sport during those evenings on the Severn River in the Academy's blue-hulled, unsinkable Knockabouts used to train midshipmen.

"We need to get our own sailboat," I said to Sue upon our passing the course with flying colors.

"That would be nice, but we can't afford one," she replied, ever the practical one in the family.

"Maybe we can find a used one someplace under a thousand bucks," I suggested.

After several weeks of searching classified ads and checking out a few inexpensive derelicts, we found our first boat. She was a homemade knock-off of the classic Chesapeake 20. Except that she wasn't a *true* member of that venerable class: she had a mast and boom from a Celebrity-class boat and ill-fitting sails from some other vessel. The hull was made of wood; the sails were made of cotton and had shrunk so much that they failed to reach the top of the spruce mast. She came with a trailer constructed from the chassis of a 1952 Chevy. That was the bad news. The good news? The asking price was six hundred dollars. We had found the only sailboat we could afford.

When we docked her at the Naval Academy on College Creek, she had a fancy French name, *Coup d'Essai*. Not only did we have no idea what that meant but, after several months, we decided that another name— *Dilemma*— would be most appropriate. She earned the moniker that now adorned her transom by leaking like a sieve. When underway, water poured in around the rudder post. Many layers of sealant failed to fix the problem.

During the next sailing season, I devoted more time to making repairs than to sailing. When we did go out on the water, we did not dare sail *Dilemma* past the spider buoy marking the entrance to the Severn River. After a second winter of labor, attempting to make the boat seaworthy, we launched *Dilemma* and sailed her out into the Chesapeake Bay. I held my breath. Lo and behold, the leaks seemed to have stopped and there appeared to be no other problems. However, I had already come to a conclusion.

"Guys," I announced to Sue and David at the dinner table. "Wooden boats are for people who either have lots of time on their hands or are rich enough to have someone make constant repairs. We don't qualify. We need a fiberglass boat!"

Four-year-old David agreed enthusiastically. Adult Sue was a bit more reluctant because, once again, she wondered if we could afford such a luxury. Nevertheless, we decided to put *Dilemma* up for sale and to see if someone might bite. We were shocked when a retired Navy captain wrote a check for eight hundred dollars after a short test sail. Two hundred bucks more than we had paid for her! As we watched the captain and *Dilemma* disappear past the spider buoy and out into the Chesapeake Bay, I was stricken with guilt.

"God, I hope we don't read in the paper tomorrow that a retired naval officer died when his boat sank off Thomas Point Light," I said to Sue and David. We searched next day's newspaper, but there was no story about a disaster on the Bay. We breathed a collective sigh of relief.

We named our first fiberglass baby—a Venture 21—*Christie*, after an old skiing turn technique. She had a cabin, and now we could cruise the Bay, anchor at night, and sleep in the v-berth. Her accommodations were not exactly luxurious. The cabin was so small that only one of us could go below at a time. He or she would settle for the night in the v-berth before the other one could enter. And cooking on the tiny, one-burner stove had to be done on one's knees because the headroom was only four feet. Fortunately, we did not know any better and were happy as could be. Moreover, little David became hooked on sailing and began taking the helm in calm weather. It was a great confidence-builder for our son.

Our satisfaction with *Christie* was diminished one day when we went on a weekend sail to the West River along with our friends, Mike and Nancy Saarlas and their son, Scott. They arrived first in the anchorage and dropped a hook off the bow of their Catalina 22. We tied up alongside. When it came time to go ashore to dinner at Pirate's Cove restaurant, Sue slithered into our cabin and struggled to change her clothes while David and I awaited our turns in the cockpit. I looked over at Saarlas' boat, expecting them to be going through the same ritual—after all, they must have the same problem since their boat was only a foot longer than ours.

"Look, David," I shouted, shocked by what I saw. "All three of them are down below at the same time!"

"Dad," answered my observant son, "they have a pop-top."

I stared at the Catalina and noticed, for the first time, that Mike had raised the cabin top more than a foot and a skirt dropped down to close the gap between it and the hull.

"Do you guys have standing headroom down there?" I called over.

"Yeah, it's great!" Mike replied. "Why don't you come over and change your clothes here after we get done?"

When they climbed out of the cabin, David and I clambered over the boats' lifelines and went down below. Wow! I was actually able to stand up and pull on a clean pair of pants.What luxury! Sue came over and admired this unprecedented phenomenon.

"Our next boat is gonna have standing headroom!" I

announced at dinner that night. From that moment on, sailor disease—yearning for a bigger boat—set in.

It did not happen immediately. Sue was busy teaching, and I was completing my doctorate at Catholic University while on the Naval Academy faculty. We sailed *Christie* whenever possible, although we limited ourselves to day sails, rather than subjecting our bodies to overnights at anchor. We bought David a 420 racing dinghy, and he went through the progression of the junior sailing program at the Severn Sailing Association (SSA). He was becoming a fine sailor, while Sue and I too continued to progress in our boat-handling skills.

It was around this time that I gave up sports car racing and was introduced to sailboat racing by John Gebhardt. John had purchased an International 14 from well-known sailor, Sam Merrick, and asked me to crew for him. It took me a microsecond to sign on.

Our first regatta was on a windy Saturday in April. We had not practiced together, so John and I went out early in order to do tacking, jibing, and spinnaker-setting drills on the way out to the starting line. We managed to capsize three times— *before* the first race! The first capsize was the scariest. I had never before hung out outside a boat in a trapeze. I was out there, on the windward side, during a prolonged wind gust. When the puff died, I should have scrambled into the boat. Instead, I stayed out on the wire. Suddenly, I saw the mast coming toward me, as my wet suit grazed the waves. Then, boom! I was in the water and the mast and sail were on top of me. I broke away from the trapeze and swam to the surface, just in time to see my lunch—a sandwich and an orange in a clear plastic bag—heading up the Severn River. The next two capsizes were to leeward—to the side away from the wind, and thus away from me out on the wire. Instead of being in the water and under sails and rigging, I stood on the submerged hull, trying to figure out what to do next. John talked me through the procedure of righting a capsized boat, and we got under way and raced all day without another mishap. Under John's tutelage, I was a quick study. We never capsized again while I crewed on his 14. Moreover, I had discovered racing—and it was a blast! I was anxious to try it in my own boat someday.

We found one in October 1971 at the US Sailboat Show in Annapolis. She was a gorgeous Catalina 27, white hull with a red cove stripe and a blue bottom. She was on the hard at the City Dock, and we knew she would be our next boat as soon as the president of Catalina Yachts, Frank Butler, gave us a sales pitch. We first saw her on Thursday and bought her on Friday. Seven-year-old David stood guard during the remainder of the show, warning boarding visitors that she was "our boat" and that they needed to take off their shoes before going down below into the cabin—the cabin with six feet of headroom!

We named her *Serene*, and she spent her first winter in the yard of the local dealer, Dick Parham. It was there that we met a number of sailors who had also purchased new Catalina 27s: Bill and Bev Miles named their C-27 *4 Miles Away*; Paul and Margy Barrett had *Paldemar*; two German immigrants, Olaf Tom Felde and Rainer Wetzling, named their new boats *Flitzer* and *Wetzer*, respectively. In the spring, several other brand new Catalinas arrived in Annapolis, and we decided to form a club. We discovered the existence of the National Catalina 27 Association and applied for membership. Soon, we were its Fleet 8, and I was elected its first commodore. By then, we had a large contingent of Catalina owners—and lots of other new friends. Among those early adapters were Rich Krebs, Jim Troutman, Gary and Karen Rossow, Ed and Eileen Mowle, and Larry and Bev Westerlund. Bill Miles would become my lifelong closest friend.

Racing on the Chesapeake Bay takes place under the auspices of the Chesapeake Bay Yacht Racing Association, CBYRA. Sailboats compete in classes divided into two general categories: one-design and handicap. One-design classes are made up of identical boats, whereas handicap classes allow boats of different manufacture and various sizes to race and to have, at least theoretically, equal opportunities to win. We applied for one-design class status, and sponsoring yacht clubs on the Bay soon gave us starts.

We raced nearly every weekend during the season. But my favorite day of the week was Wednesday. As CEO of a high-tech startup company, CADCOM, I usually left the office around eight or nine o'clock in the evening. But on Wednesdays, I headed out in time to arrive at the dock at five o'clock, so that I could have our boat ready by the time the crew arrived, and we would be on time for the start of the Wednesday Night Series, an Annapolis Yacht Club tradition of many years. Despite frequent travel while generating business and searching for investment capital, I would miss only two Wednesday night races in thirty years.

A sailboat race was not much different from my day at the office. First came planning: calculations of wind speed; current location, strength, and direction; the favored end of the starting line. Then came execution: attempt at a perfect start, staying upwind of the competition, avoiding unfavorable currents. Along with it, there was leadership: I delegated various duties, called the tactics, and coordinated the actions of our team. The entire experience was a mirror image of leading and guiding a team of engineers, computer program-mers, and sales people toward a common goal. In business and in sailboat racing, all of us had one goal in mind: annihilate the competition while enjoying the experience!

Cruising was quite different because it was a time for my family and me to relax on a sailboat. Despite the fact that we raced every sailboat going in our direction—usually without the occupants of the other vessel knowing that they were competing against us—we did it with drinks in our hands. We loved the creeks, rivers, and coves of Maryland's Eastern

Shore. Nothing I had ever experienced in my life, with the exception of cross-country skiing, was as soothing as silently cutting through the water of the Wye, Choptank or Chester Rivers while the pastoral scenes of farms and grazing livestock slowly slipped by. At the end of each day, we anchored in some quiet cove, swam, watched blue herons hunting for their dinners, and listened to music while gazing into a dark, starry sky unencumbered by city lights. These were times when our small family truly bonded. For me, it was a respite from a fiercely competitive business life and certainly a diversion from pushing the boat to go faster around a race course.

Our social life, too, revolved around sailing. Nearly all our friends were fellow sailors. We partied together, visited each other's homes, and vacationed by cruising the Bay in groups and rafting up at the end of each day. Often, we cruised with the Miles family—Bill, Bev and their children, Vicky and Geoff. David and Geoff were close in age and became good friends.

The highlight of every year for most Annapolis sailors was the US Sailboat Show, the world's first and largest in-the-water boat show. Every October, manufacturers, dealers, and vendors from all over the world descended on our town for a five-day sailors' love fest. For many of us, it became a yearly reunion, a chance to see the latest and greatest in boats and gear, and an opportunity to exchange stories of our adventures on the water at various parties.

In 1974, at one such party hosted by the British Embassy, Sue and I met a couple who would become our good friends despite the expanse of the Atlantic Ocean separating us. John and Doreen McIntosh were exhibiting a pretty, twenty-four-foot-long, red boat, with the brand name Foxhound, at the show. Their company built the sloops, designed by, and named for, famous naval architect Uffa Fox, on England's Isle of Wight. They had come to Annapolis hoping to find a distributor or dealer to import their boats to the United States. Finding immediate rapport with John and Doreen, we invited them to our home, and spent much of our time with them during the show.

"I've been unable to find a distributor or a dealer," John said to me on Columbus Day, the last day of the show. "It's quite frustrating."

I was well aware of the old adage: never make your hobby your business. Yet, I succumbed to the desire to become part of the marine industry.

"John," I said. "Sue and I are no experts at this, and we'll have to do it on a part-time basis, but we'll be your US distributors, if you're interested."

John was elated, and we shook hands to seal the deal. Several months later, we formed a company and named it Starboard Sailing Products. We would wait until the following year's sailboat show to start selling Foxhounds.

The first of October of 1975, a sleek blue sloop arrived at the Port of Baltimore in time for the boat show. When the show gates opened, having proudly changed our status from attendees to exhibitors, we waited for orders to come in from buyers. Thursday through Sunday, we entertained many "tire-kickers," but no one bought. On Monday, the final day of the show, desperation began to set in.

"We haven't taken a single order," I said to Sue. "And what will happen if we don't even sell the boat-show boat? We have no place to keep her. Tonight, they will require all boats to be moved from City Dock. Where the hell are we gonna go?"

Around five o'clock, a man and his wife returned for the third time to examine the Foxhound. Hope springs eternal! We invited them into the cabin and went through the specifications and detailed pricing. At ten minutes to six, a woman's voice announced over the PA system:

"The show will close in ten minutes!" just as the new owner of the blue Foxhound was signing a check. We popped the cork on a bottle of wine that had been ageing in a cooler and celebrated.

Sadly, that was the one and only Foxhound we would sell. Our problem was timing. While Europeans still favored smaller boats like the Foxhound, Americans were buying bigger boats. As it turned out, the Hellers were no exception.

My entry in the log of our Catalina 27, *Serene*, dated July 5, 1980—the last day of a holiday cruise to Langford Creek on Maryland's Eastern Shore—reads:

On this cruise, there was talk of a larger boat. Even Sammy talked about it. What will the future bring?

The future brought both sadness, as we parted with our beloved *Serene*, and excitement as we welcomed a new family member. I had long admired the sleek lines, and racing success, of sailboats made by a Canadian manufacturer located in Niagara-On-the-Lake, Ontario: C&C Yachts. We decided that we would be on the lookout for a used C&C, one at least thirty feet long. During the fall of 1980, we found our next baby. She was a blue C&C 30, owned by a Coast Guard captain and named *Blue Jacket*. She was longer and beamier than *Serene* and had more amenities, including an inboard engine, a step up from *Serene's* outboard.

Her blue gelcoat was a bit faded, so with the help of our friend Dom Ciuffreda, we painted her a gorgeous dark blue with yellow and orange cove stripes. On the sides of her gleaming hull, we added huge decals depicting a downhill skier in a tuck position, and we named her *Blue Ice*. During our thirty years of racing, we had our greatest successes with her. We won numerous races on the Chesapeake Bay, competing in a Performance Handicap Racing Formula (PHRF) class, and we took home so many plaques in the Annapolis Yacht Club Wednesday Night Races that they filled the walls of our sun room.

Then, at the 1985 US Sailboat Show, I was approached by a representative of C&C Yachts.

"We've followed your successes racing an old C&C 30 on the Bay," said the Canadian executive. "Would you be interested in sailing an even more competitive boat?"

"What do you have in mind?" I asked.

"During the summer, Canada held its offshore one-design championship," he said. "It was sailed in five C&C 35 Mark IIIs. We provided them with six boats, the sixth one to be used only in case of a problem with one of the competing boats. The spare one was never used. It's essentially a brand new boat, with all sorts of special equipment and amenities down below."

"That sounds interesting," I said, beginning to smell a deal I could not refuse.

"We'd like to introduce the Mark III to the Chesapeake Bay," he continued. "It would be great if you'd race it successfully and give it exposure here in the Mid-Atlantic."

Having appealed both to my ego and my pocketbook, he sold me. On a cold December day, our shrink-wrapped baby arrived in back of a truck at the AYC Sailing Center. We had already decided on a name. Although boats are considered feminine, she would be named after a very masculine person, the mascot of my beloved alma mater, Oklahoma State University. "She" would be *Pistol Pete*. Pistol Pete Eaton had been a real Oklahoma lawman and his fierce-looking, mustachioed, orange-and-black figure—complete with two six-guns—adorns all things OSU. Now, he would aim those pistols at our competition on the race course.

As soon as the winter snows disappeared, we began practicing and becoming accustomed to the boat. *Pete* was considerably more tender (heeled more when the wind popped up) than *Blue Ice* had been. This, as well as larger sails, greater loads on sheets, and more complex controls, steepened the learning curve for crew and skipper. We did not do well in the season's early races, but we were improving as we became more familiar with the new boat's peculiarities.

During the winter, while *Pete* had been on the hard in a marina, I met another new C&C owner, one who had bought a 41-footer and named her *Motley*, after his squad in the Vietnam War that had called itself "The Motley Crew." In late spring of 1990, while we were breaking in *Pistol Pete*, *Motley's* skipper phoned me.

"We've decided to do the Annapolis-to-Bermuda Race," he said. "But we have a problem. We're not experienced racers. You guys are. Would you and your crew like to do the race with us?"

I received a resounding, and unanimous, "NO!" when I polled our crew. They had seen the upcoming race schedule for *Pistol Pete*, and they knew that, by the time of the ocean race to Bermuda in June, they would be close to burned out. When I informed the *Motley* captain, he was ready with a counteroffer.

"In that case, how about we race the boat and you guys bring her back from Bermuda?" he asked. "We'll buy round-trip airplane tickets—you use them to fly to Bermuda, and we'll use them to fly home."

This time, the offer was met with enthusiasm. Six of us, with visions of a leisurely cruise on a smooth sea and under a sunny sky, signed on. Sue, David, and I, along with three friends—Dom Ciuffreda, Lou Corletto, and Sandy Morse—flew to Bermuda, where we spent two enjoyable days prior to weighing anchor.

"There's a large depression off Newport, Rhode Island, and a small one off Charleston, South Carolina, but neither one will affect you," a meteorologist at the US Naval Station in Bermuda assured me the morning of our departure. "You'll have nothing but good weather and smooth seas between here and the Chesapeake Bay."

It did start out as a brilliant, warm day, with a glassy sea as we sailed out of St. George's harbor. A light breeze helped to push the 41-foot sloop toward its destination—Annapolis, Maryland. So it went for the first few hours of the journey. I steered *Motley* on a northwesterly course while the crew relaxed, occasionally trimming sails to adjust for small wind shifts.

"We really made a good choice," said Lou Corletto, "deciding to cruise the boat back, rather than racing from Annapolis to Bermuda. I've been looking forward to catching up on my reading and working on my tan."

And this was how I got us to the situation we were in— terrified of losing my life, as well as those of my wife, son, and friends. Seemingly out of nowhere, the sky turned a dark gray, and the wind rose to thirty knots. Within minutes, huge twenty-foot waves began crashing onto the deck. *Motley*, which only a few moments ago had been cutting gracefully through a smooth blue sea, was suddenly but a toy to the mountains of water that tossed her from crest to trough. The boat shuddered with each wave, and the eighty-foot mast bent, twisted, and vibrated from each shock.

David crawled onto the pitching foredeck and replaced the genoa with a small storm jib. We reduced the mainsail area with a double-reef, and I turned on the engine. Although all of us except Lou had many years' experience of racing and cruising on the Bay, our ocean sailing expertise was limited. Anxiety and tension set in. By dusk, we were climbing mountains.

"Dad," said my wide-eyed, twenty-two-year-old son, "these are forty-foot waves!" observing that the depth of each trough plus the height of each wave added up to *Motley's* length. Indeed, the waves were gigantic and steep, with spray blowing off their tops as they broke over our bow. The formerly blue sea became a boiling green cauldron topped off with white foam. As both captain and father, I had to appear confident and calm, so I simply nodded to David, as I maneuvered *Motley* through the monsters.

Back on the Chesapeake Bay, where we had raced successfully on three different boats, David and I had an unenviable reputation. An obedient and courteous son on land, David became a know-it-all monster once the gun went off to start a race. His skipper father, too, became belligerent and the two of us screamed at one another to the discomfort of the crew. Now, out in the Atlantic, we needed to work calmly and as a team.

Steering took an enormous amount of strength and, by now, Dom, Lou, and Sandy were seasick, while Sue was not strong enough to help. Only David and I could helm the boat, taking twenty-minute shifts at the oversize wheel. Any movement by the crew became nearly impossible. All of us were in foul-weather gear and wearing life jackets and harnesses that allowed us to attach ourselves to wire jacklines running the length of the boat. I instructed everyone to stay clipped in at all times.

By dusk, we managed to get *Motley* under some degree of control, although the crew was now even sicker. Then things got worse. Around eight o'clock, the effects of the second, smaller, depression—eight-foot waves hitting us broadside as we slid off the mountains—kicked in. Now we were really in trouble. The boat slammed down with overwhelming force after every wave, and I feared that, at any moment, the eighty-foot rig would crash down on us.

The night was particularly terrifying, with its uniquely scary sights and sounds. The howling of the wind in the rigging seemed louder. The gurgling noise of the hull plowing through the water, along with the eerily green stern-wake we were leaving behind as we stirred up thousands of the ocean's phosphorescent organisms, and a pungent salty smell, created a frightening scene. It was clear that, should anyone be swept overboard, there would be no hope of survival. This angry sea would simply laugh at the unfortunate sailor's weapons against it—life jacket, strobe light, whistle, and a Dacron lifeline to the boat—and swallow him or her.

For one-and-a-half days, we went virtually without sleep. Water was pouring into the cabin around the mast, and all our belongings were soaked. One by one, things were breaking—topping lift, lines, shift lever, life-ring support—and David was repairing them under near-impossible conditions while I steered. Rest was out of the question due to the violent motions of the boat and the noise and smell down below. When we managed to lie down in the cabin, we were fully dressed in foul-weather gear and wet boots. We kept our life jackets on because they cushioned the impact of being slammed against the hull and bulkhead.

A trip to the head was an adventure. I would spend a full ten minutes planning the journey of about twenty feet from the quarter-berth in which David and I were hot-bunking, strategizing the synchronization of steps with the motions of the boat. When I reached the toilet and closed the door behind me, I propped my head against the overhead, while using my hands to take care of business. Then, just as I would get ready to pee, invariably a wave would crash over the bow and salt water would pour in through the closed hatch above my head.

Both David and I were dog tired, but we managed until late afternoon of our second day at sea. The two of us had communicated wordlessly and worked to keep *Motley* together and her crew safe. Miraculously, despite the terrible punishment she had taken, the boat had held up. However, I was already dreading the thought of another night of terror facing us in just a few hours. The hull and the rigging could not take much more punishment. I feared that a monstrous wave was out there, just waiting to crumple our protective fiberglass cocoon. Moreover, we had been blown far from Bermuda, too distant to be rescued by a helicopter from the island. Dreadful thoughts of drowning came rushing at me. What had I done, bringing my wife, son, and three friends out here? Were we going to die?

Then, just as suddenly as it had hit us, the storm subsided. In a matter of minutes, the sea smoothed out and we began to sail in a fifteen-knot breeze. We looked at one another in disbelief.

"I think God hit the off switch," said Lou Corletto.

Once we realized that the storm had really passed, we took inventory of the damage. Most distressing was the discovery that all our navigation equipment except the Satellite Navigation System (SatNav) had been shorted out by seawater or destroyed by flying objects. As we began to recover, dry out, and make repairs, we realized that we would have to navigate by compass and sextant, just like the ancient mariners. The SatNav would give us one reading a day, but we did not trust its accuracy. Nevertheless, we felt confident that, as long as we kept heading west, eventually we would run into North America.

Our second night out was in sharp contrast to the terror of the first night. The crew had recovered from seasickness and, despite being sleep-deprived, all of us chose to sit in the cockpit until well past midnight. The sky was filled with stars, and the boat was gliding smoothly through the water. The scary bioluminescence in our wake from the previous night became a beautiful greenish glow, and we cheered when the occasional flying fish landed in the cockpit.

Prior to leaving Bermuda, all of us had attached scopolamine patches behind our ears in order to prevent seasickness. Obviously, they had not done much for Sandy, Dom or Lou, but they seemed to have worked for Sue, David and me. However, one of the potential side effects of the patches, according to the directions, was hallucination. Mine came on at night, and it provided great entertainment for the rest of the crew. Starting with our second night out, and continuing throughout the trip, I steered the boat when, suddenly, a beautiful woman in a red dress appeared next to the mast. She and I carried on conversations lasting ten to fifteen minutes. Of course, my shipmates heard only my end of the dialogue, but they enjoyed it immensely. Their laughter failed to stop the discourse. On another occasion during the night, I spotted a fleet of J/24 sailboats off in the distance, and I began racing against them. Just as in weekend races on the Chesapeake Bay, I asked the crew periodically whether we were gaining on the fleet or losing ground. With tongues in cheek, they gave me status reports.

We did not do a very good job of navigating by the stars. Every time our navigator, Sandy, attempted to get a sight, the sky clouded over. After experiencing a bit of stormy weather in the Gulf Stream, and late on the fourth day at sea, we were scheduled to see the light marking the entrance to the Chesapeake Bay. About two hours after our dead reckoning had predicted that we should see the navigation aid, there was nothing but open ocean around us.

As evening approached, I began to worry: *If we keep heading west, we may run aground in the dark.* Everyone was tired and still beaten up from the early storm, and the last thing I wanted to do was to turn east, back out to the open sea, and thus add more time and distance to the journey. As I sat and silently considered my options as captain, Sue's voice penetrated the stillness.

"Lights on the horizon!" Several vertical white lights far in the distance indicated that a ship was approaching. I ran below and grabbed the VHF microphone. Before I had a chance to speak, a voice came over the ship-to-ship channel.

"Captain, we're on a collision course. Which way are you going to pass me—to port or starboard? Over."

"Neither one, Captain," I answered. "We're heading right for you because we need your help getting out of here. We're lost. Over."

"Where are you headed? Over."

"We're headed for Annapolis and trying to find the entrance to the Chesapeake Bay. Over."

"You're a bit south of there, Captain," he said. "You're north of Cape Fear, North Carolina. But, you're in luck. This tug is headed for Norfolk. So you can just follow us. Over."

"Fantastic. Thanks, Captain. We'll wait till you pass us and then follow behind you. Out."

We cracked open cans of beer and celebrated our luck while we waited in the calm sea. The tug passed us around six in the evening, and we got into her wake and followed under power, with our 45-horsepower diesel engine turning maximum RPMs. After an hour, the gap between our vessels had opened up to nearly half a mile, and I got on the radio again.

"Captain, our top speed is six-and-a-half knots, and you seem to be doing about ten. Would it be possible for you to slow down? Over," I begged.

"No problem. I'm slowing down to your speed. Out."

He waited till we got closer and then proceeded at our speed for the next two hours. We were enjoying the ride and finally felt that we would soon be in the familiar waters of the Chesapeake, when Dom said:

"Oh, shit! Look at the fuel gauge! We're just about empty."

"Now what do we do?" Sue asked.

"Let's see if the tugboat has any spare diesel fuel," suggested David.

I was reluctant to ask another favor of the captain of a commercial vessel, for whom time means money, but I had no choice. I went below again and picked up the radio mic.

"Captain, I hate to ask this, but we're just about out of fuel. Is there any way we could get some diesel fuel from you? Over."

"No problem, Captain," he replied. "I'll stop the engines, and you come and tie up alongside. We'll give you enough fuel to get you home. Out."

So there, about fifty miles offshore in the Atlantic Ocean was a sight that would have caused a few laughs among our sailing friends at home: a 41-foot sailboat sitting low in the water tied up to a high 120-foot steel tug. The crew of the tug filled our fuel tank and gave us a jerry can full of diesel as reserve. In return, we gave them a case of Heineken beer and a canned Polish ham. They thought they had gotten the better of the deal, while we were thanking our lucky stars for having found such kind folks out at sea.

With no further complications, we followed the tug over the Chesapeake Bay Bridge-Tunnel and expressed our gratitude to its crew, as we left them for the remainder of our journey up the Bay. Tacking into a northwesterly breeze and making our way toward home, we reminisced about the journey. We recounted the many incidents, the scary moments, the broken equipment, and how we had managed to come through it all. With each reminiscence of how we had overcome a problem, one name kept coming up over and over again—that of David. He had steered the boat through some of the roughest seas; he repaired rigging when it broke; he seemed to have a ready solution for every problem we encountered. Lou Corletto, an executive with the Washington Capitals of the National Hockey League, came up with a sports-inspired idea.

"Let's give David the Most Valuable Player award," he said.

The vote was unanimous. With *Motley* off Point No Point, near the mouth of the Potomac River, David was celebrated with a burgee of the club that had hosted us in Bermuda, St. George's Yacht Club, one we inscribed with the letters "MVP." Suddenly, it dawned on me: our boy had become a man. He had gained the respect of his teammates. Without him, we might not have survived. I was overcome by a sense of pride and satisfaction. Moreover, I knew that, in the future, father and son would remember the ordeal they had overcome together and treat each other with respect onboard a sailboat.

A few months later, having survived our Bermuda Triangle ordeal, we were ready to take on the Atlantic Ocean again, this time in our own boat.

"Dad, you're not working hundred-hour weeks anymore,"

David said, referring to the fact that I had cashed out of my company and accepted a position at the University of Maryland College Park as its Director of Industrial Research. "Do you think we could do the Newport Race next year?"

Annapolis-to-Newport is a venerable, often grueling, 473-mile contest, with the fleet starting from Annapolis and heading south in the Chesapeake Bay and into the Atlantic Ocean, rounding that same light we had found elusive on our sail from Bermuda. From there, the boats turn north, eventually rounding the eastern tip of Long Island, passing Block Island, and finishing outside of Newport, Rhode Island. Unaware of the amount of work—and money—it would take to prepare for the race, I agreed. We had six months to get ready; the magic day would be Saturday, June 13, 1987.

It did not take long to discover that preparation would be at least as difficult as the race itself. Even today, as I thumb through the log book, the list of required acquisitions boggles the mind. There were major (translation: expensive) items: seven-person life raft, EPIRB (a tracking device which emits a continuous signal), man-overboard pole and light, radio direction finder, three new sails, various charts, and a "going-away kit" (a bag with necessities one would take along if forced to abandon ship). Among hundreds of small items were flares of various colors, wooden plugs to stop leaking through-hulls, a parachute-like device called a drogue, and a fog horn. In addition to hundreds of hours of physical labor involved in getting *Pistol Pete* ready, a ton of arrangements had to be made: get the boat certified for blue-water racing; reserve hotel rooms for the crew in Newport; make provisions for docking in Rhode Island; and make travel plans for those crew members who would not be sailing back to Annapolis after the race.

Oh, yes, the crew—the most crucial missing piece. I was not about to cross the starting line without an accomplished and compatible team. Most of the crew members who raced

Pete with us on weekends and Wednesday nights had little or no offshore experience. Ordinarily, we sailed on the Bay with a crew of seven, and we decided on the same number for Newport. We needed to recruit four sailing friends who had been there and done it before. A critical requirement, in addition to sailing expertise, was a congenial personality. We would be spending several days and nights together in the tight confines of a 35-foot boat, so we had to be compatible.

Several weeks of telephone interviews and meetings resulted in a strong team that consisted of: Wayne "Dee" D'Ambrosio, Bill Lockwood, Sandy Morse, Rick Porea, and, of course, Sue, David, and me. Dee was a strong guy, a former Naval Academy football player with lots of sailing experience. Bill was a long-time friend and successful racer against whom we had competed in Catalinas. Sandy had been our navigator during the "perfect storm" sail from Bermuda; he was an ideal choice because of his knowledge of celestial navigation as well as the use of modern technology. We did not know Rick, but he came highly recommended by Bill, for whom he had been crewing. The team was set.

We spent the spring practicing and preparing the boat. Finally, June 13 arrived. The starting area was ringed by boats with hundreds of spectators as we watched the first two classes cross the line while anxiously awaiting the 12:20 p.m. start of our IMS (International Measurement System) class. We hit the line almost simultaneously with the sound of the gun and headed down the Bay in a fifteen-knot southwesterly breeze. In perfect conditions for our boat, we tacked our way into the lead position in our class. We held our lead throughout the afternoon and into the evening, with me at the helm. We would begin a watch system at nine o'clock in the evening and maintain it all the way to Newport.

At dusk, we could see dark clouds on the western horizon. The weather radio began warning of a strong squall headed for the Chesapeake. We were near the mouth of the Patuxent

River, still leading our class and surrounded by several larger boats from other classes when it came time for me to give up the helm to Bill Lockwood as we initiated the watch system. I caught sight of the approaching thunderstorm as I climbed down into the cabin for a short rest. Suddenly all hell broke loose. The storm was upon us. I got to the companionway just in time to see lightning hit the water, perhaps a quarter mile away. Next, I saw a bolt of lightning strike the mast of a nearby boat.

"Holy shit!" someone in the cockpit exclaimed. "I think that was one of the Navy 44s!"

In the darkness between lightning strikes, there was pandemonium all around us. The wind was swirling, and boats were going in every direction. People were screaming, as skippers and crews attempted to avoid collisions.

Then—the world turned white. It was as if a giant strobe light had flashed and, simultaneously, a grenade had gone off inside our boat.

"Damn!" I heard Bill Lockwood scream. "I just got hit in the head."

As we sat in stunned silence, the world became quiet; the storm moved east and we realized what had happened. We had taken a direct lightning hit. David climbed to the foredeck where he discovered a pile of ashes from what had been a fiberglass whip antenna at the top of the mast. At the navigation station, Sandy found that all our instruments, with the exception of the VHF radio, were dead. I ordered the sails to be dropped, and we sat dead in the water. I had to make a quick decision: to go on with the race or to retire. I ignored the arguments pro and con raised by the crew and recalled a long-ago sailing club meeting, to which a skipper had brought a piece of his rigging that had been struck by lightning.

"Lightning hit the mast and came down the shrouds and stays," I remembered him telling us. "I work at Westinghouse, and I took pieces of the rigging to work with me for testing.

We found that the steel had become annealed and lost almost fifty percent of its tensile strength."

Our shrouds and stays were made of stainless steel rod. Although I had not used my education as a structural engineer for some time, I knew what superheating could do to the strength of the material.

"Guys," I announced, after minutes of contemplation, "we can't go on. We don't know if the lightning compromised the structural integrity of the boat. As skipper, I can't take the chance of taking us all out into the ocean when we're not sure. If we got into trouble out there, there'd be no place to run. We have to withdraw."

No one said a word. We turned on the engine and aimed the bow north toward Annapolis. The conversation was quiet and awkward, as we spent the night steaming toward home. Throughout the night, two lights—one green and the other red—followed us up the Bay. With the first light of dawn near the mouth of the Severn River, we saw that the other casualty of the storm, a Navy 44 sloop, had been our companion.

At the Maryland Capital Yacht Club dock, we unloaded our five-day supply of food and drinks. Bill Lockwood took a case of Heineken and a Styrofoam container of Sue's painstakingly prepared meals.

"The guys and I are going to get on *Auf Ghets* and go cruising," Bill said. "We'll get out of town for a couple of days." *Auf Ghets* was a Peterson 34 which Bill co-owned with former Catalina sailor and friend, Rainer Wetzling.

Sue, David, and I drove home. After my wife and son went to sleep, I locked myself in the bathroom, sat down on the toilet, and lost it. Tears of frustration and anger rolled down my cheeks, as I smashed a magazine and a bar of soap against the wall.

All that work, and thousands of dollars—down the goddam drain! We were as well prepared as anybody could be. How could this have happened to us?

In my despair, I forgot to contact the Annapolis-to-Newport race committee and to notify them of our withdrawal from the race. I would discover later in the week, after all the boats in our class had finished and we were unaccounted for, that the Coast Guard was sent out to search for *Pistol Pete*. Fortunately, someone at the Annapolis Yacht Club had heard that we had returned home and notified Newport. The search was terminated, but I was further embarrassed.

On Monday, we had *Pistol Pete* hauled at a marina, so that we could inspect the damage with the assistance of a marine surveyor. We concluded that the lightning hit the top of the mast and came down two ways. It traveled down the backstay and jumped to the helmsman's head. Fortunately, Bill Lockwood had been wearing a rubber sou'wester hat, which possibly saved his life. The lightning then hopped from Bill's body to the instrument panel and from there traveled through the engine to the shaft, to the prop, and finally into the water. At the same time, the lightning raced down the aluminum mast, burning up all wiring along the way and frying all instruments that contained chips or transistors. The mast was stepped on the keel, and the lightning, seeking an exit to the water, went through a stainless-steel bolt and out through the interface between a fiberglass stub to which the lead keel was attached. The evidence of the latter was obvious. With the boat out of the water, we could see hundreds of tiny, nearly microscopic, holes around the periphery of the stub-keel interface, created when the powerful lightning bolt blew out into the Chesapeake Bay.

From the moment I announced to the crew that we were withdrawing from the race, I had been wondering silently whether or not I had made the right decision. Seeing the damage, I knew I had.

Over the next several weeks, *Pistol Pete* stayed on the hard, while repairs were taking place. The good news was that insurance covered nearly all the damage and that the standing rigging had remained structurally sound. By early August, the boat was back in the water, and we began racing and cruising again. For the remainder of our sailboat racing life, we remained inside the usually friendly confines of the Chesapeake Bay.

CHAPTER TWENTY

DEEP POWDER

Long before I stepped aboard a sailboat—or heard of a game called basketball—I became addicted to another sport. When I was three years old, my father took me to the woods overlooking our village, Kojetice, in pre-war Czechoslovakia. He placed a pair of short hickory skis in the snow and strapped my boots into bear-trap bindings—so called because, once the leather straps over the toes and around the heel were fastened, one was trapped. Despite frequent falls and face-plants, I delighted in the experience of gravity pulling me down small hills. The rest of that winter, I spent many days skiing down the gentle slope from the St. Vitus church across the street from our home.

Then my life changed abruptly. In March 1939, German troops occupied our country. As one of Europe's so-called "hidden children," skiing was the furthest thing from my mind during winters of Nazi tyranny. For six years, the fun and games of my early childhood were supplanted by a sustained effort to survive. In May 1945, the war finally ended, and I was reunited with my parents. For a short time, we resumed a normal life, despite the fact that twenty-five of our family members had perished in what would become known as the Holocaust.

Now nine years old, I accompanied Mother, Papa, and their friends on frequent ski trips to the Krkonoše mountains in northern Bohemia, as well as the spectacular Tatra range in Slovakia. I became an accomplished skier and even dreamed of becoming a competitive ski jumper after completing a series of lessons on a junior jumping hill.

However, once again an apocalyptic event interrupted my skiing life. We were forced to flee Czechoslovakia when the Communists took over the government and declared my parents enemies of the state. Life in refugee camps, followed by a period of near-poverty once we landed in America, was not conducive to spending holidays in Chamonix or Davos. Eleven years elapsed before I schussed down a mountain again.

Actually, "schussing" and "mountain" are monumental exaggerations of that first skiing experience in America. Along with my father and Sue, I began to learn all over again on a two-rope-tow, 270-foot-high, ant hill located in a skiing mecca called New Jersey. Years later, we would watch a grainy 8-mm movie my father made that first day. Seeing a clumsy figure snowplowing on wooden skis two feet longer than he, wearing baggy wool pants, a long blue nylon parka, and a hat which could have been borrowed from a Rolls Royce chauffeur prompted David to erupt:

"Look! It's Charlie Chaplin on skis!"

Although the film would provide hilarity to our family audience in the future, I was dead serious that day on the hill called Craigmeur. I learned to ski all over again and began a love affair that would last me a lifetime. I found that nothing compared to the euphoria I felt when standing on top of a mountain, surrounded by pristine untracked snow. With skis at the ready and taking in the majestic views of the countryside, I was on top of the world—whether that world was made of the deep powder of Utah, the sunshine of New Mexico, the deep bowls of Idaho, the serenity of Montana, the nearby slopes of Pennsylvania and West Virginia, or the ice and wind of Vermont and New Hampshire.

I was lucky enough to combine two love affairs—skiing and writing—when I became a ski columnist. More on that later, except to explain here that, as a writer, I was privileged not only to be comped with lift tickets and free lodging, but to ski with resort presidents, instructors, and patrollers—often out-of-bounds in pristine and avalanche-prone areas, places where the paying public was not permitted. There were many other benefits. I skied Whitetail Mountain with the incredible Diana Golden, a one-legged skier who won a gold medal at the Calgary Winter Olympics. I attended ski instructor school at Pennsylvania's Liberty Mountain with no intention to become a teacher of skiing, but in order to write about the experience. In the middle of a cold, starry night at Utah's Solitude Mountain Resort, I rode in a grooming vehicle down a slope so steep that the snow cat had to be tethered to a stout aspen tree at the top of the run. And at the crack of dawn, I ascended Alta's peak with ski patrollers who used long poles to break off dangerous cornices. Formed by overnight snowfall and wind, these overhangs had to be smashed each morning in order to eliminate avalanche danger by the time the lifts opened to the general public.

In addition to combining my love of writing with that of skiing, I was even able to apply my education to the sport. Head Ski Company, a firm that revolutionized skiing by introducing the first metal skis (until then, skis were made of wood), hired me as a consultant. I used my knowledge of structural mechanics to design the Head 240, a ski for the European market.

One of the most exhilarating experiences I ever had on skis began early one morning in 1989 when twelve of us, including

Sue and David, met our two guides at the base lodge of Park City Ski Area. They would lead us on a tour called "Utah Interconnect," one that would enable us to ski five world-class mountains—Park City, Solitude, Brighton, Alta, and Snowbird—in a single day.

The day began on an auspicious note. We were handed hold harmless agreements, stating that we understood the dangers of skiing out-of-bounds in the Wasatch Mountains. When I saw the words "avalanche" and "death," I stopped reading, hid the document from my wife and son, and signed quickly on behalf of the Heller family. Next, we were issued transmitters to be strapped to our chests. These would emit a signal in case we were buried by an avalanche. *Whoa, baby! I thought this was going to be fun!*

A group that had been smiling and chatty a short time before was now somber as it started up the Ski Team chairlift. At the top, we skied to the base of a high-speed quad under the watchful eyes of our guides. Only later did we find out that this was a test of our respective skiing abilities. Apparently, since no one was turned back, everybody was considered strong enough for the upcoming trek.

Two more chairlift rides took us to the top of 10,000-foot Jupiter Bowl peak. It was snowing lightly, so visibility was somewhat limited. Nevertheless, my first experience of skiing out-of-bounds in thirteen feet of pristine powder was one I will never forget. Crisscrossing graceful S-shaped tracks with David, who was ahead of me, I felt my internal body parts rushing toward my head as I plunged down the steep wall of Big Cottonwood Canyon. I held my hands high in order to free my poles from snow that rushed under my armpits. I had admired scenes such as this in Warren Miller films and in advertisements for helicopter skiing. Now, I was floating on white clouds just like those movie guys! Whooping and hollering, our little group was on a deep-powder high by the time it reached bottom, across the road from my favorite of all ski areas, Solitude.

We walked across the road, knocked down cups of hot chocolate in the cafeteria, and then took two chairlift rides to the top of Solitude. Once again, we went outside the area boundary and floated through bottomless powder down a steep face toward neighboring Brighton Ski Resort. Suddenly, the sun peeked through the clouds, and I could look across the canyon. There, I saw the graceful tracks we had made earlier while bombing down from the top of Jupiter. What a spectacular sight!

We entered Brighton, took one run, and headed back to Solitude. Three ski areas, and the morning was not even half over! When we sat down for lunch at the base lodge, the guide named Greg Cayeis addressed the group:

"Get some nourishment, guys," he said. "You'll need it because your test of stamina and courage is coming up."

Since he was smiling, we failed to take him seriously. Soon we would find out that he had not been joking. Once again, we rode to the top of Solitude, this time in preparation for crossing into neighboring Little Cottonwood Canyon, home of Alta and Snowbird. Once at the summit, we crossed the area boundary. We turned the corner, and—suddenly—we were confronted by a huge, impossibly steep, treeless, snowfield. It resembled an arctic tundra tilted at a sixty-degree angle.

"Well, gang, welcome to Highway to Heaven. We have to get to the other side," Greg announced. "I'm going to cross first on my telemark skis and cut a track. You'll see that I'm going to shuffle very slowly in order not to cause an avalanche. You will follow in my track, just as slowly, at 75-yard intervals. Be extremely careful and patient!"

With that he pushed off, painstakingly making a narrow track across the 300-yard-wide expanse. Sue followed the prescribed distance behind him and found the experience frightening. Unbeknownst to me, she was sobbing by the time Greg pulled her to safety on the other side. After watching

David and our companions take tiny steps in the single track, finally it was my turn.

As I followed the track, I forced myself to focus my eyes on the tips of my Olin Kinetics. When I made the mistake of looking to the right and up, my mind immediately conjured up a picture of a small stone breaking loose, picking up snow and speed as it hurtled down, and becoming a full-fledged avalanche by the time it reached me. *That's why I'm wearing the beeper*, I thought in a panic. Turning left and looking down the incline brought a more disconcerting thought: *If I slip and slide down to the bottom of the canyon, the beeper won't do me much good. They'll find my body in July!*

The trek across Highway to Heaven seemed to last hours. When I made it to the other side, actually in about fifteen minutes, I was greeted by my fellow skiers—exhausted, but proud of our joint accomplishment—pounding me on the back.

"Now, you guys will see why it was worth the ordeal," said Rod Keller, our second guide, who had crossed last, behind me.

This turned out to be an understatement. What awaited us was the most incredible skiing I would ever experience. We floated down Grizzly Gulch in feathery powder that appeared a mile deep. Each of us picked his or her own line and created graceful curves, sometimes wide and sometimes narrow, in the seemingly endless white expanse. Occasionally, the mono-chromatic scene was interrupted by a stand of aspens, only to open up on the other side to another pure, white tundra. Time seemed to stand still as gravity pulled me toward the bottom of Little Cottonwood Canyon. When I reached the base, I extracted my small writer's notebook out of the pocket of my yellow powder suit.

I crossed the Highway and arrived in Heaven! I wrote in it.

By now, our group was on such a high that each of us felt that we could tackle anything the mountains threw at us. We rode Alta's Wildcat chair to the top and from there skied a combination of steep, mogulled, chutes and narrow paths through trees until we reached our final destination area— Snowbird.

At this point, Sue and a couple of others packed it in. They were simply too exhausted to continue. They walked to a van that had come to bring us back to Park City. The rest of us piled into Snowbird's tram for its last ride of the day. Being jammed in with 125 skiers was quite a come-down after the solitude and serenity of our powder runs. I was tired before embarking— exhausted and in pain. Now I was also pissed off about the culture shock.

Adding to my anger and aches, a blizzard and gale-force wind greeted us upon disembarking at the top. With my legs and body sending SOS signals to my brain, my only goal became to make it to the bottom in one piece. I managed it only because our guides took pity on their worn-out survivors and actually mixed a few intermediate runs among the expert ones, as we made our way to the waiting van. David had to pull me through the door of the vehicle, and I plopped down— totally wiped out— next to Sue, who was fast asleep. The last frames of a Warren Miller ski movie are marked by the words, "The End." Not this movie. I would relive the Utah Interconnect adventure hundreds of times in my mind.

While the Utah Interconnect qualifies as the most exciting adventure I have experienced on alpine (downhill) skis, an excursion into Yellowstone National Park is the most memorable of my nordic (cross-country) escapades. It was the winter of 1993, and Sue, David and I were guests of Big Sky, a fabulous downhill mecca co-founded by the late television newscaster, Chet Huntley. We alternated skiing downhill at Big Sky with trips down the road to the top-ranked nordic center in the Rockies, the Lone Mountain Ranch.

Early one morning, we hopped aboard a small bus which

took us from Lone Mountain Ranch to West Yellowstone, Montana. The town resembled a western movie set straight out of Universal Studios. I would not have been surprised to see John Wayne walk out of one of the saloons, ready to duel with a bad guy in the street. Yet, something was strange. The "horses" tied up outside the stores, bars, and hotels were red, green, blue, and yellow, with names like Yamaha, Arctic Cat, Polaris, and Eagle inscribed on their sides. The streets were unplowed and the motorized horses were buzzing up and down West Yellowstone's main drag.

Our small group transferred to two snow coaches: egg-shaped vehicles with steering skis in the front and powering tracks in the rear. As we headed toward the entrance to the park, we fell into line behind a line of snowmobiles. Our guides called their drivers "bubbleheads," for their distinctive helmets, and were displeased by the fact that these noisy, stinking, motorcycles on skis were allowed into the national park, where they disturbed and disrupted animals and brought air pollution to a once-pristine place.

On our way to the Norris area, we learned from the guides that Yellowstone has a volcanic history. The last eruption, some 600,000 years ago, caused the formation of a 28- by 47-mile basin, called a caldera. The magmatic heat powering that eruption still creates the park's famous hot springs, geysers, and mud pots.

Once in the Norris area, we dismounted, put on our skis, and headed for the backcountry of Yellowstone. Within minutes, we were confronted by a herd of about fifty bison.

"Stop!" ordered Mike, our guide. "Anytime you see a herd, look for the biggest bull. He's the leader, and he protects the herd. You watch his tail. If he raises it, he's going to do one of two things: charge or discharge. Pray that it's the latter."

Mike went on to warn that people who get too close to the lead bull are sometimes mauled, and he ordered us to keep a distance of at least fifty feet between ourselves and any herd.

We skied around the bison and, with every eye trained on him, the boss bull raised his tail, as if on cue. I heard several of my fellow skiers gasp. I looked for an escape route and hoped that Sue, David, and I could kick and glide faster than our companions. Then, to our relief, the bull discharged. We breathed a collective sigh of relief.

We made our way across the expanse of the park, skiing on a couple of feet of snow, which disappeared completely every time we approached a warm-water stream or a hot spring. Over and over, we took off our skis in order to cross, only to put them back on again once on the other side. A couple of miles into the trip, we came upon a herd of elk, none of whom took an interest in a small band of two-legged creatures sliding along on skinny boards.

Every few minutes, an eagle soared above us in the clear, blue sky. A flock of trumpeter swans flew overhead and landed near a steaming hot spring, perhaps for their weekly bath. Over the next couple of hours, while gliding silently along the caldera, we saw more bison and elk, coyotes, geese, and ducks. As a hidden child during the war, books were often my sole companions. One I cherished above all others told of the adventures of Norwegian explorer Roald Amundsen, who led his party on skis into Antarctica. I dreamed of someday gliding in his tracks. Now, in this wild, wide and desolate place, I felt as if I had achieved that childhood dream of emulating my hero.

As breathtakingly beautiful as our surroundings were, we could see the results of the disastrous fire of 1988, during which thirty-five percent of Yellowstone had burned. Because of the deadfall—trees that had burned and fallen to the ground—we were forced to take many detours in the backcountry. Along the way, we circled around hundreds of hot springs, as well as areas of dangerous quicksand. We stared in disbelief at the remains of a bison who had fallen through the snow into a hot spring. Large and small bubbles rose and popped around the whitened bones; steam, like smoke from a crematorium, ascended toward the sky. This served as a graphic warning to stay with the guide at all times. The aftermath of the fire was not entirely negative. For one thing, the dead trees had their own, stark beauty. For another, new vistas of far-off mountain ranges were created by the disaster.

When we ended our tour near Old Faithful, I concluded that the Yellowstone adventure was unlike any I had ever experienced before. It helped me appreciate the enormity and diversity of this country. To be able to enjoy such breathtaking beauty on skis brought us closer to this incredible place than would have been possible any other way.

The best skier I ever had the privilege of following down a mountain was the man who became something of a big brother to me when we came to America. Tom Eisner, the elder son of our sponsors when we immigrated to America, was born in Prague on March 10, 1931, and came to this country nine years later with his parents and younger brother, Steve. Tom became a successful builder and developer, and he and his family lived in Fort Worth. They owned a vacation home in Taos, New Mexico, not far from Taos Ski Valley, one of the steepest and most difficult ski venues in the West. Tom was a fixture on the mountain, not only for his acrobatics on the snow, but also for the outrageous outfits he wore while doing it.

Some days, he skied in greasy, orange airplane mechanic's overalls to which he attached a kite that followed him down the mountain. On special days, such as Easter Sunday, he wore a black brocaded tuxedo, ruffled shirt, an opera cape lined with red satin, and a top hat. When he bombed down the mountain, executing royal christies and helicopters—all the time either whistling or singing a tune as a metronome for his turns—everyone's eyes were on him. I followed at a distance great enough not to be compared to him. I was a pretty good skier, but a rather ordinary one in comparison to Tom.

Sue and I were scheduled to spend a ski week in Taos with the Eisners in late February 1992. Two weeks before our scheduled arrival, I received a phone call from Tom's 33-year-old son, Stephen.

"Daddy was killed in a skiing accident," he cried.

"Oh my God, what happened?" I asked after catching my breath.

"On the last run of the day, he went airborne off a mogul and landed on his head. He broke his neck. A patroller saw the accident. Once stabilized, Daddy was helicoptered to a hospital in Santa Fe. But the damage was too massive and there was nothing that could be done to save him. The day before Valentine's Day, our family decided to turn off the respirator."

I was devastated. The Hellers and the Eisners, though unrelated by blood, considered themselves one family. Of course, our vacation plans would be cancelled, as we awaited word of the upcoming funeral. Then a few days later, Stephen called again.

"I hope you're still planning to come to Taos," he said.

"No way, Stephen. We can't come and ski and play as if nothing happened."

"Please, Charlie," Stephen pleaded. "You have to come. I grew up skiing Taos. Skiing is a part of our family. If I don't go ski there now, and if I don't ski the run where Daddy was killed, I'll never be able to go back there again. And he'll come back and kick my butt! I need you to ski it with me. Please!" Of course I agreed, and Sue and I arrived as scheduled.

With tears obstructing my vision, I followed Stephen down a mogul-laden slope called Zagava. We tried to imagine the line Tommy would have taken on that last run. Stephen skied it as beautifully as I imagined Tommy had done. When we reached the bottom, we hugged and cried on each other's shoulders. That gray, snowy day at Taos marked the saddest experience of my skiing life.

Throughout my life, I have been fortunate to befriend many wonderful, interesting people. One such friend was Allan Isen, whom I met through our respective activities in venture capital, but with whom I bonded over our mutual love of skiing. Ten years older than I, Allan was the son of Eastern European immigrants. In the 1950s, he was one of the few Jewish students admitted to Columbia University, where he became president of his class and obtained both an undergraduate degree and a professional diploma in optometry. As an optometrist, his claim to fame was his discovery of a soft plastic material invented in Communist Czechoslovakia. He obtained US rights to it and sold a license to Bausch & Lomb, which used it to produce the first soft contact lens. Allan's pioneering work with contact lenses came to the attention of President Lyndon Baines Johnson, and the president not only made Allan his personal optometrist, but he moved him into a White House office, where he became LBJ's confidant and advisor.

When I met Allan, he had moved to Sun Valley, Idaho, and married Wendy, his second wife. Sue and I became regular guests in the Isens' home and fell in love with the slopes of Sun Valley. There, we skied with a group of friends—Brent and Bev Robinson, Chuck and Wanda Parker, Janet Ross-Heiner— and communicated via walkie-talkies as we spread out over two mountains and their bowls, slopes, and trails. Evenings, Allen entertained us with stories of his travels with LBJ, in-between heated discussions of politics and international affairs.

Upon our departure from Sun Valley on our last visit, Allan handed us a key to his house.

"The house is yours anytime you want to come—winter,

spring, summer or fall."

Sadly, we never had the opportunity to use the key. Allan passed away on December 8, 2005, following a three-year struggle with prostate cancer. The key to his Sun Valley house is a treasured reminder of a wonderful friend.

In early 1989, Sue and I spent the weekend with Bill Miles and Louise, the wonderful lady he had married recently, at their vacation home in West Virginia. With the small ski area near their place lacking sufficient snow, we hoped to find an alternative.

"There's a place called Canaan Valley about an hour from here," said Louise, a native of the Almost Heaven State. "It's at a higher elevation and may have snow."

Louise's simple suggestion would lead to another love affair. We drove to Canaan (pronounced "Kah-**neyn**") Valley and, sure enough, they had plenty of snow. With a vertical drop of 850 feet, the hill was no match for the western and New England mountains we were accustomed to skiing. But it was fun, with a variety of runs, from green (easy) to double-black (very difficult).

The following winter, the four of us decided to return for a long weekend. Louise made reservations at a condominium resort called Beaver Ridge, at the north end of the valley. During our stay, we discovered that there was a second downhill ski area in the valley, this one called Timberline, with a vertical drop of a thousand feet. Moreover, there was a nordic center, White Grass, with fifty kilometers of cross-country trails surrounding Canaan Valley's original downhill run, Weiss Slope. We found out that Canaan, at 3,300 feet above sea level, was the highest-elevation valley east of the Rockies. And, most importantly, that it was the recipient of lake-effect snow—a narrow band originating over Lake Erie, one that dumped about two hundred inches of the beautiful white stuff on the area each year.

"This would be a great place to have a vacation home," I speculated one evening during dinner at the Oriskany Inn. "It's only a four-hour drive from home. We could come for weekends and vacations."

Sue agreed that we should check it out, and the next day I walked over to the Beaver Ridge rental office. There, a congenial man named Terry Smoot, who had been a football star at Virginia Tech and a running back for the Pittsburgh Steelers, introduced himself as the resort manager and gave me a sales pitch. He presented me with an idealized cash-flow print-out, showing how much money we would make by renting out a two-bedroom unit. I told him that I would study it upon our return home and would get back to him.

The following Wednesday evening back in Maryland, I played tennis at the Big Vanilla indoor arena near our home. Following our match, my playing partner, Knut Aarsand, and I had our customary beers in the bar above the court.

"Hey, Knut," I said, suddenly remembering that he had gone to college in West Virginia. "Are you familiar with a place called Canaan Valley?"

"Yeah, sure. Why?"

"We're thinking of buying a vacation condo there."

"Really? Where's the condo?" asked Knut.

"A place called Beaver Ridge Resort," I replied.

Knut set down his beer glass, wiped the foam from his lips, and laughed for the next thirty seconds.

"What the hell's so funny?"

"Believe it or not, I just bought all the unsold Beaver Ridge units at a bankruptcy auction," he explained. "I've sold several of them, but some are still available. You'd better hurry up and buy one from me because they're going fast."

In May 1990, Sue, David and I became proud owners of Unit 122, a two-bedroom/two-bath condo, on the top floor of Ash Lodge, the lower of two lodges at the north end of Canaan

Valley. Although we bought the condo with the intention of using it primarily in the winter, we soon found out how wonderful summers are in "Almost Heaven." There are hundreds of miles of hiking trails in the region, kayaking on the Blackwater River, and the fairways and greens of Canaan Valley State Park, where we re-discovered our long-forgotten passion for golf.

CHAPTER TWENTY-ONE

FORE!

At an Annapolis Rotary Club lunch, at the peak of a period during which my life outside of work revolved around sailboat racing, I had struck up a conversation with an old friend. I knew that Dick was the best golfer in Rotary, and I inquired how he had gotten his start in the game. He explained that he learned as a youngster at a course in his hometown and then played on his high school and university teams.

"Where do you play now?" I asked. He named a nearby country club. Recalling my father's comment back when we were newly-arrived immigrants living near the poverty line that only rich people belong to country clubs, I continued my questioning.

"How much does it cost to belong to a country club?"

"The initiation fee was around twenty-five thousand dollars," he said, "and the monthly dues are five hundred."

"You must be kidding!" I blurted out and nearly choked on my fried chicken. "You paid twenty-five thousand bucks to join, and now you pay another six thousand bucks a year just to play golf?"

He set down his knife and fork and looked me in the eye. "I'm just as passionate about golf as you are about sailing. How much does it cost you to race your boat?"

I had never given thought to the annual cost of pursuing my obsession. I pushed away my plate, pulled a pen from my pocket, and began to write on a paper napkin:

Slip fee: $5,000; insurance: $300; yacht club dues...

I continued to list annual costs of repair and maintenance, one new sail each year, weekly bottom-cleaning by a diver, race entry fees, and more. When I finished and added up the numbers, I was dumbfounded.

"Okay," said Dick, grinning like a Cheshire cat. "What's the number?"

"More than seventeen thousand bucks a year," I said. "Hard to believe!"

"That's almost three times as much as I pay to play golf, and we're not done yet," he replied. "I paid twenty-five thousand dollars to get started at my club. How much did you pay for your boat?"

I did not need a pen and napkin to come up with the number. "A hundred thousand more than your initiation fee. I surrender. Golf is a hell of a bargain, compared to sailboat racing."

Now, a couple of years after that conversation, we were at the Canaan Valley golf course, some ten minutes from our new vacation home. Sue and I had not played golf for nearly thirty years, having determined back then that we had to choose between it and sailing—the two sports are too time-consuming to be compatible. We chose sailing.

"That was fun," said Sue, following that first round at Canaan. "It would be nice to start playing golf again,"

Back home, we discussed it at length and decided that both of us were burned out from racing. Training new crew members each year was getting old. For the first time, we realized that a busy race schedule precluded us from partaking in any other social activities. Perhaps most importantly, David was no longer living at home; he was going to college and working, and he had a girlfriend. Our days as a sailing family seemed numbered. We sold *Pistol Pete* to a man in Havre de Grace, Maryland. We heard that our beautiful OSU-inspired artwork had been replaced by an ugly spider web. Our baby was racing in the northern Chesapeake Bay as *Charlotte's Web*.

We took up golf in earnest. One of the most wonderful things about the game is that one can play it for the rest of his or her life. I found that I enjoyed it more—and was more passionate about it—than I had when I was young. Restarting then, and lasting till today, I came to value the freedom, the companionship, and the joy of being out in God's nature. I have come especially to appreciate the complex mysteries of the game.

I had actually started playing golf several years before first stepping aboard a sailboat. It was a rather inauspicious beginning to a sport about which I am just as passionate today as I once was about sailing.

One of my parents' first purchases in America was a 1949 Studebaker Champion. We took weekend drives around the North Jersey countryside, as we began to familiarize ourselves with our new home. On one of our drives, we encountered a sign: "Spring Brook Country Club, Members Only Beyond This Point." My father stopped the car, and we stared at the beautiful green expanse in front of us. Meticulously cut lawns spreading out as far as the eye could see, occasionally dotted with areas containing white sand and crossed by narrow streams. In the distance, we observed small flags fluttering atop short, thin poles.

"It's a golf course," my father explained. "I saw several during the war when I was stationed in England. Here comes a group of golfers now. Watch. The idea is for them to hit a little white ball into a hole at the bottom of that flagstick."

We observed as the men withdrew sticks from their bags and launched their balls toward the waving flag. I had always been a good athlete, excelling in soccer, tennis, skiing, and hockey in Czechoslovakia. Now I was learning to play American sports: baseball, basketball, and football. Golf looked like fun, too.

"I'd like to try to play golf," I said. "It looks easy."

Papa and Mother laughed. "That's a rich man's sport," my father said. "There is no way we could afford to buy those sticks called golf clubs or to pay a fee to play on a golf course. Maybe someday you'll be rich enough to play."

Our first home in America was a two-bedroom apartment on the second floor of a brick building in Franklin Village, a complex of garden apartments in Morristown, New Jersey. From one of our neighbors there, I was able to acquire my first "set" of golf clubs. It consisted of five irons made up of wooden shafts, rusty metal heads, and black electrical tape that passed for grips. I knew I could hit the little ball that came with the clubs as well as those country club guys, and I could not wait to prove it.

The following weekend, I carried my clubs to the baseball field across the street. I placed the ball in the outfield grass, gripped a club with the word "Brassie" engraved on its blade, and swung. Swish! The ball was still sitting in the grass. Several more swings and, finally, I began advancing the ball. But its flight was a far cry from what I had seen at the country club. The ball never left the ground and rolled perhaps ten yards.

"What are you doing?" I turned around and discovered a middle-aged man dressed in a maroon sweat suit standing behind me and laughing.

"I'm playing golf," I answered in my halting English.

"But why are you swinging a right-handed club left-handed?" he asked.

Although I am right-handed, I had always held everything

where two hands were involved—a hockey stick, a baseball bat, a shovel, a rake—left-handed. Now, it turned out, I was doing the same thing with the golf club, without realizing that it was intended to be swung from the other side.

The man picked up one of the clubs lying on the ground, gripped it with his right hand low and left hand high, and swung. The ball flew on a gorgeous arc toward the backstop on the other side of the baseball field. I ran after the ball and brought it back. The stranger showed me how to place my hands on the club and told me to swing. I hit the ball. This time, it went into the air and settled perhaps fifty yards away.

"There you go," said the man. "Now you're a golfer." He smiled and walked away.

Swinging right-handed did not come naturally, and I spent a great deal of time practicing on that baseball field. The following year, my parents bought a house in nearby Morris Plains, where we became close friends with our neighbors, Jack and Lynne Geils and their son Jay. Lynne decided that she wanted to learn to play golf, and, on several occasions, she brought Jay and me along to play at Canary Cottage Golf Club. I brought my wooden-handle, five-club "set" and attempted to coax the little white ball from tee to hole—not very success-fully. Eventually, I retired the antique clubs to our attic, where they remained until my parents threw them out during a spring-cleaning weekend while I was away at college.

Thereafter, my only attempts at golf throughout high school and college were occasional trips to driving ranges with friends. Because the only clubs provided by the ranges in those days were right-handed, once again I was forced to take unnatural cuts at the balls. The results were unimpressive—often comical—but none of us were golfers, so my ugly slices and feeble worm-burners did not stand out.

When Sue and I settled in Santa Monica, California, following graduation and marriage, circumstances dictated that I make a serious attempt to become a golfer. My employer, the Missiles & Space Division of Douglas Aircraft Company, sponsored a Thursday evening, nine-hole, twilight league at nearby Fox Hills/Baldwin Hills golf courses. Most of my fellow engineers played.

For the first time in my immigrant life, I had some spending money, and for a hundred dollars, I purchased a set of J. C. Higgins clubs from Sears & Roebuck. Right-handed, of course. In those days, lefties had to have their clubs custom-made, and that I could not afford.

My game was beyond terrible. I swung and missed often and, when I managed to hit the ball, the little white dimpled sphere reacted in one of two ways: either it hopped forward like some crazed rabbit, never rising more than six inches off the ground or it soared toward the sky in a left-to-right arc resembling a gigantic banana, often hiding behind a palm tree or mired inside shrubbery. My nine-hole scores were comparable to those achieved every weekend by golfers on the PGA Tour, except that theirs were for *eighteen* holes. But, I enjoyed the camaraderie of the game and I was improving, albeit slowly. Mostly, I looked forward to getting together with my teammates and opponents in the clubhouse at the end of each round. We sat around a large semicircular bar and relived our adventures on the golf course.

"Man, on number seven, I laced a two-hundred-and-fifty-yard drive down the middle of the fairway," one of my friends would brag.

"I got down in two from the green-side bunker on number three," another would claim.

I provided comic relief with stories about my slices into never-never land, shanks in the fairways, and futile attempts to escape from sand traps.

One evening about a month into the season, a guy about our age, dressed in golf clothes like the rest of us, but otherwise quite unlike us in appearance, sat down at the opposite end of the bar and ordered a beer. What attracted our stares was the length of his sandy hair. Defying the early-1960s fashion of close-cropped hair, the visitor's locks nearly reached his shoulders. He was alone, and, as soon as he emptied his glass and paid the bartender, he departed. He reappeared the following Thursday and left just as quickly. When he took his customary seat for the third consecutive Thursday, I walked over to him.

"Hi, my name is Charlie," I said to him. "Why don't you come over and join us?"

"Yeah, hi. My name is Clint," he replied. "I'd like that."

I introduced the handsome, rugged, soft-spoken guy to my friends, and he sat down on a stool on our side of the bar. He joined in the banter about our golf rounds, although it turned out that he played each Thursday afternoon alone and on the other course from the one we were playing that day. After that evening, Clint joined us at the bar whenever he encountered us there. During those times, the beer-drinking conversation never seemed to veer away from golf, and we knew as little about Clint as he did about us.

One evening, Sue and I were sitting on the living-room floor of our apartment in Santa Monica, watching one of television's most popular shows on our fifteen-inch black-and-white screen, a weekly western saga called "Rawhide." Several cowboys on horseback were driving a herd of cattle through a mountain pass. The camera panned the stampeding throng of cows and then, slowly, it zoomed in on the trail foreman. I jumped to my feet and stared at the image in disbelief.

"Holy crap!" I screamed, startling Sue. "That's Clint!"

I explained to Sue that the guy playing Rowdy Yates was the same friendly, long-haired golfer who joined us for beers most Thursday evenings at Fox Hills. Judging by her questions, I knew that she had her doubts. The next morning at work, I told my golfing friends about my discovery. They too were skeptical and threatened to prove me wrong by questioning Clint at our next get-together at the bar.

As luck would have it, and as if Clint had a premonition that his identity had been uncovered, he did not show up the following Thursday. Or a week later, or the week after that... We never saw him again. The only good news was that my friends no longer doubted me. They tuned in to "Rawhide" and confirmed the fact that our drinking buddy had been Clint Eastwood.

Following our eastward move across the country in 1962, Sue decided that she, too, would start playing golf. We took lessons from the head pro, Jimmy Flattery, at Forest Park Golf Club on the west side of Baltimore. Our respective games improved to a point where we no longer felt embarrassed to tee it up on crowded weekends.

"You're an engineer," Jimmy said to me one day. "You should use the latest and greatest technology to help your game. The days of steel shafts are numbered." I did not tell him that, after starting out with wooden shafts, I considered steel state-of-the-art.

He opened a box and pulled out a set of four woods with shafts made of aluminum tubes wrapped in super-strong filament winding. The gleaming white sticks resembled the exotic fiberglass structures with which we had experimented in the space program at Douglas in California. I had to have them! I do not know if I was the first golfer to play with a predecessor of today's graphite shafts, but Jimmy claimed I was the first in the state of Maryland. While my game did not improve a great deal, my clubs were the envy of every golfer who spotted me on the tee of any of Baltimore area's public courses.

In September 1963, I began teaching at the Naval Academy. I commuted from Baltimore for the first couple of months, but as soon as we moved into the Admiral Farragut apartments in Annapolis, we joined the Naval Academy Golf

Club. The course, designed by Bill Flynn in 1916, is owned and operated by the Naval Academy Athletic Association and located across the Severn River from the school. It is quite difficult, with long holes, undulating fairways, and multiple-break greens.

Sue and I played a few rounds at Navy before her pregnancy put her golf on hold and cold weather brought a halt to mine. David was born in April 1964, and our lives now revolved around the little guy. It was another year before either of us picked up our sticks again. When we did, we made rapid progress. Sue became a competitive player in the Naval Academy eighteen-hole women's group, and I improved steadily, eventually bringing my handicap down to a fourteen—meaning that I was shooting regularly in the mid-eighties.

But the waters of the Severn River and nearby Chesapeake Bay proved to be bigger magnets than the green grass of the Navy golf course. We got hooked on sailing. Once we became proficient at the new sport, we bought a competitive boat, and began racing. That is when we discovered that people with full-time jobs cannot be both golfers and sailboat racers. Each activity is so time-consuming that the two cannot coexist. Golf lost. It would remain a distant memory for nearly thirty years.

That brings us back to Canaan Valley and 1990. At the south end of the valley, in the middle of a state park, lies the eighteen-hole course that brought us back to the game.

It did not take long to become hooked. We bought new clubs, took lessons, and joined a private club—Walden Country Club in Crofton, Maryland. Each week, we participated in a Friday evening couples scrambles with our friends, Jill Warrington and Basil Duncan, and Sunday afternoon rounds became part of our weekly routine. Our social life, which had revolved around sailing for so many years, now focused on golf. But the transition also triggered a sad realization. My father had dabbled at golf while he was still working. Once he retired, he began playing regularly, usually with a neighbor friend. With the exception of a few rounds on joint vacations with my parents at Lake George and the Poconos, Sue and I had not played golf with my parents. I had been so wrapped up in work and sailboat racing that it had never occurred to me that Papa would be pleased to spend time with his son on the golf course. I had never offered to join him. And now he was gone.

Some years later, I would read James Dodson's *Final Rounds: a Father, a Son, the Golf Journey of a Lifetime*. When the author discovers that his father has two months to live, the two of them travel to Scotland, where they play the world's most famous courses. During those few days, father and son develop a new relationship and discover that they are one another's best friend. If I could turn the clock back today, I would gladly give up sailing in order to experience such special times on fairways with my Papa.

As Director of the Dingman Center for Entrepreneurship at the University of Maryland, I accepted a number of invitations to play in corporate and charitable tournaments. In 1996, Lillian Lincoln, CEO of Centennial One, asked me to participate in her company's outing at her club, The Country Club at Woodmore, in Mitchellville, Maryland. Lillian's life story is an amazing tale of chasing, and realizing, the proverbial American Dream. Born poor in the segregated South, she worked her way through Howard University and became the first Black woman to graduate from Harvard Business School. In 1976, she founded Centennial One in her garage. I met her only after she had grown it to 1,200 employees, and a few months before she sold it. A few years later, she would tell her remarkable tale in a book titled, *The*

Road to Someplace Better.

Lillian's invitation led to a new love affair. The Woodmore golf course was one of the most beautiful I had ever played. No wonder *Golf Digest* magazine rated it among the state's best year after year. When Lillian offered to sponsor Sue and me for membership, we jumped at the chance and, over the next twelve years, were active there. Besides participating in many competitions, both of us took on roles in various club management functions.

One of the members of my Dingman Center board was a partner in the accounting firm, Ernst & Young. Bill Cole's connection to our organization was a natural one because he ran E&Y's entrepreneurial practice out of the Baltimore office. Outside of our professional association, Bill and I became good friends and often played golf together. In the spring of 1997, Bill asked me to join a golf group he had formed a few years before.

"We call ourselves Team Mulligan," he explained, "and we go on golf trips to different resorts every April."

"Why the name, Team Mulligan?" I asked.

"Mulligan" is a common term for a do-over sometimes offered to a golfer who hits a poor shot off the first tee. Bill informed me that his group had a special rule: whenever every player in a foursome hits a poor shot off a tee, all are permitted do-overs—they take a "Team Mulligan."

I joined Bill's group on a trip to TPC Sawgrass, near Jacksonville, Florida. On that junket, my roommate was another rookie, Lee McGee, Chief Financial Officer of Sylvan Learning Systems. Thus, another friendship was born. Eventually, Sylvan split into two companies. One of them, Laureate, became a holding company for a number of domestic and international for-profit colleges and universities. Upon Lee's introduction, I would join the boards of directors of two of them, Walden University and the NewSchool of Architecture and Design. Our son, David, would become an information technology manager at Laureate's headquarters in Baltimore.

Belonging to Team Mulligan afforded me the opportunity to play golf courses throughout the country: Myrtle Beach, Kiawah Island, Orlando, Pinehurst, Scottsdale, and the Robert Trent Jones Golf Trail in Alabama, among other golfing meccas. Even more importantly, the association led to the start of many lasting friendships. When we added an annual fall golf weekend on Maryland's Eastern Shore with our wives, Sue became a card-carrying Team Mulligan member, and our circle of friends expanded.

The Great Recession of 2008-2009 brought upheaval to The Country Club at Woodmore. Many members faced financial crises in their respective businesses and paying dues to a country club became a luxury they could no longer afford. Like many private clubs throughout the country, Woodmore was in trouble. Eventually, it was bailed out by a private equity firm, which began to rebuild the membership. However, during the crisis period, many of the golfers with whom I had played regularly resigned. The seniors (men fifty-five and older), a group which at one time numbered more than twenty, whittled down to a foursome or two.

Meanwhile, the only private golf club in Annapolis was thriving. Naval Academy Golf Association had been immune to the fiscal problems of its industry. As a long-time resident of the area, I had many friends who belonged to Navy, and several of them urged me to join. The only problem was that Navy had a two-year-long waiting list for membership. Despite that, I applied and, in January 2015, rejoined the club to which Sue and I had belonged forty-five years earlier.

In 2011, we sold our beloved house on a hill and moved into a condo in Annapolis. Our community, Heritage Harbour, has a lovely nine-hole, par-three course practically across the street from our home. The club professional, Jon Magarace, runs an active tournament schedule and we participate as much as we can.

Despite my advancing age and diminished power, my game has continued to improve—due to better equipment and the coaching of Jon Magarace. My handicap is nearly at the same level where it had peaked some years back, and I have even won three club championships at Heritage Harbour, as well as my age group at the Navy Senior Championship, and I have had six holes-in-one in the past nine years.

Most importantly, I find golf a completely fulfilling sport because it is so difficult, so challenging, so competitive. The sport combines the enjoyment of being out in nature, coping with weather, battling with one's self, and making tough choices.

While I continue to flog myself for having failed to play with my father, our son David has unwittingly made much of the pain go away. At the mid-century mark of his life, he has decided to take up golf. Much to my delight, he is not doing it half-heartedly. He takes lessons and practices as much as his work and family obligations permit. I am seldom happier than when he and I walk, golf bags slung over our shoulders, along a lush green fairway on our way to our next shots. David has never been a great communicator, but on the golf course, we converse like good friends: about work, the children, politics, and life.

I am grateful for being able to participate in this wonderful game, one my father once hoped I would be sufficiently wealthy to play.

CHAPTER TWENTY-TWO

VELVET REVOLUTION

Back in 1970, a little more than two years after the Soviets and their Warsaw Pact serfs crushed Czechoslovakia's brief period of freedom, my family and I visited my native land—the only time I set foot on the other side of the Iron Curtain. By then, those of us who had escaped with the "class of 1948," were no longer considered enemies of the state. Thus, when the National Academy of Sciences asked me to go on an official visit, I jumped at the chance. My parents were petrified, convinced that I would never return. When I informed them that Sue and six-year-old David would accompany me, Mother became hysterical, and Papa begged me not to subject them to such danger.

Despite their objections—and, I must admit, my own last-minute trepidation—we went. As guests of the Czechoslovak Academy of Sciences, we were housed in a comfortable, government-run—and government-bugged—apartment. By day, I spent my time lecturing and mentoring Czech research-ers about computer-aided design, a technology totally foreign to highly educated Czech researchers who were deprived by their government and their Russian masters of modern computers and forbidden to read scientific and technical papers written by western authors.

Outside of work, our three weeks in Prague were a mixture of delight and sorrow. Delight because we spent the majority of our time with my parents' closest friends, the Hahns. Uncle Viktor, Aunt Aša, and their daughter Sylva introduced us to the historical wonders of Prague. Delight because I was able to show my wife and son Kojetice, the village where I grew up and where I had spent many months hiding from the Nazis. Delight because we and the Hahns paid several visits to Mother's and Papa's favorite spot: the Lobkowitz castle high on a hill in Mělník, sipping Ludmila wine while gazing at one of the country's grandest sights, the convergence of Czechoslovakia's two great rivers, Vltava and Labe.

However, all the while, it was impossible not to feel sad—sad for my fellow Czechs who were prisoners in their own country. They were deprived of many of their freedoms—of speech, of the press, of foreign travel, of economic and educational opportunities. I felt embarrassed when they questioned me about life in America, and I had to tell them about our house, our two cars, our freedom to travel, our freedom to criticize our government, and the fact that in America hard work and persistence could lead to both emotional and material success.

When we boarded a British Air flight for London, I was torn between joyful relief because we were returning to the free world and a terrible sadness for those we were leaving behind in the somber, gray, joyless place called Czechoslovakia. As the airplane's wheels left the ground, I prayed for them all.

When we returned to the United States, pressures of running CADCOM, a growing high-tech company, took immediate precedence, and soon Czechoslovakia faded into the background. Nineteen years went by before that tiny flame of Czech patriotism began to burn brightly once again.

The year was 1989, and the walls of the Soviet empire began to crumble. Its downfall had begun with strikes and nonviolent civil disobedience in Poland. Then the Berlin Wall that had separated democratic West Germany from Communist East Germany came tumbling down. In Prague, students chose November 17, the fiftieth anniversary of the murders of Czech students by Nazi troops, to organize a protest against the Communist regime. On November 28, following daily protests and worker strikes, the Communists capitulated. The bloodless coup, labeled the "Velvet Revolution," led to the election of playwright Václav Havel as president of the newly democratic Czechoslovakia.

I was elated, although my one great regret was the fact that my father was not alive to see the change. Sadly, he had passed away less than two years before, in January 1988. Mother had mixed emotions about her native country. She was happy because she despised the Communist thugs who had driven us out. And she was overjoyed that her best friend, Aunt Aša Hahnová, would be free and that she might be able to see her again. At the same time, Mother's memories of World War II were different from mine. While my primary residue of the war was a loathing of Germans, Mother was unable to forget or forgive the cruel acts of some Czech Nazi collaborators—experiences which she did not disclose to me until several years later. Mother considered herself an American, and she had no interest in returning to Czechoslovakia or in attempting to reclaim properties that the Communists had stolen from us.

Thus, Mother was unmoved when our friend at the Czechoslovak embassy in Washington, Irena Zíková, informed us that, under a newly passed restitution law, we were eligible to get back those properties or to receive financial compensation. The new law covered properties that had been nationalized by the government back in 1948.

"You're on your own," Mother told me when I asked her to join me in filing for restitution. "I'm the heir to all this, but I'll assign everything to you. I'll be rooting for you, but please keep me out of it."

By now, my family and I were quite comfortable financially, and my interest in getting back Heller/Neumann properties had nothing to do with money. My attitude was: *The bastards robbed us of everything we had. I'm going after them!* And I did, with help.

With the assistance of our Czech lawyer, Jiří "George" Bedrna, our good friend, Jitka Thomasová, and a bank account used to bribe corrupt government officials, we managed to get back nearly everything stolen from us by the government of the now-defunct Czechoslovak Socialistic Republic. I became the owner of a clothing factory and a couple of single-family homes, and I received minimal cash restitution for houses I declined to take over. But one obstacle remained.

The restitution laws enacted by Parliament applied only to properties that had been taken over by the Czechoslovak government. Our family had owned a seven-story apartment building in Prague, one in which my parents and I were living prior to our escape, one that was taken over by the Secretariat of the Communist Party. They converted it to an office building and made it their headquarters for a section of the capital city.

"The Communist Party is still legal in this country," Bedrna told me. "They still own the building. The only way to get it back is by suing them."

"OK, let's do it," I said.

"It's not so simple. We don't have any proof that your grandfather and great-uncle built the building or that your family ever owned it. I haven't been able to find the deed or any other proof of your ownership."

We had escaped in a rush, and the last thing my parents

wanted to carry out with them were documents showing that they owned properties in a land to which they had no intention of returning. The last legal owners, prior to the Nazis and then the Communists stealing the building, were my grandfather and his brother. Both had been murdered by Germans while trying to escape through Yugoslavia. Bedrna managed to convince the court that the two Neumann brothers had been the builders and owners. However, he was told by the judge that we could present our case to the court only if we could produce death certificates proving that they were dead and thus, that Mother is the sole legal heir. Fine, but how do we manage that?

My entrepreneurial skills—and a lack of conscience when it came to dealing with thieves—came to the rescue. I forged a letter from my grandfather to his daughter, Mother, informing her that his brother had been shot the previous day and that he was holed up in a farmhouse in Yugoslavia, surrounded by German soldiers. He expected to die at any moment.

I informed Bedrna of my "amazing find," and sent it to him. He took it to a government officer who, with the assistance of a bribe, promised to produce the death certificates. However, Mother and I had to appear before him in person to sign some papers.

The trial was scheduled for the Friday following Easter in 1994. Reluctantly, Mother agreed to accompany me, and we arrived in Prague on Easter Sunday. On Monday morning, along with Bedrna, we drove to the ministry to get the death certificates. Horrors! The bribed official had been promoted the previous week, and a short, plump, surly woman had taken his place.

Following a half-hour lecture on the unfairness of "rich Americans" coming back to their native country to get back their properties, she said: "You'll get your death certificates. But you'll have to wait sixty days, like everyone else." The fact that the trial would take place on Friday was no concern of hers.

So, now the cold and rain were an appropriate reflection of our collective mood as we stood on the courthouse steps under umbrellas. Our chances of winning the suit and getting our building back were somewhere between slim and none. Suddenly, one of our Communist adversaries, who were standing on the other side of the steps, approached.

"Why do we have to fight like this?" he asked Bedrna in Czech and put his arm around his shoulder. It turned out that the two had been classmates in law school. "Can't we settle this amicably?"

Bedrna and I had a long-standing agreement that, in order to give me time to think, we would pretend in all our negotiations that I did not understand Czech. He translated the Communist's words into English for me.

Oh, the slimeballs don't realize that we don't have any proof of ownership, I realized as soon as I heard the question asked in Czech.

"What do they suggest?" I asked George in English.

"What kind of settlement do you have in mind?" George asked in Czech.

"We have no place to go with our headquarters. We need to be able to rent three floors of your building for two years at a reasonable rate," the Communist replied.

Your building—all right! I cheered silently. George translated, but my answer was ready.

"Two floors, one year," I blurted out in English.

George translated my offer into Czech and the lawyer joined his fellow henchmen who huddled under umbrellas on the other side of the steps. Despite the cold, I was sweating profusely while trying to appear calm and in total control of the negotiation. Finally, the Communist lawyer walked back toward us. As he approached, he extended his hand to me.

"Deal," he said in English.

"*No, tak dobře,*" ("Well, OK,") I replied in Czech, and shook his hand. His eyes opened wide in surprise at my perfect pronunciation. Mother transferred title to me, and, for the next year, I was landlord to the sleazeballs of the Communist Party of Czechoslovakia.

Our friend, Jitka Thomasová, introduced me to a high-ranking officer of the nation's second largest bank. As luck would have it, they were expanding their operations in Prague 8, the section in which our building was located. They signed a fifteen-year lease. Despite having to make major improvements—new elevator, installation of a T1 line, conversion from coal to gas—we had an unexpected revenue flow for the next fifteen years.

Soon after the termination of the lease, I sold the building to a telecommunications company. What had begun as an act of revenge, one not motivated by economics, turned out to be a financial windfall. Eventually, I also sold the factory and a single-family home, as well. Today, the only piece of my native country I own is a plot of land outside my native village, Kojetice, and I plan to donate it to the town.

A major highlight of my return to my native country has been the resurrection of a friendship that had been interrupted by the calamity that brought about forty-one years of Communist repression. Vladimír "Vláďa" Svoboda was my best boyhood friend during the short period between the end of the war and my family's escape from Czechoslovakia. We were classmates in elementary school and gymnasium, and we were inseparable: playing street hockey, skiing, riding street cars throughout Prague, and swimming in the Vltava River. Following the Velvet Revolution, Vláďa and I reconnected, proving that true friends can grow separately without really growing apart, despite the passage of time. A true test of friendship is whether two people can pick up where they had left off, and we passed it with flying colors. Twice, he and his wife Marie have visited us here in Maryland, and Sue and I have spent much of our time with them each time we have visited the Czech Republic.

My frequent trips to the Czech Republic—nearly always accompanied by Sue, once by Mother, and once by the entire Heller family—have helped me come to grips with my ethnicity and instilled in me a sense of pride in being a Czech-American. At the same time, hearing the stories of life under Communism from Vláďa and others made me more appreciative of the bounties America offered me. My adopted country allowed me to leave the past behind and to erase the remnants of war and the Holocaust. Visits to the Czech Republic helped me realize that, although I still love the country of my birth, my heart belongs to America.

CHAPTER TWENTY-THREE

WORDSMITH

Back in 1979, I met a man named Frank Young, publisher and editor of a semi-monthly newspaper called *The Public Enterprise.*

"I understand you're an expert skier and sailor," he said to me at a party in Eastport, a peninsula between Spa and Back Creeks in Annapolis.

"I'm not sure I'm an expert," I said, trying to appear modest.

"Can you also write?"

"I love to write. It's been my hobby for years."

"Sounds like we may be a perfect match for each other," he said. "I'm looking for someone to write a skiing column in the winter and a sailing column in the summer. Are you interested?"

"That sounds great," I replied, "but I'm running a software company and working a hundred hours a week. I don't know how I'd find the time."

"We publish twice a month. Surely, you could find a couple of hours to write two 800-word columns a month on your favorite pastimes."

"That may sound easy to you but, as much as I enjoy writing and would love to combine it with my passion for skiing and sailing, I'm not sure I can commit."

"I'll tell you what," Frank said, following a long pause. "Let's do it on a trial basis. It's winter, so why don't you write two ski columns in February, two in March, and one in April? I have another person who can write the sailing columns, and she can start that toward the end of April. If she works out, we'll keep her on, and you'll just be the ski columnist. If she doesn't work out, you can decide at that time if you want to take on sailing, as well. What do you think?"

I told Frank he had a deal. My first column, titled "Blue Knob—Challenges and Complaints," appeared in the February (first half) 1979 issue of TPE. It was the predecessor of sketches of ski areas in the region, in New England, in the western United States, and in Europe that would be published under my byline in a column called "The Annapolis Skier" for many years.

When the 1978-79 ski season ended, I thought I would have a writing hiatus until snowflakes began to fall in November. But then Frank called me one day in my office:

"I fired the sailing columnist. Are you interested in taking over that column, too?"

My first "Annapolis Sailor" column, dated September (first half) 1979 was an embarrassment. Writing about unsafe sailboat design that led to a tragedy during the recent Fastnet Race in England, I wrote about masts that had a tendency to break under severe wind conditions. The only problem was that the typesetter dropped two lines and the paper's proofreader failed to detect the error. Thus, my carefully researched description made no sense. The editor apologized and made the correction in the next issue. It was then that I discovered a newspaper columnist, no matter how meticulously he or she prepares a piece, is subject to the whims of an editor, headline-writer, and typesetter. Yet, it is always his or her name that gets associated with any goof.

Twice each month for the next eight years, I devoted a Sunday evening to writing exactly 800 words about sailing or skiing, depending on the season. Since this was in ancient times before the general adoption of word processors and desktop computers, I handwrote and edited each column on a yellow legal pad and then typed it on my Smith Corona portable typewriter. The next day, I deposited my pages into an aluminum box on Frank Young's porch on Van Buren Street in the Eastport section of Annapolis.

One of our neighbors in the Rugby Hall community was Phil Merrill, owner of Capital-Gazette newspapers, the oldest newspaper publishing firm in the nation. Their major paper was a daily, *The Capital*, headquartered in Annapolis. Phil had written about our firm's use of computers in the design of skis for Head Ski Company and was familiar with my columns in *The Public Enterprise*.

"How would you like to move your 'Annapolis Skier' column to *The Capital*?" he asked me at a business meeting in the summer of 1987.

"Phil, I write the skier column in the winter and the sailor column in the summer. The two are pretty much inseparable. I'll consider it if you want me to move both of them to your paper."

"I'm afraid that won't work," he said. "I already have one of the most famous sailors in the country, Gary Jobson, writing a sailing column."

I told Phil that I was sorry, but I would stay with *The Public Enterprise*. I added that, should things ever change, we could discuss it again. That time came much sooner than either of us expected.

"Gary Jobson is going off to sail with Ted Turner in the America's Cup," Phil phoned. "He's going to have to give up writing for *The Capital*."

I met with Phil Merrill and executive editor Ed Casey, and we agreed that my columns would run in the Sunday sports section each week. I would begin with an "Annapolis Skier" column in November 1987, and transition to "Annapolis Sailor" the first Sunday in April 1988. There was one more thing I wanted to discuss.

"I've been writing for *The Public Enterprise* for free," I told Merrill and Casey. "But I do have travel expenses associated with my writing. I don't expect you to cover my expenses, and I don't need the money, but you have to pay me something, so that I can claim writing as a business and start taking deductions on my tax returns. I need to show some income."

"We don't pay our outside columnists anything," said Casey. "What do you think, Phil?"

Following a long pause, Merrill spoke: "I think we can make an exception. How about $75 per column, Charlie?"

We shook hands, and I was a legitimate, professional columnist. However, I should have paid attention to a conversation that followed, when Merrill took me to the rear of the newsroom to introduce me to the sports staff. I met Jerry Jackson, who edited the Sunday sports section. Merrill departed and Jerry introduced me to *The Capital's* sports editor, Joe Gross. After we exchanged a few sports stories, Joe left me with a warning.

"Our publisher, Phil Merrill, knows absolutely nothing about sports. He doesn't know who's playing in the World Series, and he has no clue about the Super Bowl. But he considers himself an expert on two sports—sailing and skiing. I'm afraid you're in deep doo-doo."

It took a while for me to discover that Joe was not kidding. During the first couple of years, I wrote about the activities of local ski clubs and area sketches of nearby ski mountains. My sailing columns were primarily about racing on the Chesapeake Bay and other stories of local interest.

In year three, I began writing about our ski trips to New

England and out west—to Vermont, New Hampshire, Utah, New Mexico, and Montana. Phil Merrill, who had remained silent until then, called me on a Monday, a day after his paper had run my story about skiing Solitude in Utah.

"What the hell are you doing?" he screamed into the phone. "This is a local paper, and people want to read about local stuff!"

"Phil, there are no ski areas in Anne Arundel County," I replied. "What do you want me to do, invent them?"

"I don't give a shit! Every column you write has to have a local flavor. Otherwise, I'm shutting it down."

"Phil, when Gary Jobson was writing the sailing column, he wrote about his sailing experiences all over the world. How are my columns about skiing different?"

"Gary Jobson won the f...ing America's Cup," he screamed. "When did you win a f...ing gold medal in skiing at the Olympics?"

Exasperated, I promised that my columns would—some-how—maintain a local flavor. By now, I had developed a minor national reputation as a ski writer—I freelanced for a couple of ski magazines—and I was receiving frequent invitations to ski and stay at major areas around the country. Sue and I, and often David, enjoyed free skiing with free slopeside lodging all over New England and out West. I had become a member of the prestigious North American Snowsports Journalists Association. I was not about to let that end! But how would I deal with the "local flavor" issue? Driving home from my University of Maryland office one day in 1990, I came up with a solution. I could not wait to get home to begin to implement it.

I sat down with a telephone directory of Anne Arundel County and a spiral-bound notebook. In the notebook, I drew two columns, one for first names and the other for last names. Next, I began thumbing through the directory and randomly picking out last names. I wrote them in the right-hand column until I had fifty names. Then I opened the book again and randomly selected first names, writing fifty of them in the left-hand column. When I finished, I had fifty fictitious people of both genders as my "skier database." I would meet these phantom citizens of our readership area on mountains throughout the United States—and occasionally, I would even throw in the names of real people who really were there.

While I considered my ruse silly—and even funny—I never felt that I was being dishonest with my readers. Every week, I gave them straight information about ski areas through vignettes of my personal experiences. Judging by messages I received as well as letters to the editor of *The Capital*, readers of my columns appreciated and enjoyed the stories. I assumed that they could not care less whether or not a "Don Vance of Severna Park" was a real person or some ghost. For five years, the only people aware of the weekly farce were Sue and David, and both were sworn to secrecy.

But then it came to an end. In early March 1995, Sue and I enjoyed several glorious days of spring skiing in Vermont. On the last day, we skied Okemo Mountain, near the town of Ludlow. I loved the challenge of the steep terrain, the variety, the friendliness of the staff, and I wrote a glowing report that appeared in the paper on Sunday, March 12, 1995. The only problem: I forgot to insert the names of ghost skiers from Maryland. My office phone rang the next morning.

"That's the last piece of shit about some Podunk hill hundreds of miles from here I'm gonna allow in my paper!" Phil Merrill screamed. "You're fired!"

I was both disappointed and relieved. Relieved, because I would no longer have to refer to my "database" of phony names as a final, repugnant edit of a weekly labor of love. But disappointed for two reasons. For years, I had been able to escape the stress of the workplace by combining my love for writing with my passion for skiing and sailing. At the same time, I had established a relationship with my readers, one that I would miss going forward.

For a short time, I wrote a sailing column for the *Baltimore News-American*. However, the newspaper which traced its lineage all the way back to 1773, went out of business a few months after I started. I turned to freelancing for skiing and sailing magazines and the new medium of online blogs.

But I abandoned writing about my favorite sports when I was asked to become a columnist for two prestigious publications, the *Washington Business Journal* and Baltimore's *Daily Record*. I had developed a reputation as an entrepreneur and as Director of the Dingman Center for Entrepreneurship at the University of Maryland. The managing editors of both publications asked me to write regularly about all aspects of entrepreneurship, from raising startup money to growing a successful high-tech company.

My career as an author of books began in a rather unforeseen manner. While studying toward my doctorate at the University of Maryland (prior to transferring to The Catholic University of America) in the 1960s, I chose Russian as one of two foreign languages required for graduation. PhD candidates in engineering had to demonstrate the ability to translate a chapter from a book in their respective disciplines—in my case, engineering mechanics. I knew the Cyrillic alphabet from having taken Russian as a required subject in Communist Czechoslovakia, and I had a limited knowledge of conversational Russian. However, I was unfamiliar with technical terms. So, in preparation for the exam, I began to compile a list of specialized Russian words and their English translations. By the end of six months, I had a handwritten dictionary in a spiral-bound notebook.

"Well, are you ready to take the Russian exam?" asked my advisor during one of our weekly meetings.

"Yes, sir. I've been studying for a long time." I showed him my notebook.

"Holy cow!" he said. "That's quite a piece of work. I don't think anything like that exists in the literature. It could be useful to American researchers because the Russians have done a lot of important work in engineering mechanics. You should think about publishing it as a book."

"I wouldn't know how to go about doing that," I replied.

"I'll tell you what. I'll contact the company that publishes my books to see if they might be interested," he said.

By the time I walked out of his office, I had already forgotten about a book. I could not have cared less. I just wanted to pass the damned exam. Thus, it came as a total surprise when my phone rang a few days later.

"Hi," said the voice of a man whose name I do not recall. "I'm an acquisitions editor with Elsevier. I understand you have a technical dictionary we might be interested in publishing."

A couple of months later, I signed a book contract and received a small advance. After several months of writing introductory chapters and organizing the content, my first book baby was born. *Dictionary of Engineering Mechanics: Russian-English*, printed in The Netherlands by Elsevier Publishing Company, came out in May 1965. Far from a best seller, my cumulative royalties over the years are measured in three figures. Amazingly though, used copies of the little book were still available on Amazon some fifty years later!

Following the ouster of its Communist oppressors in November 1989 after forty-one years, Czechoslovakia became of interest to Americans, some of whom invited me to speak to groups large and small, not only about my native country, but about my experiences. After years of suppressing my memories of terror while hiding from the Nazis, the murders of my family members, our harrowing escape from Czech

Communists, life in refugee camps, and our struggle as a poor immigrant family in America, I began to open up—to myself and to others. And, much to my amazement, everywhere I went, I heard the same refrain.

"You must write a book!"

At first, I ignored the comments, thinking that my life story was nothing extraordinary. But over the next few months, the clamor of others, the existence of Holocaust deniers, the ignorance of the war and the Holocaust by young people, and my mother's having filled in most of the holes in our family story, pushed me over the edge. I would write a book.

I took writing courses, joined critique groups, did research, and signed a contract with a famous literary agent in New York. Six years later, I had the first draft of a memoir. When my agent announced her retirement, I contacted my friend Lillian Lincoln Lambert, who had recently published a wonderful memoir titled, *The Road to Someplace Better*. She introduced me to her agent in Boston. The latter informed me that my book was not suitable for her agency, but she gave me an invaluable piece of advice.

"Several writers with stories similar to yours have gone back to their countries of origin," she told me. "They had their books translated into their native language and published there. You should do that. If the book sells, American publishers will be all over you. And great news for you: European publishers generally prefer to deal directly with authors and don't want agents involved."

I hung up the phone, inspired by her suggestion—a route I had not considered previously. But, as I contemplated my next step, I ran into a wall. I did not know a soul in the Czech publishing industry, and neither did any of my Czech friends. So, I turned to the last weapon in the arsenal of a salesman— the cold call. I Googled, "five largest publishers in Czech Republic," found the list, and sent query emails to the respective acquisitions editors. Publishers two through five never responded. Amazingly, I heard back almost immediately from number one. Antonín (Tony) Kočí, Program Director of the Book Division of Mladá Fronta, emailed to say that my topic was in his firm's sweet spot. He requested the manuscript.

A couple of months later, over breakfast in Prague, we agreed on a book contract. I used a portion of my advance to pay our good friend and professional translator and interpreter, Irena Zíková, to convert the manuscript to Czech. Together, Irena and I hired a Czech author to edit the translations. As this was taking place, I was floored by an email from Tony.

"Arnošt Lustig has agreed to write the Foreword to your book," he wrote. "That will get the attention of thousands of readers."

Arnošt Lustig was the most famous contemporary Czech author. He had spent time in three Nazi concentration camps: Terezín, Auschwitz, and Buchenwald. He escaped when the transport carrying him and other prisoners to a fourth, Dachau, was hit by American fighter-bombers. After the war, he wrote fiction and screenplays, and he played a leading role in what became known as "Czech New Wave Cinema." He left Czechoslovakia following the 1968 Soviet invasion and continued his writing career while teaching at American University in Washington. His best-known books are *Indecent Dreams, Lovely Green Eyes, Darkness Casts No Shadow*, and *Diamonds of the Night*. Following the Velvet Revolution, Lustig returned to Prague, where he was given an apartment in Prague Castle by President Václav Havel and was honored with the nation's Franz Kafka and Karel Čapek Prizes.

Wow! I thought. *With his name on the cover, my book is bound to hit the best-seller list!*

Sadly, that euphoria did not last long.

"Arnošt is in the hospital with cancer again," wrote Tony

Koči in January 2011. I had read that the great author had been battling Hodgkin lymphoma for more than five years. "But he assures me that he's dictating your Foreword from the hospital bed, and that his daughter is writing it."

Then, one cold February morning, there it was, in the Metro section of the *Washington Post*: Arnošt Lustig's obituary. Three days later, Tony wrote that, unfortunately, Lustig had been unable to complete the Foreword to my book. I was devastated, not only because his name would not share the cover with mine, but even more by the fact that I had not had the opportunity to meet the great man. At the same time, I felt honored because he had agreed to partner with me on *Dlouhá cesta domů* (*Long Journey Home*).

On Easter Sunday, April 24, 2011, Sue and I landed in Prague. The big moment came immediately after we checked into our favorite hotel, the Marriott on V Celnici Street. Jiří, the bellman, rolled a cart out of the baggage room. It was stacked with books—my books. There they were, wrapped in clear plastic, four to a package. I wanted to grab the top pack and tear it open right there in the hotel lobby. But then I thought: *Is that what Pat Conroy would do?* Of course not! I acted casual, pretending that I did this every day. As he wheeled the carrier into the elevator, Jiří spotted my face staring at him from the back cover.

"*Vy?* (You?)" he asked.

I gave him my Pat Conroy smile. "*Ano* (Yes)."

As soon as he departed from room 551, I turned into the rookie author, tearing off the wrapping and examining the product of seventy-five years of living, six years of writing, and another two years of begging for someone to publish it. Sue unpacked calmly and stored her clothes, as if this were just another of our regular visits to Prague, while I—overwhelmed with emotion—was unable to move from my chair. Staring at the cover, I found it difficult to believe that there, above a sepia shot of Prague, was my name: Charles Ota Heller.

Take that, you dumbass American agents and publishers who have either ignored my queries or sent me inane boilerplate rejections!

Two days later, Sue and I met my editor, Tony Kočí, and Mladá fronta marketing director, Magdalena Potměšilová, for breakfast. We went over the schedule of appearances and interviews packed into the week ahead, beginning in two hours with a national TV program called "CT24," modeled after America's "Today" show. Although there would be many interviews by TV, radio, newspaper, and magazine reporters, this one would prove to be the most difficult—and not only because it was the first.

The show's hostess, Patricie Strouhalová, a pretty, stocky blonde, met me in the green room.

"We will be on for ten minutes," she explained. "I will ask you about your book and something about current events."

As I followed her into the studio, I began to panic: *Why the hell am I being asked to discuss current events? I'm a rather opinionated person, but I must stay away from anything that might be considered controversial. After all, this is a live telecast, and whatever I say can't be changed. Moreover, I'm here to sell my book!*

The hostess and I sat down behind desks—she on the right and I on the left as the viewer would see us—with my book standing between us, cover facing camera. Suddenly, the red light was on, and Patricie was asking me about my life. I understood every Czech word and began to respond in Czech. Then I heard the interpreter's gentle voice in my ear, reminding me that I was to answer in English and he would translate. *Oh, shit! We haven't even started, and I've screwed up already.* Settling in now, all began to go well. The questions were softballs and on point. I relaxed and kept a smile on my face for the camera. Then, out of the blue, the moderator picked up the book, turned to a page with photographs, and threw me a curveball.

"Here is a photograph of your father in a British Army uniform, taken in Tobruk," she said. "That's in Libya. How would you compare the war in which your father fought there to the war that is going on in Libya now?"

What kind of a dumb question is that? Why the hell don't you stick to my book? Then I remembered her comment about "current affairs" and the fact that NATO airplanes, led by those of the United States, had begun bombing Libya just a few days before.

"During World War II," I said in a voice as calm as I could muster, "it was a strategic battle for a Mediterranean port crucial to both the Allies and the Nazis. Today's war is one for the freedom of the Libyan people." I wanted to add: *Now shut the hell up and get back to my book.*

I glanced at the clock and saw that, thankfully, our ten minutes were up. I looked forward to being released, but Patricie Strouhalová was not finished with me—yet.

"As the war was coming to an end, you were nine years old," she said, smiling for the camera. "You shot an escaping Nazi." She paused and looked directly at me.

"Are you sorry?"

I stared back at her.

"*Ne!*" I reverted to the negative in Czech, making it clear that no explanation was forthcoming. The show was over.

I was not happy about the way the show ended, but Sue congratulated me in the green room, where she had been watching. For the remainder of the week in Prague, hundreds of strangers echoed Sue's compliments while asking rhetorically why I had been asked such ridiculous questions. Ironically and unintentionally, Ms. Strouhalová had managed to make me a celebrity and, more importantly, unwittingly provided nationwide publicity for my book.

The remainder of the book tour was a blur of meetings, talks, signings, and interviews, highlighted by the official launch at the Luxor bookstore on Wenceslas Square. The event was particularly sweet because so many people precious to Sue and me attended.

My boyhood best friend, Vláďa Svoboda and his wife Marie came from their mountain home and were joined by their daughter Jitka and grandchildren Dalibor and little Jitka. My distant cousin Sylva Pustina and her husband Karel drove down from Germany. Seated next to Sue was our family's dear friend, Jitka Thomasová, who had come with her brother Honza. The son of my favorite nanny, Lubomír Věchet, sat in the second row with our family's attorneys, Jiří and Míša Bedrna, and our village historian, Jarda Kučera, and his family. Stan and Marie Kotrčka came from Tábor with Jana Šípová. My book's translator, Irena Zíková, sat alongside me and the publisher's representatives while her husband, Dick, watched from the back row, not far from another friend, Štěpánka Matesová. Even a former classmate of Vláďa's and mine, Pepa Tomásek, whom I had seen only once before in the past fifty years, joined the large crowd at Luxor.

Following formal speeches by my editor and Alexander "Saša" Turkovič, who was representing all Czech and Slovak Rotary clubs, I read from the book. The audience seemed astounded that I spoke Czech without a trace of an accent. Friends and strangers lined up to buy *Dlouhá cesta domů,* and I signed for what seemed like hours. I was amazed when several people who had been waiting in line placed blank pieces of paper, and not my book, in front of me and asked me to sign.

"Why do you want me to sign a piece of paper?" I asked in Czech.

"We're autograph collectors," one of them informed me.

Now I was really full of myself. *Damn! I'm so important that collectors are after my autograph! Doesn't Pete Rose charge five bucks for signing?* No need—the ego trip was sufficient.

Finally, everyone was gone except for three of us—Sue and

I, and our good friend, Jitka Thomasová.

"We have so many friends in the Czech Republic," Sue commented. "Yet until tonight, most of them had never met. All had heard us speak about the others, but they had never been in one place at the same time."

"That's true," I said. "When I looked up from signing, I saw them greeting one another like old friends."

That alone had made the evening worthwhile.

At the end of a hectic week, only one more event was on the schedule: a talk to members of the American Center of the US Embassy in Prague. An hour before we were due there, Tony Kočí arrived at the hotel along with "that redheaded girl," as he referred to the young reporter from the nation's largest and most widely read newspaper, *Lidové noviny*. She informed me that she writes a daily article about "important people." Naturally, I was flattered. The redheaded girl, Judita Matyášová, and I developed immediate rapport, resulting in my running late for the embassy event. To complete her interview, Judita jumped in a taxi with Sue, Tony and me, as we headed for my last gig. When we arrived, Judita informed me that the article would run in the paper on Monday, May 2, the day of our departure for the States.

Early that last morning, Vláďa picked us up at four o'clock to drive us to the airport. As we rolled through the dark, empty streets of Prague, I asked him to turn on the radio so that we could hear the weather forecast.

"During the night," came the solemn voice of the announcer, "American Navy SEALs shot and killed the notorious international terrorist, Osama bin Laden, in Pakistan."

"Fantastic!" Vláďa and I exclaimed simultaneously in two languages and slapped hands.

"Barack Obama got rid of that bastard after Bush just managed to talk big for eight years and did nothing," I said to Sue as I translated the news.

A few moments later, I had a second, selfish, reaction, one

that I kept to myself: *Shit! Why couldn't they have waited a day? Now my story is going to get pushed to page 67 of today's newspaper!*

Following a nerve-wracking interaction with ticket agents who charged us $300 for overweight baggage (courtesy of a few of my beautiful new books), and nasty security guards who practically made me strip down to my underwear, we made it finally to the inner sanctum of the airport. It was 6:15 a.m., and restaurants and shops were still closed. We could not get breakfast, and we could not purchase *Lidové noviny*, the newspaper that was to carry my story—one that would be buried somewhere near the classifieds.

Sue and I stood in the hallway, hoping that something might change. Lo and behold, at 6:30 the steel curtain guarding the newsstand was raised. At the same time, we spotted a man pushing a cart loaded with newspapers in our direction. I stayed and watched our carry-ons while Sue went exploring.

"Your picture is on the front page!" she shouted suddenly.

It was true. There I was, on the front page of the country's largest paper. There was no sign of Osama bin Laden. Obviously, the assassination had taken place too late to be included in the early-morning edition. We purchased several copies of the paper and brought them home.

"Look, I bumped Osama bin Laden off the front page," I boasted to my friends after we arrived in the United States.

I signed a book deal for the English-language version of my memoir and insisted on one important condition: the book must come out in time for the Christmas book-buying season. The publisher agreed verbally but failed to deliver. *Prague: My Long Journey Home* was released on December 27! Not only did we miss the year's most favorable selling opportunity but, as I would find out shortly, *Prague* would be excluded from several "best book" and "book-of-the-year" competitions in 2012 because it was classified as "a 2011 book." Had it been launched a mere five days later, it would have been a different story.

Despite that, I was ecstatic when *Writer's Digest* gave the book its "Mark of Quality" for literary excellence. Later in the year, *Prague* was chosen among the best new memoirs at the Los Angeles Book Fair, and it was a finalist for the 2012 Independent Book Awards.

More satisfying than the awards have been my interactions with readers all over the world. I have spoken and signed for groups as small as a ten-member book club in Annapolis and as large as six hundred doctoral university students in Orlando. I have met Holocaust survivors and their children, Americans of Czech and Slovak ancestry, World War II history buffs, and hundreds of other readers simply interested in a good story. I have received a profusion of emails and web-site comments from people who have read my book and are anxious to tell me their own family stories. Several folks named Heller have attempted to prove that we are related—unsuccessfully, I am sad to report. My good friend Bart Childs, Professor Emeritus at Texas A&M, arranged a book tour of Czech and Slovak communities in Texas, as well as a speaking gig at the George H. W. Bush Presidential Library. Since 2012, I have crisscrossed the country and told my story hundreds of times.

For the past few years, I have been part of a Holocaust survivor group sponsored by the Baltimore Jewish Council (BJC). Along with my friend Herb Hane, I am one of two oddballs in this group—Catholics whom the Nazis labeled Jews because we had Jewish fathers. As much as I have enjoyed the connections to many people and the friendships I have forged with many readers of *Prague*, the most satisfying interactions I have had—and continue to have—are with students. As part of the BJC's speaker bureau, I have had the opportunity to tell my story at a number of elementary, middle, and high schools. Much to my surprise, many schools include the Holocaust in their curricula. Even more surprising to me, this is especially true of Catholic schools. Some, such as John Carroll School in Bel Air, Maryland, annually devote an entire week of the senior year to a study of the Holocaust.

Probing and intelligent questions by these smart, interested young people have kept me on my toes and given me hope that the world will be in good hands with this generation. At times, I have been touched by the reactions of students. One that stands out in my mind took place at Mount de Sales Academy, an all-girls Catholic high school in Baltimore. At the end of our question and answer session, a tiny blond-haired sophomore came up to me. She placed her small hand on my arm.

"Don't worry," she said as she looked into my eyes. "We won't let it happen again." With that, she walked out of the room, while I stood there with tears cascading down my cheeks.

Back when I decided to write a book, I wrote an outline that included not only my experiences as a World War II hidden child and my later reconnection with my ethnicity and nationality, but also described the trials, tribulations, and triumphs of an immigrant entrepreneur chasing the proverbial American Dream.

When my agent read what I had written to date and then analyzed the outline for the remainder of the book, she was flabbergasted.

"This looks like a quarter-million-word manuscript," she said. "We'd have to publish it in three volumes. That won't fly. You have to cut it way down. You need to aim at 75,000 to 80,000 words."

"My God!" I cried. "What do you want me to cut out?"

"Everything that doesn't pertain to your life as a hidden child and your eventual reconnection with your past and your native country."

"You mean I shouldn't include my life as an immigrant in America?"

"Right. That should be another book."

While she may have failed me in many other ways, it turned out that my agent's edict was a blessing. Not only was I able to focus the book and cut it to an industry sweet-spot size of 77,000 words, but I was left with hundreds of pages that would constitute material for three additional books, including this one.

Following the publication of *Prague* and after much contemplation, exchanges with members of my two writers' groups, and changes of mind, I decided to turn my attention to two phases of my life in the United States. One would describe my many struggles and occasional triumphs as an entrepreneur; the other would constitute this immigrant's "coming-to-America" story. The goal became a memoir trilogy.

As I worked on the two manuscripts simultaneously, my memory and the journals I have kept for many years kept unearthing anecdotes about famous, and near-famous, people I have been lucky enough to encounter since coming to America as a boy.

Upon reading the earliest of the stories—about Clint Eastwood, Dr. Ruth Westheimer, Larry Doby, and Wernher von Braun—to my writer friends, they jokingly accused me of being a name-dropper. As I added vignettes starring such notables as Monika Lewinsky and Earl Weaver, my colleagues' quips turned into compliments.

"These are great stories," they said. "You have to include them in your next books."

I tried. But there was a problem. If I compiled all these anecdotes into a single chapter, the section would be much too long. Moreover, because the stories span a period of more than fifty years, placing them into a single chapter would destroy the continuity of the book. As a second possibility, I attempted to disperse the tales into various sections of the book, where they might fit chronologically. This attempt, too, failed. Although some of them bore a direct relationship to my overall themes, most did not.

Finally, after a great deal of head-scratching, I concluded that it would be best to keep the stories together, but to separate them from the upcoming memoirs and to publish them as a short book. Yet, I worried that a book like this might be considered an exercise in vanity, something I attempt to avoid in my writing. But my writers' group friends put me at ease. All of them—Karen Cain, Paul Harrell, and Marilyn Recknor—gave their enthusiastic approval and even suggested a title.

"You should call it *Name-droppings,*" Karen advised, implying that my grandiloquence resembles the spreading of scat. I liked the image and went to work. Thus was born a second book, titled *Name-droppings: Close Encounters with the Famous and Near-Famous*, published in 2013.

After that, I decided to tackle the entrepreneurship memoir. I thought I had come up with a clever title that would attract readers. In my teaching and mentoring of entrepreneurs, I often used the phrase "ready, fire, aim" to emphasize how a startup company must operate in a competitive environment.

"Before a large, established company enters a new market or decides on building a new product," I would explain, "it has the luxury of forming focus groups and holding fifty meetings in order to explore all the pros and cons. As an entrepreneur, you have neither time nor money to do that. You make a decision, go for it, and worry about the consequences later. Any decision—right or wrong—is better than no decision. Staying nimble and flexible gives you an advantage over the big guys. Sometimes you have to fire—and aim later."

After parting company with a second literary agent, I discovered that a new form of publishing was entering the marketplace. Known as "hybrid" publishing, it is a cross between the traditional and self-publishing models. Many of the hybrid publishers are as selective as their traditional brethren in terms of literary quality and market potential, and they provide the same level of editing. They differ from the "big boys" in that they require the author to share some of the financial risk and they pay no advances. The business model seemed perfect for me. Following six rounds of edits, the WriteLife imprint of BQB Publishing launched *Ready, Fire, Aim! An Immigrant's Tales of Entrepreneurial Terror* on June 1, 2017.

After *Prague: My Long Journey Home*; *Name-droppings: Close Encounters with the Famous and Near-Famous*; and now, *Ready, Fire, Aim*, the only "memoir stuff" remaining was the "coming to America" story—that of the life of a refugee seeking the good life in America. Being uprooted from one's native land and landing in another country with no material possessions, no friends, and an inability to communicate is hard. Yet, it has been experienced by millions of people who make up this great land. Many books have been written on the subject; *Cowboy from Prague: An Immigrant's Pursuit of the American Dream* is one of them.

CHAPTER TWENTY-FOUR

FRUIT ON THE FAMILY TREE

On October 27, 1994, as both best man and father of the groom, I made a short speech at the reception that followed the wedding of our son David and Elizabeth Roberta ("Bobbi") Bass. I spoke about the fact that Sue and I are only children, and David is an only child. Thus, with both of my parents also having been only children, the Heller family tree had been reduced to a single root—David. I expressed my elation at the addition of Bobbi to this tree and the hope that sometime in the not-too-distant future, there would be fruit growing on that expanded tree—our grandchildren.

Bobbi and David did not disappoint. On February 25, 1996, Samuel Heller came into this world. Not only were Sue and I thrilled to have a grandson, but I was grateful for his parents' choice of Sam's middle name—Neumann, my mother's maiden name, a name he will carry throughout his life in honor of all the Neumann members of our family who were murdered by the Nazis during World War II. I only hope that Sam will not "Americanize" it by pronouncing his middle name "New-man," but that he adheres to his family's Czech tradition and proudly announces himself as "**Noy**-mon."

Some two-and-a-half years later, on August 8, 1999, Sue and I were playing golf at Walden Country Club when I received a call from David.

"Bobbi just gave birth to a girl," he said. We rushed off the course and to the hospital, where we met a beautiful little girl, whom her parents named Sarah Katherine. Another joy brought into our lives!

2001 was a difficult year. As soon as school ended for Sue, we flew to Prague for a week's vacation. Prior to leaving, Sue had met with the principal of the Naval Academy Primary School—where she had been teaching for the past thirty years—to discuss our grandson Sam's behavior problems in his just-concluded pre-kindergarten year. For the upcoming year, Sue offered to have him in her kindergarten class, where she would be able to control the situation and help Sam learn to get along with other children. She assumed that the principal had agreed. But it was not to be. One evening in Prague, our hotel room phone rang.

"Sam will not be allowed to return to the Primary School next year," David informed us. "The principal called us today." As if that was not enough to spoil the remainder of our holiday in Prague, David called again the next evening with even more devastating news.

"Bobbi was diagnosed with Hodgkin Disease." I spent much of the night with my laptop, learning about this form of cancer. I was slightly relieved that Hodgkin was a lymphoma that can be cured with radiation and chemotherapy treatments. However, when morning arrived and we got over the initial shock and began to think more clearly, we realized that there was a major complication: Bobbi was pregnant.

When we returned home, Bobbi informed us that she and her doctor had decided to hold off on treatment until the baby was born. We were horrified because the due date was still four months away.

While dealing with the fear for Bobbi's health, as well as that of the little human forming inside her body, Sue was determined to resolve Sam's school problem. She met with the principal, hoping to change her mind by convincing her that having Sam in her class would resolve any potential behavior issues. Sadly, she failed. She felt betrayed and unappreciated for having served for thirty years while being paid one half of what she could have earned in a public school. As gut-wrenching as the decision was for her, she felt that she had no choice but to resign.

After a summer of apprehension and fear for our daughter-in-law, the month of September arrived. On a beautiful, sunny, Tuesday morning—a day which will be known forever as "nine-eleven"—terrorists attacked the United States. Later that week, while the nation mourned and Americans wondered about their future, something wonderful happened to our family. On Saturday, September 15, Bobbi gave birth to a baby girl. She was named Caroline Ilona—her middle name an homage to my mother, who was thrilled. Our family was beyond relieved and grateful when doctors declared Caroline healthy.

Bobbi began treatments that winter and a few months later was declared "clean" of cancer. A five-year period followed during which doctors monitor a Hodgkin patient. At the end of the period, she remained cancer-free.

David, who had begun working with computers as a child, received an Associate's degree from Anne Arundel Community College and then continued his education at the University of Maryland University College (today, University of Maryland Global Campus) part-time, while working full-time as a computer-aided design (CAD) technician. Once he earned his undergraduate degree in information technology, he embarked on a career in IT project management, working for a number of companies and government agencies.

Bobbi, who is a graduate of the US Naval Academy, decided

to follow in her father's footsteps in real estate. Once the children were sufficiently old, she studied for, and eventually earned, certification as a real estate appraiser. A few years later, she used her knowledge and experience to join the federal government as a property manager, first at the FBI and then at the Veterans Administration in Washington, DC. At the same time, she obtained a master's degree from Georgetown University.

Sam, that little kid who disrupted a pre-kindergarten class, grew into a 6'4" smart, well-mannered, athletic young man. While in high school, he decided to try rowing, never having even seen a rowing shell previously. That was in March of his junior year. By May, he was rowing in the junior national championship in Tennessee, and eventually was selected for the pre-Olympic development team. Unfortunately, the rigors of engineering studies at Massachusetts Maritime Academy forced him to forego rowing at the college level. Today, Sam is an officer in the US Coast Guard, married to Bethany, and living outside of Seattle where he is stationed.

Cute little Sarah is now a mature, intelligent, and immensely kind young lady. She played basketball throughout elementary and high school and, when she entered college, her goal was to go on to medical school in order to become a physician. However, she and chemistry were not on good terms during her freshman year at Virginia Tech, so she switched majors. Today, she is majoring in psychology, intends to attend graduate school and then build a successful career, perhaps as a psychologist.

Our youngest grandchild, Caroline, is both an athlete and a scholar. Following in her brother's footsteps, she excelled as a rower with Annapolis Junior Rowing—so well that she was recruited by a number of schools and accepted an athletic scholarship to Manhattan College. She is a dogged student whom the New York City school also rewarded with an academic scholarship. However, after the pandemic of 2020-

21 kept her away from campus and forced her to attend classes online, she changed course. She completed training as an Emergency Medical Technician (EMT) at a local community college and, following a summer as a life guard, she enrolled in a nursing program at the University of Central Florida.

Sadly, the marriage of David and Bobbi came to an end in 2016. Sue and I recognized the cracks in their relationship some time before. I have always prided myself as a problem-solver, but as I grieved and recognized areas that needed fixing, I had to come to grips with the fact that, as a father and father-in-law, I could not interfere. To the best of my know-ledge, there had never been a divorce in the Heller/Neumann families, so this was a new experience for me. The good news is that both parents love their children, and the children love them.

Like other families throughout the world, ours was affected by the pandemic of 2020-21. Our granddaughters' university experiences consisted of staring at computer screens, learning online, and missing the social interactions that are such a vital part of college life. Most of us form our strongest, often lifelong, friendships as college students. The girls did not have the same opportunities during the pan-demic.

Their parents and grandparents, too, have had to adapt. Bobbi began working from home at the start of the pandemic. David spent many months looking for a new job in a difficult Covid-affected market. For Sue and me, the pandemic crushed a number of travel plans but, most importantly, it robbed us of the pleasures of hugs and kisses with our family.

In August 2014, I brought our entire family—all seven of us—to my native country. With some trepidation, expecting pushback from three bored grandkids—I planned an itinerary loaded with visits to places of historical importance, to locales where I had both thrived and suffered as a child, to the homes of friends. As the date of our departure approached, I began to worry.

Would they care about the history of their Heller family? Would these Christian kids be shocked to discover that a fraction of their blood is Jewish? Would they ignore or embrace their Czech identity? My obsession with gaining the respect of strangers in America was now surpassed by a consuming passion to leave a legacy for my family, along with their admiration for the courage, suffering, and accomplishments of their ancestors.

Thus, I was amazed and delighted when eighteen-year-old Sam, fifteen-year-old Sarah, and twelve-year-old Caroline embraced their family's history and fell in love with the Czech Republic and expressed great pride in their heritage. Upon our return home, the children wrote me letters that described their feelings:

Sam: ...*From the day we arrived in Prague to the day we left, I felt astounded by the sights we had seen. It was incredible to get the opportunity to view all the places you and our family have been. Visiting all these places opened my eyes to our past... It gave me passion for our family's home country and makes me want to return... Thank you for giving me the opportunity to visit such an amazing place.*

Sarah: ...*Knowing that the people I am related to were involved in the Holocaust makes me even more proud of our history, and that is why I was so grateful that you and Nana took us to the Czech Republic... When we went to the Jewish cemetery, I felt extremely privileged to be there. I still feel that way and I think I always will. Having that experience impacted me significantly and, if I could, I would bring everyone I know there because it is really just amazing to see what the human race is capable of, if we let it... I feel like it is my duty as a person to continue to educate myself and those around me, so that there will not be any more mass graves to look at, or lists that go on for miles of families that have been destroyed... I will never forget the trip we took and hope to soon return...*

Caroline: *...you took us to a wonderful place where we learned about how great somewhere else can be. You took us to a place where you grew up, where you lived and suffered. I am so grateful because something to desire is to know your family tree... Now my family, as well as I, knows the town, the country, the continent where our family was created... I have fallen in love with this amazing place... I appreciated learning about the Holocaust from you and by seeing Terezín. This is something everyone should know about because it was one of the times when society was at its worst... Thank you for this overwhelmingly amazing experience. I will always remember it...*

I could not have been prouder of our grandchildren. Their letters fulfilled my most fervent dreams. Yet, as pleased as I was with the unexpected success of the trip, I was almost brought to my knees by a shocking revelation that followed the visit.

Although three years had passed since the triumphant launch of my Czech-language memoir, *Dlouhá cesta domů (Long Journey Home)* in Prague, I was still sought out by journalists for interviews during our 2014 visit. Because our program was chockful, and I was not about to interrupt our grandchildren's learning experience, I declined respectfully— until the day before our departure. On that day, I received a call in our hotel room.

"My name is Michaela Čaňková," a lady introduced herself in English. "We are compiling stories of famous Czechs who emigrated after the Communist take-over."

Having had my ego stroked by being called a "famous Czech," I agreed to meet her before our family's farewell dinner. Now, the pretty, middle-aged lady was sitting across a table from me.

"I've read your book, so I know your history. But there is

one major gap I'd like to fill in," she said.

"Fire away, Ms. Čaňková," I said.

"Please, call me Míša."

"Thank you, Míša. I'm Charlie."

"OK. The gap I found concerns your maternal grand-mother, Marie Kozušníková. You write that she was a Sudeten German Catholic when your Jewish grandfather met her in Vienna. They never married and, when they had a daughter—your mother, Ilona—Marie had Ilona baptized in a Catholic church in Vienna. Two weeks later, your grandfather adopted your mother and brought her home with him. Your grand-mother returned to her home near Ostrava, and, as far as you know, she stayed there. After you came into this world, you never met her."

"I may have, but I don't remember ever meeting her," I said.

"Now, things become interesting—and a bit mysterious," said Míša. "You write that, after the occupation and the round-up of Jews for death camps, your mother lied in racial court by telling the Nazis that both her parents were Catholics. If the Nazis would buy the story, she would be considered a Christian and both of you would be safe. Since her Jewish father had escaped from Czechoslovakia, your mother needed her mother to corroborate the story. She dispatched her best friend, the lady you called Aunt Aša, to Ostrava, where Aša attempted to persuade Marie to come to Prague and to lie in court. At first, she refused. After Aša's second visit, she finally agreed to do it."

"That's correct," I said.

"OK—now the mystery," she said. "Here is what you wrote in your book:

...my parents' silence allowed no discussion of my maternal grandmother, Marie Kozušníková... Since she was a Sudeten German living in Czechoslovakia, I wonder today if she was among the 2.5 million ethnic Germans who were deported after

the war. I hope and pray that she was not, and that my father was able to use his influence as a war hero and that my mother was able to testify as to Grandma's antifascist activities... Sadly, I have been unable to learn her fate.

"What have you done to try to find out what happened to her?" Míša asked.

"I contacted the municipal authorities in Ostrava and in the small town of Frýdek, where she was born. All I was able to learn was the date of her birth: June 24, 1888, and that she was one of eight children."

"Is it possible that your mother had close friends in the Czech Republic, in whom she may have confided the story of her mother?"

I took a few minutes to ponder the question, one that had not occurred to me when I researched our family's story.

"There's one possibility," I said finally. "Mother had a close friend, who is also a very good friend of Sue and me, Jitka Thomasová. Since we've only known her for the past twenty years, I didn't use her as a source. But I know that she and Mother had many intimate conversations. Unfortunately, we're leaving Prague tomorrow, and I won't be able to speak to Jitka until we get back to the States. I'll get back to you if I find out anything."

A few days later, I heard Jitka's voice from the other side of the Atlantic.

"Charlie, of course I read your book—several times—and I have to tell you that I cringed when I read about your fond feelings for your grandmother. I had no intention of ever speaking to you about this, but you've asked. So, I must."

"I appreciate that, Jitka."

"I'm not so sure you'll appreciate it," she replied. "But here we go. When your mother's friend, your Aunt Aša, tried to persuade Marie Kozušníková to testify, the woman refused to even admit that Ilona was her daughter. But apparently, Aša eventually applied some kind of blackmail to force her to come to Prague and to lie to the racial court. So, she wasn't the kind, brave lady that you thought she was."

"Why do you suppose she refused at first to admit that Mother was her daughter?" I asked.

"Because she was afraid that her husband would find out. Now, are you ready for this?" Jitka asked but did not wait for my response. "Her husband was a member of the Waffen SS— the worst kind of murdering Nazi."

The news was so staggering that I remained speechless for a long time. Politely, Jitka remained silent at the other end of the line. Finally, I thanked her and hung up the phone.

The Waffen SS ran the concentration and extermination camps. They oversaw the murder of more than six million people, twenty-five of whom were members of my family. Now I discovered that my maternal grandmother was married to one of these gangsters! The thought that I may have distant cousins somewhere out there, cousins who have traces of the same blood as I, mixed with the blood of a Nazi murderer, made me ill.

As promised, I rushed off an email to Míša: "I found out about my grandmother," I wrote. "This is one part of my family story I want to forget."

CHAPTER TWENTY-FIVE

SOMETHING HAPPENED

Something happened to me back in 1988, during the memorial service for my hero—my father. It happened while I was only half-listening to a rabbi who did not know Papa and was reciting words I had written for him. Sitting in the front row of the chapel with my mother, my wife, and my son—and with tears streaming down my cheeks—I felt a mental jolt with the voltage of a lightning bolt.

I've never before attended the funeral of a family member. During my fifty-two years on this earth, twenty-five members of my family have died. But until now, not a single one had died a natural death. Every single one—all twenty-five—had been murdered by the Nazis in some far-off place. Rather than being honored at the ends of their lives, they were dismissed as inconsequential, and their bodies were thrown into ovens or mass-burial holes in the ground.

I had been brought up a Roman Catholic and, along with my Catholic mother, attended church faithfully prior to the war. Because the Jewish men in our household—my father, great-grandfather, grandfather, and great-uncle—were secular and celebrated Christmas and Easter with us, I knew nothing of my Semitic ancestry. In fact, I had no idea what a Jew was.

During the war under Nazi occupation in Czechoslovakia, whenever I asked why I had to hide when the Gestapo or its Czech collaborators came looking for me, why I was not allowed to attend school with my former friends, why I had been stoned in my only foray outside the farm walls, why I was always hungry, the answer was always the same: "because your father is fighting against the Germans."

I was unaware that Mother had no idea if Papa was even alive, much less that he was really fighting against the Nazis (which, it turned out, he was—as a member of the Czecho-slovak Brigade of the British army). The truth was that the Germans' Nuremberg Laws classified me—a six-year-old Catholic boy—as a Jew because I had three Jewish grand-parents. But I believed Mother's explanation and took my suffering as a point of pride. If Papa was shooting Germans, I would help him win the war by being brave and silent.

My parents and I were reunited after the war, the only survivors of the combined Heller-Neumann family. Although I had no cousins, uncles, aunts or grandparents, I began living the life of which I had dreamed during months in hiding. However, that lasted all of two-and-a-half years, before the Russians and their Czech Communist puppets took over the government and declared my parents "enemies of the state." We were forced to escape and spent fifteen months in refugee camps, waiting for permission to emigrate to the United States.

When we landed on America's shores, my father gave me strict instructions: forget everything that had happened to me on the other side of the Atlantic. In 1949, when a European father gave an order, his son saluted smartly and said, "Yes sir." I did not salute, but I did say "Yes sir," in Czech, of course. For the next forty years, I followed his edict and devoted myself to becoming an assimilated American, achieving academic and athletic success, building a respected career as a businessman and academic, and—most importantly—creating a wonderful American family. I had no time to reflect on the horrors of the past; they remained in the Old World. But then—something happened.

That "something"—the figurative jolt of lightning in that sad memorial chapel—changed my life by initiating a long search for my identity. Long before, I had stopped attending church and, in fact, disavowed all organized religion. I did not need a priest, a minister, an imam, or a rabbi to tell me how to converse with God. And I had no interest in mouthing prayers or singing hymns written by others. I had my own voice—my very personal way of worship. Yet, there were all those Holocaust victims in my family, about whom I now thought every day. And, of course, there was my late father. I began to wonder: *Am I Jewish?* I knew next to nothing about the Jewish religion, yet I felt a strong bond with Jews.

My struggle with ethnicity and identity continued after the Velvet Revolution that ended forty-one years of oppressive Communism in my native country. In 1990, on my first visit to free Prague, Aunt Aša led me to the city's ancient Jewish ghetto. Inside a stone building, she gripped my hand and guided me through large chambers whose white walls and vaulted ceilings were filled with beautifully scribed names.

"There are more than 77,000 names here," Aša explained. "Czech victims of the Holocaust, listed by their hometowns. Some of them are your family."

My eyes scanned the walls until they rested on "Kralupy nad Vltavou," my father's hometown. The name "Hellerová, Otilie" seemed to fly off the wall and slap me in the face. It was my grandmother's name, and suddenly the enormity of the Holocaust became very personal. I froze in place as I read the names of my great aunt, my great uncle, and my cousins.

I broke away from Aša's grip and set out in search of my boyhood home. Finally, there it was: "Kojetice u Prahy!" And there was the name—"Neumann, Gustav"—that of my great grandfather. I called him *Dědeček*, and he had been my best friend while we were being sheltered from the Nazis on a farm. I closed my eyes and saw *Dědeček* standing by the front door with a battered suitcase by his side and a yellow star sewn to his lapel. He was on his way out of my life and ultimately to the Treblinka death camp.

When I opened my eyes, tears blurred the letters of his name. I leaned in closer. Involuntarily, I reached across the railing and ran my finger back-and-forth along the wall. "What are you doing, Otíku?" asked Aunt Aša quietly, using the diminutive form of my Czech name.

"I don't know," I replied, snapping out of a momentary trance.

But I did know. I had been searching for a name: "Heller, Ota Karel," my full name prior to its Americanization. My mind had played a trick on me. It whispered that I could have—and perhaps should have—been one of the 77,000 victims.

Another moment of introspection came on my first trip to Israel, when I visited a sacred place near Jerusalem called Yad Vashem. There, I entered an underground cavern. In contrast to the bright sunshine and oppressive heat of the outer gardens, the chamber was dark and cool. It was deathly silent, except for a hushed drone:

"Riva Arbitman."

"Edit Berger."

"Ester Grisman."

"Tomi Singer."

Suddenly, I understood the significance. These were names of Holocaust victims, read in a continuous recording. I stood mesmerized for more than an hour, listening intently. Why was I crying? Why was I waiting to hear my own name?

In the past, I had never reacted this way, even at the end of the war. My parents and I had survived and were reunited. We waited for my great grandfather, grandparents, uncles, aunts, and cousins to return. None did. Although I was nine years old and vaguely aware of the atrocities the Germans and their collaborators had committed, I failed to connect our loss of twenty-five family members with the cataclysm that would one day be called the Holocaust. Along with Mother, I resumed my life as a church-going Catholic.

Once in America, I did as I was told: I dressed like an American and spoke without an accent within a year of our arrival. But when he ordered me to forget everything that happened to us in Europe, Papa may have been thinking beyond that and to this country's anti-Semitic past. No doubt, he had read about the German-American Bund and the Silver Shirts, America's pro-Nazi organizations of the 1930s. He may have been told about workplace quotas, and even hiring prohibitions, of Jews—some of which he would experience personally in the coming years. He may have wanted to shield me from such potential impediments to achieving my American Dream. Accordingly, having driven memories of the war into some deep recess of my soul, there could be no introspection about my roots or my ethnicity.

For years in my new country, to my friends, colleagues, teammates, co-workers—indeed, to myself—I was an over-reaching immigrant who at various times was a decent student, good athlete, dedicated teacher, successful entrepreneur, and devoted husband and father. People bestowed a number of awards on me, and some called me a "Renaissance Man."

But since my epiphany, every aspect of my life seemed to be affected by a new consciousness. An avid sports fan and former collegiate athlete, now I found myself checking players' names and wondering if they were Jewish. Devouring stories about one of baseball's greatest homerun hitters, Hank Greenberg, and finest pitchers, Sandy Koufax, became a subliminal act, as was cheering for golfers Amy Alcott, Corey Pavin, and Morgan Pressel, and for two of the finest female basketball players of all time, Nancy Lieberman and Sue Bird.

Beyond the seemingly inconsequential realm of sports, I found myself admiring the vast contributions of Jews to society as a whole—in science, medicine, art, music, and literature. I realized that millions of parents are indebted to Jonas Salk and Albert Sabin for discoveries that made it possible for children to grow up without the likelihood of being struck down by polio. Albert Einstein's theory of relativity forever revolutionized physics and mathematics. Marc Chagall's contributions to the world of art, and those of Franz Kafka, Philip Roth, Hannah Arendt, and Elie Wiesel to literature, struck me as priceless. I connected these achievements with Jewish culture's emphasis on scholarship, and I related it to our family's near-fanatical devotion to education.

Another pivotal moment came during my second visit to Israel. Walking through the Holocaust museum at Yad Vashem, I struggled unsuccessfully to hold back tears while staring at photos of bearded Jews being slapped by German soldiers, naked women being herded into showers of gas, and dead bodies being thrown onto piles of other skeletal figures. I was overcome with grief when I rounded a corner and suddenly came upon a group of Israeli soldiers. Swarthy young men and women in uniform, with Uzis strapped to their backs, they were listening intently to their guide. A force seemed to pull me toward them. I could not understand the guide's Hebrew lecture, but I did not need to. The sight of the soldiers mesmerized me. They were strong, good-looking, athletic— and tough. I looked from one to the other and felt a strange sense of pride and tranquility. Like the Israelites of biblical times, these Sabras would stand up to any enemy and fight. They would not be led to slaughter like their relatives, and mine, during the Second World War. I wiped my eyes and managed a smile.

It will never happen to us again, I said to myself. Did I really say "us"? I stopped abruptly when I stepped out into the bright sunshine.

Soon after I returned from that trip to Israel, I attended a lecture at the United States Holocaust Memorial Museum in Washington. At one point, the speaker asked if there were any Holocaust survivors in the audience. Six or seven hands were raised and, when the survivors were asked to stand, I applauded along with the rest of the audience.

"Why didn't you raise your hand back there?" asked a lady who introduced herself as a Museum staff member at a reception following the lecture.

"Because I'm not a Holocaust survivor," I replied.

"Oh, yes, you are!" she said. She explained to me that until 1991, children who had survived the war in hiding were not recognized as Holocaust survivors. "Then, on Memorial Day 1991, at the Marriott Marquis Hotel in New York City, the Anti-Defamation League convened a conference during which it acknowledged the error. On that day, they formed the Hidden Child Foundation to reveal stories like yours to the world."

So, now I was officially a Holocaust survivor, despite the fact that I am not a Jew. Yet, it dawned on me that I feel an affinity with Jews that I do not have with people of other faiths. It is possible that this feeling has been there throughout my adult life and that it remained below the surface until my father's death brought it out into the open. I may not be able to differentiate a Shabbat from a Pasach, and I have no desire to convert to Judaism, but something did happen to me.

That "something" is a realization that I have a Jewish soul.

CHAPTER TWENTY-SIX

THEY'RE GONE...

Throughout both our lives together, I had made a few promises to Mother—and kept most of them. Those that I could not keep, such as becoming the first baseball player in history to make a hundred thousand dollars a year, usually were based on silly boyhood dreams. However, there was one unkept promise that pains me to this day.

Following surgery to remove a blood clot in his carotid artery, Sue's father Ed Holsten was moved to Future Care for rehabilitation. Located near Anne Arundel Community College in Arnold, Maryland, Future Care was a facility that was part rehab for patients such as Ed, recovering from illness or injury, and part nursing home for permanent residents requiring constant care.

One fall day in 1996, I visited Ed at the facility. On my way out, passing through the nursing home section, I was dumb-struck by the sadness of the place. The hallway and lobby were filled with poor souls in wheelchairs, some asleep and others staring blankly into space. When the nurse provided me with a combination to punch in at the exit, I realized that these downtrodden humans were imprisoned there. Feeling despondent, I quickened my step toward the door.

"Please take me out of here!" pleaded a tiny, barefoot lady in a nightgown, as she grasped my arm.

"I'm sorry. I can't do that," I said, shedding her grip and heading out the door and into the cool autumn air. *My God,* I thought. *How could I have done that to the poor lady? It was cruel, but what could I do?*

I hurried across the parking lot and into my car. Behind the wheel, I took a deep breath and pulled out my phone. I dialed Mother's number in New Jersey.

"Mother, I just left a nursing home. I promise you that I will never allow anyone to put you in a place like this," I said, intending never to break the promise. Sadly, less than ten years later, I would do just that.

In November 2005, our family celebrated Mother's ninetieth birthday, along with a number of her friends from Sunrise, an independent living home in Severna Park, located a mere ten minutes from our house. As had become tradition, seven of us—Sue and I, plus David, Bobbi, Sam, Sarah, and Caroline—departed immediately after Christmas for a week's skiing vacation in Canaan Valley. As always, I called Mother each day to make certain that she was OK. Although she assured me each time that she was, a visit immediately after our arrival at home revealed that all was not well. Mother's heart condition, one that had been monitored closely by her cardiologist, Dr. Barbara Hutchinson, had deteriorated due to an error Mother had made in her daily dosages of the blood thinner, Coumadin.

After a short hospital stay, Mother was feeling better, and she was sent for therapy to the Heritage Harbour facility—the same type of nursing home/therapy center that I had vowed she would never enter. Despite the broken promise, Mother improved a bit each day—until disaster struck. During a morning walk in the hall, Mother suffered a massive stroke.

After a lengthy stay at Anne Arundel Medical Center, her doctor hit me with a bomb shell.

"I don't see any improvement, and I don't expect any," she whispered to me in the hospital hallway. "You need to prepare to let go."

"Letting go" has a specific meaning in the medical world: All heroic attempts to keep her alive would be stopped, and she would be kept as pain-free as possible until the end. Following several sleepless nights, arguments with myself and consultations with family, I agreed to heed the doctor's advice. It was the saddest day of my life.

Mother was taken off all medications except pain-killers and transported to a nursing home for her last days. But she had one surprise left for us. Suddenly, she began to improve. She became more alert, ate a little each day, and, although unable to speak, she communicated with facial gestures and hand signals. We were ecstatic. The beautiful lady who had beaten the Nazis and the Communists, and who had achieved great success in America after starting from nothing, was not about to give in easily. Then came a phone call at 7:16 am on March 3, 2006.

"I regret to inform you that your mother took her last breath at 6:29 this morning." The call came from a nurse at Mother's last place of residence: Future Care in Arnold—the same place from which I had called her ten years earlier and promised that "I will never allow anyone to put you in a place like this." The memory of a broken promise made the tragedy of Mother's death even more difficult.

Ilona Heller was the last of Sue's and my parents to leave the Earth. My father, Rudolph Heller, had been the first. Following his escape from the Nazis, Papa became one of the first volunteers in the Czechoslovak Brigade of the British army. He saw more than five years of combat—in North Africa, during D-Day, at Dunkirk, and during the triumphant march through Germany into western Czechoslovakia while assigned to General George Patton's US Third Army.

While fighting in the African desert, Papa had contracted malaria. This affected his heart, a condition that grew worse as he aged. In late 1987, soon after his seventy-seventh birthday, his cardiologist called me from New Jersey.

"Your dad is on a downhill course," he informed me. "He needs open-heart surgery to replace a valve and to cut away a thickening heart muscle." He informed me that there were only two surgeons in the United States who were considered experts in doing this procedure at that time. I recognized the name of one—Dr. Denton Cooley—because he was world-famous for his pioneering work in heart transplants. A few days later, on my fifty-second birthday, Papa, Mother, and I were on our way to the Texas Heart Institute at St. Luke's Hospital in Houston.

Two days later, Cooley informed us that he had success-fully replaced the valve and cut away a portion of the heart muscle. Mother and I spent a sleepless night in a hotel, awaiting word that Papa's recovery was going well. At ten o'clock in the morning of January 28, the phone in Mother's room rang. I answered it.

"Dr. Heller," said the woman on the other end. "I'm terribly sorry to tell you that your father passed away a few minutes ago. The surgery was successful, but he was simply too weak to survive it. I'm so sorry."

Mother and I held each other and cried for a very long time. Finally, we walked to the hospital, where a nurse pulled away a white sheet to reveal Papa's pale, but tranquil, face.

"Goodbye, Papa. I love you," I whispered as I kissed his cold lips. I held Mother's hand as she gave her beloved Rudy a final kiss. I watched through my tears as my devout Catholic mother made a tiny cross with her right thumb on the forehead of my Jewish father.

Sue's parents, Edward and Viola, purchased a "double-wide" mobile home in Lady Lake, Florida, about fifty miles north of Orlando. They began spending winters there in the late 1970s, usually returning to their New Jersey home at Mt. Kemble Lake in March. Our first visit to Lady Lake was coupled with a trip to the Gator Bowl in Jacksonville, where we watched my Oklahoma State Cowboys defeat the South Carolina Game-cocks. Thereafter, Sue flew down each year with David, and I joined occasionally, whenever I could get away from work.

In early 1986, at the age of 82, Vi was diagnosed with breast cancer. Following a long-ago planned trip, she returned to New Jersey, where she underwent surgery to remove her left breast and nodules under her left arm. Despite her strong desire to remain at home close to her doctors and friends, and although she was very uncomfortable there, she gave in to Ed each of the next five years and accompanied him to Lady Lake for the winter.

Before six o'clock the morning of March 20, 1991, I was awakened by a ringing phone on my night table. It was Sue's father, Ed.

"Vi passed away last night," he said simply.

While in Florida that winter, Vi's cancer had metastasized. Sue managed a couple of short visits while her mother was in the hospital. As a teacher, she found it impossible to be away from her students for longer, or more frequent, trips to Florida.

Following Vi's passing, Ed remained in Lady Lake for a time before returning home to Mt. Kemble Lake. We bade a sad goodbye to Viola Holsten later that spring at a service held at the First Methodist Church in Basking Ridge, New Jersey.

Now that Ed was alone, we attempted to convince him to sell both the New Jersey and Florida homes and to move closer to us in Maryland. However, his stubborn German genes kicked in, and he refused. He spent the next two summers up north, with the in-between winter in the south. In both places, he devoted the majority of his time to his favorite hobbies—gardening and fishing. In New Jersey at first, he managed quite well, with the assistance of several neighbors. However, as time went on, he found it more and more difficult to live alone, whether at Mt. Kemble Lake or Lady Lake. During the winter of 2002, Sue received a call from Ed's neighbor in Florida.

"I think your Dad may have had a mild stroke," he informed her. "I don't think he should be living alone."

Finally, Sue was able to convince her father to sell the mobile home. She and I flew down to help him pack up his Chevy wagon. Sue flew home, and I drove the wagon north, with Ed in the passenger seat. But convincing Ed to sell the house in Mt. Kemble Lake, where he and Vi had settled in the early 1930s, was another matter. He insisted on trying to live alone again, but it became so difficult that even he finally admitted defeat and agreed to come to Maryland to live near us.

Assisted living homes and communities were few and far between in Maryland back in the late twentieth century. The nearest one that we found satisfactory was HeartLands, located in Ellicott City—about ten miles west of Baltimore and nearly an hour's drive from our home in Arnold. We put Ed's log-cabin home on the market, and it sold quickly for the asking price because of the desirability of the Mt. Kemble Lake private community. This time, Sue drove Ed's station wagon—filled with his belongings and a large container filled with water and his beloved goldfish. The fact that HeartLands had a pond for his fish had been a critical selling point in convincing Sue's Dad to move to Maryland.

Although Ed missed his New Jersey home and friends, he adjusted to his new surroundings. However, we wanted him closer to home in order to keep an eye on him and to be available in case of an emergency. Finally, a small assisted living home in Severna Park—a mere fifteen minutes from our house—had a vacant room, and we moved Ed there, albeit without his goldfish, which remained behind. He lived out his life there in a pleasant environment until passing away on March 20, 2000, at the age of ninety-five, exactly nine years to the day after the death of his wife.

In years past, on the rare occasion that I gave thought to old age, I associated it with diminished mental and physical adroitness and with a variety of potential health issues. Thus, I was unprepared for the saddest part of having reached the autumn of one's life—the loss of those close to us. I have fought, kicking and screaming, against my own advancing age, but each time a friend has died, I have been brought to my knees. There have been so many...

In the Czech Republic, Uncle Viktor Hahn and Aunt Aša Hahnová, neither my real uncle and aunt but members of our family, are long gone. So are the Tůmas—Marie and Vladimír— who hid and saved me from the Nazis. Our dear friends, Irena Zíková, who translated my first memoir into Czech, and her husband Dick, are no longer with us. A man deprived of a great academic career by the Communists, Dr. Zdeněk Thomas, as well as our Prague attorney, Jiří Bedrna, and my hometown's historian, Jaroslav Kučera—all are gone.

The man who became my "big brother" upon our arrival in America, Tom Eisner, was killed in a skiing accident. Many high school friends from New Jersey are no longer with us, among them Pete Sheldrick, Midge Gray, and Art Toomer.

As I wrote earlier, some of life's strongest, lifelong bonds are formed during our college years. For me, they were with my two roommates, Don Gafford and Teh-Ling Lei, and with Jim Cobb and his wife LaVerna—all of whom have passed away. In refugee camps, Jan and Hana Tuma became my parents' closest friends. In the United States, Jan tutored me in mathematics and later became my mentor at Oklahoma

State University, where he rose to Chair of the School of Civil Engineering. Jan and Hana died within two weeks of one another. My OSU basketball coach, Mr. Henry Iba, and teammate Eddie Sutton—both members of the Basketball Hall of Fame—have departed.

Many professional colleagues who became close friends have departed. From my Naval Academy days, my fellow co-founders of the Aerospace Engineering Department, Dick Mathieu and Bud Carson; my second-in-command at CADCOM, Inc., Jack Cusack; and most recently, president of NewSchool of Architecture & Design in San Diego, where I served as a board member for ten years, Marvin Malecha, failed to survive a heart transplant.

Tragically, two wonderful people took their own lives. Sue misses her closest friend, Regina "Jeanne" Carpenter. My life is so much sadder without the thousand laughs provided by Bryson Goss—before he made me cry.

There were others, and I mean no disrespect by omitting their names. Intellectually, I know that all of us leave the way humans do; but emotionally, I find it difficult to cope because loved ones who depart leave holes in our lives that cannot be mended. Nonhumans, too, ultimately leave this earth. Sporty, a wonderful little Keeshond, brought much happiness to our family for thirteen years. Knowing that no dog could ever take his place, we have lived without a four-legged friend since his passing.

I live with the memories of all those who are gone. I miss them all.

CHAPTER TWENTY-SEVEN

A LONG JOURNEY HOME

How did I get here? I ask myself nearly every day.

I find it difficult to accept the fact that I am now an octogenarian. How can it be? It does not seem so long ago that I was trying to survive as a hidden child in war-torn Czechoslovakia, wondering if I would live to be a teenager. Once I made it through the war and managed to build a life in America, there came years during which the adjective "youngest" seemed to precede every accolade that came my way. I was "youngest tenured professor," "youngest high-tech CEO," and seemingly always the whippersnapper in every board room I entered. What happened?

I still work for a living, and the word "retirement" does not enter my vocabulary or my mind. I serve on boards and committees—and I am the oldest member of every one of them. I write—and I am the senior person in our writers' group. Throughout my professional career, I was a workaholic, devoting sixty to a hundred hours a week to my job. Today, my one concession to old age has been the recognition of the truth and wisdom in a saying sent to me years ago by a friend much wiser than I:

No one on his death bed ever says: 'I wish I had spent more hours at the office.'

Back then, I posted it above my desk, hoping to pay heed to the warning—but I failed. Now I do, and I have replaced the sign with:

Screw work. Play golf.

I limit my work to less than forty hours a week, and I do play golf—often. Yet, even on the golf course, I am usually the oldest player among my peers.

In 2011, we made the difficult decision to sell our house in the beautiful community of Rugby Hall on the Severn River and to downsize. Practical Sue had been pushing for this for a couple of years, but romantic me—who still thought of us in terms of Peggy Lee's long-ago song, "The Folks Who Live on the Hill"—kept resisting. I loved our house, the large wooded property surrounding it, swimming pool outside our back door, patio for soaking up the sun's rays, and my wonderful hot tub. It was this immigrant's own precious piece of America. But the turning point for me came when Hurricane Irene blew through Maryland.

"I don't need this shit anymore!" I screamed at the walls of our basement at 2:30 in the morning, while bailing ankle-deep water from the floor. "It's time to move to a condo," I said a bit more calmly.

We fell in love with the first condominium shown to us by our realtor friend, Dave Wright. The owners had never moved in despite the fact that they made many improvements. So, we purchased the brand new, three-bedroom, three-bath unit on the second floor of The Reserve, a high-rise building in Annapolis' Heritage Harbour. Today, it constitutes perfection for our lifestyle. No more worries about mowing the lawn, landscaping, shoveling snow. When a problem arises, we pick up the phone. A beautiful golf course beckons just down the street. The nearby lodge has indoor and outdoor pools, a gym, and classrooms where residents can study subjects from information technology to genealogy. I continue to hone my writing skills there under the tutelage of my long-time writing guru and friend, Susan Moger.

Heritage Harbour is a "senior community," which means that most of our neighbors are retirees. I am an anomaly: an eighty-plus-year-old guy who claims he will retire the day he is cremated. Perhaps because I was an athlete in my younger years, and since I continue to stay active as a skier, golfer, hiker, and kayaker, I have kept my body in decent condition (although Sue seldom fails to remind me that I should lose twenty pounds). Maybe because I am a voracious reader of books, newspapers, and magazines, and because I write nearly every day, my mind has stayed relatively sharp. And possibly, I have the genes of my father who, even when he was in his sixties, was often mistaken for my brother.

"No way!" people say to me. "You can't be in your eighties." They seem astonished by the fact that someone of my age has the mental capacity to write a coherent newspaper op-ed piece, or even a book.

"If I look like you and do the things you do when I get to eighty," others say, "I'll be ecstatic!"

I would be lying if I did not admit that such comments stroke my ego. Of course, the good folks who say such nice things do not know the facts. I suffer from the curse of old age: feeling young in my heart while being betrayed by my body and mind. I have macular degeneration in my left eye, arthritis in both knees, a pinched nerve in my neck, and I have a terrible time trying to remember names.

Moreover, I feel overwhelmed by my duties as a caregiver to the love of my life, Sue, whose kidneys have failed. Once athletic and strong, my wife has become frail and physically weak, and I live in fear of something happening to me that would prevent me from being here for her.

I feel as though I am being dragged into this winter of my

life, kicking and screaming. I may be flattered by others' comments about my appearance and attitude, but I resent the physical limitations age forces on me, the so-called "senior moments" I experience, and the fact that I find myself looking back more than forward. This is dangerous because I believe that, in order to remain relatively sharp, one must not fall into a nostalgia trap.

In wrapping up this last memoir, I may not have come to terms with my age, but I have made peace with my roots. I have reflected on the advice I received from my father immediately upon arriving in America as a frightened immigrant boy who spoke two words of English.

"Don't ever let anyone tell you that you're not capable of doing something," Papa instructed me. "Put your head down, and go do it! And, no matter what you do, don't ever give up!"

Papa, I hope I haven't let you down.

EPILOGUE

I am from a far-off land,
Once called Czechoslovakia, now Czech Republic.
I am from a small village called Kojetice,
And I am from a glorious city called Prague.
I am from a home with crystal chandeliers and a grand piano,
And I am from a dark closet where deep fear prevailed.

I am from wealth, happiness, and family harmony,
And I am from poverty, hunger, and loneliness.
I am from the family Neumann
And from the family Heller.
All of them Czech patriots, most of them Jews;
All but three of us murdered.

I am from refugee camps and the meadowlands of New Jersey,
I am from Ota, who became Charlie.
I am from the Oklahoma prairie and California sunshine.
And I am from Maryland, the land of pleasant living.
I am a Catholic, but one with a Jewish soul.
I am American, but I am Czech, too.

I am from the bravery of my parents
And I am from fear of the unknown.
I am from academia and entrepreneurial terror,
And I am from venture capital to writing books.
I am from "goddamn immigrant"
To Entrepreneur of the Year and two Halls of Fame.

I am from the rat-a-tat of basketballs
And the hush of the library.
I am from snowy slopes, racing sailboats, and green fairways
And from writing and learning.
I am from overachieving,
And sometimes under-believing.

I am from my wife and son,
And from our three grandchildren.
I am from the American Dream realized, but dreaming of more.
Often, I wish for too much,
But blessed with family and health,
I am from happiness and a life fulfilled.

AUTHOR'S NOTE &
ACKNOWLEDGMENTS

People who are lucky enough to have never been forced to leave their countries have no idea of the courage, risk-taking, and pain of those who leave behind family, friends, material possessions, language, and comfort of home. No one abandons his or her native country on a whim. Whether escaping tyranny, murderous gangs, poverty, or religious persecution, all refugees have one thing in common: seeking a better life. This was their driving force when my parents decided that we would escape our Communist oppressors and start from nothing in America.

Although I had written much of the material previously, I attribute the idea for *Cowboy from Prague: An Immigrant's Pursuit of the American Dream* to the events leading up to the presidential election of 2016, a period during which millions of Americans came out of the proverbial woodwork to demonize immigrants—to deny refugees access to this country and to tell immigrants who grew up here to leave. When I woke up on Wednesday, November 9, I thought of a morning some sixty-seven years before, when the beautiful Lady Liberty seemed to step forward out of the morning mist to welcome us to America. Now I wondered if the Lady had tears streaming down her face because the immigrant-haters had won.

It was at that moment that I decided that, through my own story, I needed to shout out that we immigrants are *not* a burden. We pay more in taxes than we ever claim in benefits. We start new companies and thus create jobs for others. We enlarge the labor force and increase consumer demand. Those among us who are less educated and less skilled tend to work jobs that natives don't want to take on. I wrote *Cowboy from Prague* in support of enlightened Americans—those who not only understand the economic benefits of immigration, but who believe that taking in human beings in distress is what this country has always done—whose voices will drown out the insults and bravado of the haters. That is the America about which I dreamed as a 12-year-old in a refugee camp. That is the nation which allowed me to pursue, and realize, the American Dream. That is the America about which I decided to write.

This book could not have been written without the help and support of many people. I am particularly indebted to Susan Moger, who has been my writing guru, teacher, editor, and friend for many years. Many of the stories in the book have been enriched by the comments and suggestions of my fellow writers in various workshops guided by Susan.

I turned to three good friends—John Gebhardt, Bill Miles, and Tom Strikwerda—for assistance as my beta readers. The latter provide a writer with opinions of a manuscript from the standpoint of readers. I took their comments to heart and picked up the pace in portions they considered too slow, enriched stories they thought too shallow, and deleted material they considered boring. I appreciate their having taken so much time to assist in making the book more readable.

I am truly grateful to all the kind folks who have endorsed the book. I really appreciate their having taken time out of their busy lives to read my manuscript and providing their brief comments. Their collective stamp of approval has helped me overcome doubts about the relevance of my story.

Working with the talented people at Atmosphere Press has

been a true pleasure. Their edits, comments, and suggestions have been invaluable in bringing *Cowboy from Prague* to life.

I reserve my greatest thanks to my family. I am beyond grateful to my wife, Susan Elizabeth—my Sammy—for having made more than sixty years of this journey with me, at all times tolerant of my steps and missteps while chasing the proverbial American Dream. Our son, David, and our grand-children, Sam, Sarah, and Caroline—along with the love of Sam's life, Bethany—pull me back from falling into the nostalgia trap and looking forward in hope of their untroubled futures.

ABOUT ATMOSPHERE PRESS

Atmosphere Press is an independent, full-service publisher for excellent books in all genres and for all audiences. Learn more about what we do at atmospherepress.com.

We encourage you to check out some of Atmosphere's latest releases, which are available at Amazon.com and via order from your local bookstore:

The Swing: A Muse's Memoir About Keeping the Artist Alive, by Susan Dennis

Possibilities with Parkinson's: A Fresh Look, by Dr. C

Gaining Altitude - Retirement and Beyond, by Rebecca Milliken

Out and Back: Essays on a Family in Motion, by Elizabeth Templeman

Just Be Honest, by Cindy Yates

You Crazy Vegan: Coming Out as a Vegan Intuitive, by Jessica Ang

Detour: Lose Your Way, Find Your Path, by S. Mariah Rose

To B&B or Not to B&B: Deromanticizing the Dream, by Sue Marko

Convergence: The Interconnection of Extraordinary Experiences, by Barbara Mango and Lynn Miller

Sacred Fool, by Nathan Dean Talamantez

My Place in the Spiral, by Rebecca Beardsall

My Eight Dads, by Mark Kirby

Dinner's Ready! Recipes for Working Moms, by Rebecca Cailor

Vespers' Lament: Essays Culture Critique, Future Suffering, and Christian Salvation, by Brian Howard Luce

Without Her: Memoir of a Family, by Patsy Creedy

Emotional Liberation: Life Beyond Triggers and Trauma, by GuruMeher Khalsa

ABOUT THE AUTHOR

Charles Ota Heller was born in Prague and came to the United States at the age of thirteen, following a boyhood as a "hidden child" during Nazi occupation and, later, a harrowing escape from Czechoslovakia's Communist regime. He has been an engineer, an academic, an entrepreneur founder of two companies, and a venture capitalist.

Today he is a writer, having published the award-winning *Prague: My Long Journey Home*; a lighthearted memoir, *Name-droppings: Close Encounters with the Famous and Near Famous*; and *Ready, Fire, Aim! An Immigrant's Tales of Entrepreneurial Terror*.

He earned three engineering degrees—BS and MS from Oklahoma State University and PhD from The Catholic University of America. He was recipient of Maryland's "Entrepreneur-of-the-Year" award, OSU's Lohmann Medal, and CUA's Alumni Achievement Award. He was the youngest-ever tenured professor at the Naval Academy and the first Professor of Practice in the history of the University of Maryland. In 2015, he was inducted into the Oklahoma State University Engineering Hall of Fame.

He is married, has one son and three grandchildren. He and his wife Sue live in Annapolis, Maryland. His website is www.charlesoheller.com.

Printed in the USA
CPSIA information can be obtained
at www.ICGtesting.com
LVHW090730130224
771542LV00058B/670